A CACTUS ODYSSEY

A CACTUS ODYSSEY

JOURNEYS IN THE WILDS OF BOLIVIA, PERU, AND ARGENTINA

JAMES D. MAUSETH
ROBERTO KIESLING
CARLOS OSTOLAZA

TIMBER PRESS
PORTLAND, OREGON

Frontispiece:
Opuntia pachypus
(see also page 166)

Published in 2002 by Timber Press, Inc.

The Haseltine Building

133 s.w. Second Avenue, Suite 450

Portland, Oregon 97204, U.S.A.

Printed in Hong Kong through Colorcraft Ltd.

Library of Congress Cataloging-in-Publication Data

Mauseth, James D.

A cactus odyssey: journeys in the wilds of Bolivia, Peru, and Argentina /

James D. Mauseth, Roberto Kiesling, Carlos Ostolaza.

p. cm.

Includes bibliographical references (p.).

ISBN 0-88192-526-8

1. Cactus—Bolivia. 2. Cactus—Peru. 3. Cactus—Argentina.

I. Kiesling, Roberto. II. Ostolaza, Carlos. III. Title.

QK495.C11 M382 2002

583'.56'098—dc 21

2001042535

CONTENTS

PREFACE

This book is the product of three people who have the good fortune to be not only collaborators but also friends. We met in 1986 in Salta, Argentina, at a meeting of the International Society for Succulent Plant Study. R. Kiesling was the host, and as such had the pleasure of coordinating the arrival, hotels, meals, meeting rooms, and field trips of several dozen cactus biologists from all over the world. The meeting was a tremendous success, and the participants' excitement after being introduced to the fantastic world of cacti in northwest Argentina was palpable. C. Ostolaza presented a talk and slide show about the many exotic cacti of Peru and described the plentiful opportunities that these plants presented for further studies and research. J. Mauseth merely sat in the audience and learned that cacti can grow on their own outside of test tubes in a tissue culture lab.

We went our separate ways after the meeting but kept in contact. Before long we realized that because our research methods are complimentary rather than competitive, our individual research would be more productive if we combined our efforts. We began going on joint field trips. Either together or separately, we have traveled through and studied cacti in the following countries: Argentina, Bolivia, Brazil, Chile, the Dominican Republic, Ecuador, Mexico, Panama, Paraguay, Peru, Puerto Rico, the United States of America, Uruguay, and Venezuela. This book focuses on field trips in Bolivia in March

1995; Argentina in April 1986 and March 1996; and Peru in March 1994, March and August 1997, and January 2000.

While working in the cactus habitats, as well as during many shared breakfasts, lunches, and dinners, we compared notes and swapped information about cacti. We realized, as so many field biologists do, that many fascinating aspects in the lives of plants never make it into the books written about them. Often, only the most factual, most distilled data are published, data which do not reveal the richness of the lives of these plants. Before we get your hopes up, however, we do not claim to be able to relate wonderful natural histories of all the cacti of South America, nor even of all the species we have encountered on our various trips. But we do think we know a few stories and details that you will find interesting, and we hope our observations may help make these plants come alive for readers who have not visited South America and seen these intriguing plants as they exist in their native territory. We have also included some background information for those who want to delve deeper into the features of spine clusters and cephalia, and into the relationship between the parasitic mistletoe, *Tristerix aphyllus*, and *Trichocereus chilensis*.

In writing this book, we have become more aware than ever that so much remains to be learned. For those of you who might be looking for research opportunities in cactus biology, we think this book will suggest many research possibilities you might find irresistible. And for those of you who are not cactus biologists, we hope that this book may encourage you to participate in some ecotourism. Many parts of the countries and areas we describe have excellent or at least good facilities for tourists, and the sight of an unspoiled forest of *Espostoa*, or *Neoraimondia*, or *Trichocereus* is unforgettable.

A little about us, the authors.

Among the three of us, Carlos Ostolaza's passion for cacti goes back the furthest, almost, he claims, to his birth in 1936 in Lima. He received his medical degree from San Marcos University in Lima in 1963, then specialized in abdominal surgery at one of the main Social Security Hospitals in Lima until he retired in 1990. In one of those fateful moments we never foresee but which can have such an impact on our lives, a grateful patient gave him a "German cactus" as a gift. Intrigued by the unidentified plant, Dr. Ostolaza struggled to identify his first cactus specimen only to discover that not only is there no such thing as a German cactus (all cacti are American), but the gift was a crested, monstrose form of a very popular cactus in Peru, the San Pedro, or *Trichocereus pachanoi*. Dr. Ostolaza's interest in these plants was only reinforced when he discovered there was no local expert who could help him identify plants or resolve taxonomic questions about the relationships of Peruvian cactus species.

Early in his wanderings in Peru, Dr. Ostolaza discovered a new species, *Islaya omasensis*, and his findings were published in the German cactus journal *Kakteen und andere Sukkulenten* in 1983. He founded the Peruvian Cactus and Succulent Society (SPECS) in 1987 and has also been the editor of its yearbook *Quepo* (the Spanish name for the irritating little spines of prickly pears and chollas). The research projects that have always been Dr. Ostolaza's greatest priority are those related to understanding which Peruvian cacti are endangered or threatened and in need of protection. He also investigates the ways cacti were used by the ancient Peruvians, the indigenous people who populated the lowlands, hills, and Andean slopes before the arrival of the Spaniards. Such themes are not treated frequently by other scholars, even though many pottery items discovered at archeological sites show cacti so accurately drawn that the genus can be easily recognized. Dr. Ostolaza has been invited to lecture at conventions of the Cactus and Succulent Society of America and the International Organization for Succulent Plant Study.

Roberto Kiesling, born in 1941 in Buenos Aires, has dedicated most of his life to studying the vegetation of Argentina and the adjacent regions of Paraguay and Uruguay. He studied with Dr. A. L. Cabrera beginning in 1968 and participated in many projects that focused on the flora of Argentina, receiving his Ph.D. in natural sciences in 1976 from the University of La Plata. Since that time he has been a professor of biogeography at La Plata and has also held the prestigious position of independent scientist at the Instituto de Botánica Darwinion in San Isidro, a branch of the Consejo Nacional de

Investigaciones Científicas y Técnicas of Argentina. In Dr. Kiesling's
research, cacti have played a large but not exclusive role; he has studied the
diversity of plant life of almost all of Argentina and currently is the director
and editor of a large project, *The Flora of San Juan*, which is expected to fill
four volumes when completed. The first volume was issued in 1994.
Compiling a flora is a monumental task under the best of circumstances, but
when the flora encompasses a region that is part of a country as diverse as
Argentina, the number of species, their taxonomic and ecological relationships, and other issues become all the greater.

As if that were not enough to keep Dr. Kiesling busy, he also contributes
to *The Flora of Jujuy*. For those of you not fortunate enough to have visited
Jujuy in northwestern Argentina, it contains almost every type of habitat
imaginable (from rainforest to desert, from lowlands to mountains), all
packed into one small state. In the course of his floristic research, Dr. Kiesling
has explored the length and breadth of Argentina many times, traveling the
hundreds of miles from Bolivia to Patagonia and back again, and from mountains to the ocean, examining not just cacti, but all plants that he encounters. During these travels, he has collected more than ninety-five hundred
herbarium specimens. In the last few years, his explorations have begun taking him into Brazil. His research has been published in numerous scientific
articles in various international journals. In between field trips, Dr. Kiesling
has found the time to edit *Hickenia*, the botanical journal of the Instituto
Darwinion, serve as president of the Sociedad Latinoamericana y del Caribe
de Cactáceas y Suculentas, and spend a year at Kew Gardens in London on a
fellowship. He too has been invited to lecture at conventions of the Cactus
and Succulent Society of America and the International Organization for
Succulent Plant Study.

Jim Mauseth was born in 1948 and grew up on a farm surrounded by
plants, but it was not until he went on a University of Washington field trip
from rainy Seattle to sunny Arizona that he discovered and fell in love with
cacti. Carrying out graduate student research on cacti in Seattle presented
some challenges, so he studied their growth and development in tissue cul-

ture. Dr. Mauseth did not have the chance to cultivate his favorite plants outdoors until he became a professor at the University of Texas in Austin in 1975. Most of his research continued to center on the anatomy and development of cacti, especially the ways they grow and form their tissues. Early field trips to Panama and Costa Rica taught him two things: that rainforest plants are far more wonderful and awe-inspiring than can ever be described in books and magazines, and that he does not like to be rained on every day, day after day, even to study epiphytic rainforest cacti. Dry, sunny deserts are his habitat.

While working with Gloria Montenegro at the Universidad Católica in Santiago and studying several unusual parasitic plants (one adapted to attacking cacti, the other able to spend its entire life underground), Dr. Mauseth was introduced to the superb cacti of Chile, and his book-learned images of cacti were forever transformed. Collaborative research with Maurizio Sajeva of the Botanical Gardens in Palermo stimulated his interest in how anatomy affects physiology and ecology, and a project was begun to investigate the inter-relationships between the ways that cactus anatomy has changed through evolution and how that has affected cactus diversification. Although the project initially appeared simple, it has instead occupied much of his academic career.

While he is working in South America, Dr. Mauseth often gives classes about cactus biology at local universities (the students must be very patient to listen to lectures given in really terrible Spanish). His publications have included not only scientific articles in professional journals such as the *American Journal of Botany* and the *Journal of Plant Research*, but also articles of general interest for cactus hobbyists in the *Journal of the Cactus and Succulent Society of America*. He has published two textbooks as well, *Botany, An Introduction to Plant Biology* and *Plant Anatomy*.

Before closing this preface, we want to acknowledge the help of many people and institutions who have aided us directly as well as helped the general field of cactus research. The following list is by no means complete. Dr. David Hunt of the Royal Botanical Gardens at Kew and Dr. Dieter Supthut of the Städtische Sukkulenten-Sammlung in Zürich have given unselfishly throughout their lives to aid all aspects of cactus research, generously providing data, ideas, and stimulating theories. We have been given access to various invaluable collections, and we thank the following people for their generosity: Dr. Jean-Marie Solichon of the Jardin Exotique in Monaco, Mme. Marnier-Lapostolle of Les Cèdres in Nice, Dr. Ted Anderson of the Desert Botanical Garden in Phoenix, and Dr. James Folsom of the Huntington Botanical Gardens in San Marino. These gardens and others have helped protect hundreds of species through cultivation. In several cases, the plants we observed on our field trips were either not in flower or not in good health, and several botanical gardens came to our rescue by letting us study and photograph their plants.

We could not have carried out our travels without the aid of the Museo de Historia Natural Noel Kempff Mercado in Santa Cruz, Bolivia, the Instituto de Botánica Darwinion in Argentina, and the Universidad Nacional Agraria La Molina in Lima. And special thanks and appreciation go to Gloria Montenegro of the Universidad Católica in Santiago, Chile. Finally, we want to especially thank the Cactus and Succulent Society of America, the International Organization for Succulent Plant Study, and the Institute of Latin American Studies at the University of Texas, all of whom supported us generously, funding many of our trips and research, and who, year after year, expressed confidence in our endeavors.

A CACTUS ODYSSEY

United States

Mexico

Belize

Honduras

Nicaragua

Guatemala

El Salvador

Panama

Costa Rica

Caribbean

Guyana

Suriname

Venezuela

French Guiana

Colombia

Ecuador

Galápagos
Islands

Peru

Brazil

Bolivia

Paraguay

Chile

Argentina

Uruguay

SOUTH
AMERICA

CACTI:
Introduction,
Biology,
and History

T he objective of this book is to relate some interesting findings about cacti of South America. Many aspects of their lives, their surroundings, and their interactions with animals are fascinating because they are different from the ways other plants live, and yet they also help us understand plant biology in general. For example, some South American cacti live in deserts similar to those of Arizona and California, but others inhabit rainforests, where they are bathed in almost constant fog and mist and must compete with orchids and bromeliads for space in the forest canopy. Other South American cacti are at home only at high altitudes in the Andes, where cold is a greater problem than drought. These unusual cacti of rainforests and mountain tops share many features with cacti of ordinary deserts, but they also have adaptations that permit them to thrive in areas where we might not expect to find cacti. The cactus family contains such a diverse group of plants that a look at their natural history will tell us a great deal about the ways these species are unusual in the plant world and how their unique features allow them to survive where they do.

Each cactus, like any other plant, is a living, changing, dynamic individual, carrying out the processes of obtaining food and water, defending itself against animals and fungi, and producing the flowers, fruits, and seeds that ensure another generation. We will try to relate stories about cacti as living organisms. Imagine yourself in some remote South American area,

The large masses of narrow green stems hanging from the tree branch are shoots of the cactus *Rhipsalis baccifera*. Although they do not look like real cacti at first glance, they have all the necessary features. Cacti have become adapted to many unusual habitats, including rainforests. If you look for cacti only in hot dry deserts, you would miss seeing about half the species.

having spent a long day searching for, studying, and photographing cacti. Sitting around dinner, you swap stories about these hardy creatures, sharing the things that you know about them, the things that make the plants real to you. It is these stories, which we have told each other, that we now want to share with you.

Why should we focus on South American cacti? Many people in North America and Europe are surprised to hear that there are cacti in South America at all. For most of us, Mexico and the deserts of the southwestern United States are the home of cacti. And yet the cactus family originated in South America, and in the millions of years since, they evolved rapidly and extensively, taking on diverse sizes and shapes, and becoming adapted to all sorts of environments. Much of this occurred while the North American continent, consisting of Mexico, the United States, and Canada, was not attached to South America. It is only in the last few million years that continental drift brought North and South America close enough together that birds could carry cactus seeds to Mexico, permitting them to get a toehold in the area where they would ultimately thrive. By that time, the cactus flora of South America was already old, rich, and diverse; many species and genera had come into existence, and many had already become extinct. Numerous species of South American cacti have been seen and collected only a few times, some only when they were first discovered. Even to this day, most cactus-rich wilderness areas of South America have few roads, and travel and exploration

Cactus habitats and cacti occur all over South America. This hillside near Chilecito, Argentina, contains at least five or six species of cacti, the tall columnar one being *Trichocereus terscheckii*.

are still difficult. Consequently, little is known about many cacti of South America, and even less has been written. Perhaps this book will stimulate enough interest that it encourages more people to carry out research and conservation efforts on cacti of South America.

We ask for patience from our readers. We hope for a wide audience that includes folks for whom cacti, and maybe even all plants, are a new interest, as well as for some old hands who have been cultivating, propagating, studying, and reading about cacti for longer than we have. For the newcomers, we will avoid using specialized terms unnecessarily, and when we must use a scientific word that may be unfamiliar, we will define and explain it. Do not be offended or feel excluded by terms that are unknown to you—their use is not an attempt to exclude amateurs. For the experienced specialists, we hope we have included enough new material that you do not mind reading some things that are already familiar.

WHAT ARE CACTI?
CHARACTERISTICS THAT DISTINGUISH CACTI FROM OTHER PLANTS

It is not really possible to give a short, easily understood definition of what cacti are, so how about a short answer followed by an explanation? Cacti are the group of closely related plants that have clusters of spines and that are native to North and South America. The phrase "group of closely related plants" is important: it means that all cacti alive today are descendants from one single original set of ancestral cactus plants. All those descendants fit into the cactus family, technically known as the Cactaceae (pronounced kak tay see ee), and we do not leave out any of the descendants, no matter how much they may differ from our image of a typical cactus. For example, cacti in the genus *Pereskia* have big, flat, thin leaves and stems that are not thick and succulent; most would quickly die if placed in a desert. Since the family originated in the distant past, this group has undergone few changes and still looks so much like ordinary plants that few people realize that instead of being merely related to cacti, pereskias are cacti. Because all descendants of the ancestral cacti are accepted as cacti, the pereskias are too. We are fortunate to still have living, primitive cacti like pereskias because they have helped us figure out what the early cacti looked like and what the close relatives might be. On the other hand, many members of the spurge family (the euphorbias) look so much like cacti they often fool experts, but they are not placed in the cactus family because they descended from a completely different set of ancestral plants.

How do we know the things we call cacti all have a common ancestor? The answer lies in the next part of the definition: "have clusters of spines." All cacti have spines, which are usually all too painfully obvious when we work with them. In some cacti like *Rhipsalis* and *Zygocactus* (Christmas cac-

This leafy vine, *Pereskia aculeata*,
is a true cactus native to the lowlands of the east coast of South America.
When they bloom, they have hundreds of flowers with a fragrance so wonderful
it is intoxicating. The plants tolerate light frost— they would make excellent garden
plants in the warm humid areas of Florida and California.

tus), spines are so short it would be necessary to cut a plant open and search with a magnifying glass to see them, but the spines are there. Several aspects of cactus spines are particularly distinctive. First, they occur only on stems just above the site where a leaf should be. This is easiest to see in a plant of the genus *Pereskia*, the species of which still produce big leaves. Slightly above the point where a leaf attaches to a stem, we would expect to find what is known as an axillary bud. Axillary buds are common in most plants: they produce flowers or branches when active, and until that time are covered and protected by bud scales. In all cacti, the bud scales and leaves of axillary buds have been converted by evolution into spines. This modification must have been among the first steps in cactus evolution because all cacti have these spines. The modification was probably gradual, requiring at least a couple of million years to occur, and during that time the early cacti might have had very stiff bud scales that over time became narrower, longer, and more spinelike. It would be useful if one of those early, transitional cacti were still alive so we could have an example of an organ intermediate between a bud scale and a spine, but apparently all have become extinct. All today's cacti, even the primitive pereskias, have well-developed, highly perfected spines.

Second, because cactus spines are part of an axillary bud, they occur in clusters called areoles. Areoles have various shapes and arrangements: in some species they are masses of spines that are all more or less equal in size and shape; in others each areole has longer, more massive spines in the center and shorter, thinner spines around the edges; others have spines that are hooked; and still others have straight spines. Some spines have even become modified into glands that secrete sugary nectar, although so far, this is known only for barrel cacti (*Ferocactus*) and a few of its relatives in North America, and not for any South American cacti. It is the characteristic cluster of spines—occurring as part of an axillary bud—that separates cacti from many other groups of spiny plants. Roses have thorns (there is no botanical difference between spines and thorns) arranged individually here and there along the stem, but they are never in clusters and are never part of an axillary bud. The spines of agaves and yuccas are hardened leaf tips and teeth, not the entire leaf. And the spines of those cactus-look-alikes, the euphorbias, are modified branches, not leaves. In many other prickly plants, spines are just large, tough, nasty hairs (stinging nettles) or leaf teeth (holly) that do not occur in clusters and are not the leaves of an axillary bud. Some cacti try to fool us—they have such short spines, they are virtually invisible.

Now for the last part of the definition of cacti: "are native to North and South America." To find cacti in the wild, in their natural habitat, one must look in the Americas, not on any other continent. A few species of cacti are now common in hot dry parts of the world, such as prickly pears around the Mediterranean and Australia, but we know that those plants were carried there by people, starting with Christopher Columbus, who brought them from the Americas. Plants of the New World caused a great sensation when they were brought back to Europe by the early explorers, and they were eagerly sought by wealthy gardeners; woodcut illustrations of prickly pears

Shoots of *Pereskia sacharosa* have spines above the spot where each leaf
attaches to the stem, the spot where an axillary bud would be expected.
The spines visible here, and indeed on any other cactus, are modified bud scales.

(*Opuntia*) were produced as early as 1535, and cacti were so quickly placed in
cultivation that by 1827 there were 108 species being grown in Great Britain
alone. The restriction to the Americas helps us identify whether plants are
cacti or not: if a plant is extremely cactuslike but is native to Africa,
Australia, or any other place not in the Americas, it is not a cactus. Instead
it must be a member of another group that, faced with the same problems of
desert survival, made similar adaptive modifications to its body.

What evidence do we have for the conclusion that cacti are native to
the Americas? Quite a bit actually. First, there are the areoles that all cacti
have but that non-cacti do not; areoles occur only in American plants.
Second, numerous features of flowers, fruits, and seeds are characteristic of
cacti but not of the spiny plants in other parts of the world. Third, many
microscopic features of cactus wood, mucilage, and epidermis prove that
non-American desert succulents differ from cacti in many ways. A fourth
feature is especially important: all cacti and their close relatives use a unique

set of flower pigments called betalains, and no matter how much some of the African or Australian spiny plants might resemble cacti, they use a different type of pigment in their flowers. It is only at first glance that non-American spiny plants could be confused with cacti.

It is unusual that a group as large as the cacti is native to only the Americas. Other examples of groups confined to the Americas show how unique cacti are: nasturtiums, hummingbirds, and armadillos occur naturally only in the Americas, but these are small groups, each with only a few species. In contrast, the cactus family is much larger with almost two thousand species. The only other large group that originated in, and remains confined to, our continents is the bromeliad family (Bromeliaceae).

To repeat the definition: Cacti are the group of closely related plants that have clusters of spines and that are native to North and South America. So much for theory; what about seeing a plant in a nursery or a botanical garden and wanting to know if it is a cactus or not? For that there is no easy answer; many non-cacti fool very experienced specialists, and some cacti caused botanists years of trouble trying to figure out that they are indeed cacti. After reading this book, though, you should not have much trouble.

EVOLUTIONARY CHANGES THAT CONVERTED ORDINARY PLANTS INTO CACTI

The cacti alive today are the results of tens of millions of years of evolutionary changes that allowed the plant bodies and metabolisms to survive in deserts and other stressful regions. We do not know exactly what the earliest cactus ancestors were like because they left no fossil remains, but we assume that the ancestral cacti were similar to plants in the genus *Pereskia* and resembled ordinary trees. Despite the similarities, however, the ancestral cacti were not pereskias and could not be classified in the genus *Pereskia*; it is just that the evolutionary line of plants that leads to the modern pereskias underwent very little change.

The three most obvious modifications that converted ordinary plants to desert-adapted cacti are the loss of leaves, the development of water-storing succulent tissues, and the formation of spines. Although large leaves allow a plant to produce sugars by photosynthesis more rapidly than small leaves, large leaves are a liability in desert habitats because they lose water more rapidly. Small leaves—or no leaves at all—may reduce beneficial photosynthesis, but there is greater benefit in conserving water.

The benefits of water storage tissue in cacti are easy to understand. In deserts, rain occurs episodically, often only once or twice a year, and only plants that can store water during the intervening droughts will survive. Plants of *Armatocereus* and *Browningia candelaris* grow in the bone-dry deserts of southern Peru and northern Chile and probably receive rainfall only during El Niño years—they may have to wait five to ten years from one rain to the next. Most cells of any plant's body can store water, and fortunately for the ancestral cacti, two very simple evolutionary modifications increased water storage capacity: bigger cells and more of them. Both these modifications occurred mostly in the outer stem tissues (the cortex) and to a lesser extent in the innermost stem tissues (the pith), and they produced the broad, succulent stems that are characteristic of cacti.

The final obvious modification arose out of the plant's need to protect itself from desert animals who get much of their water from the plants they eat. Bud scales and leaves of axillary buds were converted to spines, which were very effective in keeping animals away.

These three modifications, however, were not enough to convert an ordinary plant into a desert-adapted cactus. At least four additional modifications—delayed bark formation, loosening of the cortex cells, the evolution of flexible ribs, and the creation of cortical bundles—were necessary. Most plants, including pereskias, cover their stem with bark after a year or two. Bark not only stops sunlight from reaching the green photosynthetic cortex tissue, but it also prevents needed carbon dioxide from getting into the stem, where it is converted into sugar by photosynthesis. Early steps in cactus evolution included delayed bark formation and an epidermis that can remain in good condition for a hundred years or more. Cacti are somehow able to withstand full-intensity sunlight without their epidermal cells being harmed by the harsh ultraviolet rays.

Other early modifications improved the stem's capacity to carry out photosynthesis. The cells in a typical plant stem fit together so tightly that carbon dioxide cannot move quickly into the tissue from the air. Early mutations in cacti, however, enlarged the cortex cells (allowing them to store more water) and made them more rounded so that there were more air spaces between the cells. Carbon dioxide can more quickly diffuse deep into the cactus's stem and reach green tissues as rapidly as photosynthesis uses it, and oxygen, a toxic waste product for plants, is able to leave the cactus stem more quickly.

Although the creation of water storage tissue is probably easy (plants simply make more cells and make them bigger), a problem arises for the plant's epidermis as the cactus alternately swells with water after a rain and then shrinks during a drought. The plant's volume changes drastically, but its epidermis, unlike an animal's, does not stretch or shrink. Evolution provided cacti with flexible ribs. These ribs can both expand and broaden when full of water, and contract and thin during drought. Although the epidermis changes shape, none of the epidermis itself is lost or gained. A later evolutionary step divided ribs horizontally into rows of conelike structures called tubercles; a cactus plant can become taller or shorter as well as fatter or skinnier as it gains or loses water.

Although this increased flexibility in the stems allowed them to become huge (the increased succulence meant that plants such as *Soehrensia bruchii* or *Gymnocalycium saglionis* could store enough water to survive years of drought), the accompanying disadvantage is the difficulty of water movement in the stem. Water must move from stem wood outward through the cortex as rapidly as the cortex cells use it in their own metabolism and as quickly as water is being lost through the epidermis (the epidermis can never prevent all water loss). Water is carried through the roots and up into the stem by wood, but wood in cactus stems is located near the stem center. A modification that solved this problem was the evolution of water-conducting tissues called cortical bundles. These vascular bundles are located between the wood and the epidermis, and they carry water to all parts of the cortex as rapidly as

This stem of *Azureocereus viridis* shows several important adaptations—
delayed bark formation (if bark were present, the stem would be brown),
ribs, and spines—that permit cacti to survive.

water is needed. They also transport sugars away from the green tissues at the stem surface to where it can be used, such as the areoles that are producing spines or flowers. If cortical bundles did not transport this sugar quickly, it would stay in the photosynthetic cells near the stem surface, and the cactus would become irresistible to animals.

Of course there were modifications other than the seven discussed here, but they are not as universal or easy to see. The point is that numerous gradual and sequential changes occurred since the first members of the cactus family became distinct from their close relatives, the early members of the portulaca family. The conversion of leaves into spines must have been an early modification because spines are present in all cacti. Once spines appeared on the first cacti, all subsequent cacti have carried the genes that govern spine formation. Sometime later, early cacti must have separated into two lines. The first line, the pereskias, has seen very few subsequent changes. The second line's modifications (those that occur in all the non-pereskioid cacti today) included the inhibition of bark formation and the conversion of stem cortex to a better photosynthetic tissue. When the second line later separated into two subfamilies, Opuntioideae and Cactoideae, the plants likely still bore relatively large leaves, were very woody, and not especially succulent. Many members of Opuntioideae and Cactoideae still have hard, woody, non-succulent stems (for example, *Pereskiopsis* and *Acanthocereus*), and all opuntioids still produce leaves, some of which are as large as those in pereskias (such as leaves of *Quiabentia* and *Austrocylindropuntia*).

Subsequent changes to the Opuntioideae included a reduction but not an elimination of the leaves, increased stem succulence but without the development of ribs or cortical bundles, and the formation of big, white, bony seeds that are present in no other cacti. In the Cactoideae line of evolution, leaves must have been lost very early as no modern plants of this group have obvious leaves (they do have microscopic leaves, and the leaves of *Matucana aureiflora* are visible to the naked eye if examined carefully). Later mutations included the formation of vascular bundles in the cortex, increased stem succulence, and the formation of ribs and tubercles.

How much of this evolutionary diversification occurred in South America before continental drift brought North America close enough for

These plants of *Wigginsia sessiliflora* are taking the full force of the sun;
the yellow sunburned patches reflect the stress they are under.
The plant's ribs and tubercles allow them to contract down to ground level.

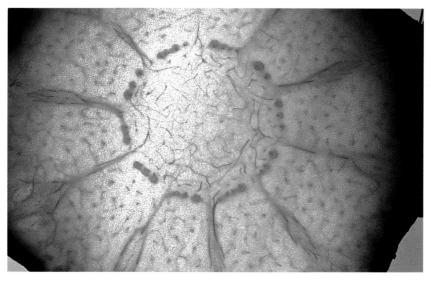

This is a thin slice of stem from *Echinopsis hammerschmidii*.
The central ring of dots is the little wood this plant makes. Tissue inside the ring is pith,
and outside the ring is cortex. The dots and squiggles in cortex are the cortical bundles,
the radiating lines transport material out to the areoles. The outermost region is dark
because it has a high concentration of chlorophyll.

cacti to migrate into Mexico, the United States, and eventually Canada? And how many types of cacti moved northward? If only a few, then many modifications might have happened twice—once in South America and again in North America. All three subfamilies occur on both continents, so there must have been at least three migrations northward. There are still many gaps in our knowledge of cactus evolution, and most concern South American cacti.

ECOLOGY: WHERE CACTI LIVE

Throughout the Americas, cacti live in just about every type of habitat— grasslands, rainforests, cold mountaintops, sea shores—but of course deserts are the most typical and common habitat. The defining feature for a desert is aridity: deserts are regions that receive less than 10 inches (25.5 cm) of rain per year. Knowing the total annual rainfall is only the beginning of under- standing a habitat and its stresses; how many people would guess that Seattle, Washington, and Austin, Texas, have about the same annual rainfall— approximately 35 inches (87.5 cm)? The two areas have such totally differ- ent vegetation that no one would ever confuse them. Seattle receives a little of its annual rainfall every week, with August and September being the most droughty months; sometimes an entire two weeks passes without rain. Austin's rains, by contrast, are episodic, and a span of two months without rain is common; native oaks (*Quercus*), junipers (*Juniperus*), and prickly pears (*Opuntia*) do not show the slightest signs of stress after a complete lack of rain lasting four or five months. This type of difference is important to cacti. If the habitat has only short dry spells between brief rains, then plants need to store enough water for a month or two, enough to get them through a rare, pro- longed drought. Many cacti of humid coastal regions, such as those of *Acanthocereus*, *Leptocereus*, and *Pereskia*, have little succulence. Cacti in habi- tats that routinely have only one period of rain a year, on the other hand, must contain large amounts of succulent tissue, not enough to last merely a year, but enough in case there are two bad years in a row. Armatocerei, copiapoas, and soehrensias survive years without rain, relying on their abundance of stored water.

The variation in rainfall pattern affects the types of surrounding vegetation that cacti compete with as well. Areas with brief dry periods have shrubs and bushes that overgrow cacti, shading them, whereas habitats that routinely have long droughts may have at most low grasses that do not interfere with cacti. And exceptional droughts lasting several years may be beneficial to cactus survival: even though cacti may be stressed by a prolonged, severe lack of rain, they would survive while competing shrubs and grasses would be killed, leaving more of the habitat available for the cacti. In many deserts, the air is dry, causing plants to lose water despite having a waxy water-resistant epidermis, but in other areas, particularly on low tropical islands and the northeastern coast of South America, the air can be very humid without dropping rain or providing mist. The humidity does not supply water to the cacti, but at least it prevents them from losing too much through their epidermis.

We may perhaps never know how many cacti are adapted to grasslands. Much as it was in the Great Plains of the United States, the fertile soil of grasslands throughout the world was plowed up and put into cultivation before native plants were studied. Many opuntias and coryphanthas can still be found in residual pockets of natural grasslands, and tales of the cowboy past sometimes mention various cacti. One report describes the horsecrippler cactus (*Homalocephala texensis*) as being so common in the grasslands of west Texas that ranchers would pile them up to make walls similar to those that people make in the Northeast by piling up rocks. There is no such abundance of cacti in present-day Texas. The farming of grasslands has been going on for even longer in South America: the highlands of Bolivia and Peru are covered from horizon to horizon with small farms that probably existed for centuries, even before the Incas. In the bits and pieces of natural grassland that remain, genera such as *Echinopsis*, *Parodia*, *Oroya*, *Tephrocactus*, and many others can still be found. Many of these cacti rely on the grasses to provide shade during the sunniest, hottest times of the year, and will sunburn if planted in a cleared area. Many are also frost tolerant but not able to withstand long periods of drought.

Tropical rainforests are home to many cacti in several lines of evolution. Most rainforest cacti live as epiphytes, their roots serving only to attach them to a branch high up in the bright, sunlit canopy of the forest. If the roots fail, the cacti fall to the ground and quickly die for lack of light. Examples of epiphytes are *Epiphyllum*, *Hatiora*, *Lepismium*, *Rhipsalis*, and *Zygocactus*. Other rainforest cacti such as *Hylocereus*, *Selenicereus*, and *Werckleocereus* are scramblers. They are usually rooted in the soil with their stems lying against a tree that they then climb, attaching themselves to the tree with short roots that penetrate crevices in the tree's bark. An interesting but not particularly convincing theory is that the branches of the host tree are basically a desert habitat: the cactus's roots run along the surface of the bark, which is moist during a rain but dries quickly afterward, and the roots become stressed for water. Perhaps—but bark is rarely dry in rainforests, and the cactus shoots have almost no water-storage succulent tissue, so they do not appear concerned with drought. And many plants growing alongside the rainforest cacti are not drought adapted: mosses, ferns, gesneriads (the African violet family), and miniature peperomias.

A simpler theory might be that cacti have moved into this habitat just as they have moved into so many others. Rather than their desert adaptations being beneficial here, they are a liability and are being lost. For example, storing water is not necessary with frequent rains, and having a big, heavy, water tank of a body makes it more likely the cactus will fall out of the tree. Many epiphytic cacti are small, with slender, lightweight stems. Lack of leaves minimizes water loss, but that too is no longer important in rainforests. What the plants need is the photosynthetic capacity of leaves. They have not been able to get their leaves back (apparently the genes were too badly mutated), but cacti have used another trick: their ribs have become taller and thinner and more leaflike. Plants of *Epiphyllum* have only two ribs protruding along the opposite sides of the narrow stem, and each stem strongly resembles a single big leaf. For some reason, rainforest cacti occur primarily in tropical rain-

Grassland cacti often lie low, allowing grasses and shrubs to protect them from the most
intense sunlight of midsummer. The body of the *Harrisia martinii* here is well hidden
by grasses, but its flowers are not. It is surprising how many cacti will sunburn
if placed in full summer sun, even though lawn, petunias, daylilies,
and other seemingly delicate plants have no trouble at all.
Perhaps cacti cannot transpire rapidly enough to keep themselves cool
because they do not have enough water.

forests ("tropical" indicates that it never freezes), and rarely in temperate
ones (where freezes occur at least occasionally). There are many temperate
rainforests in the Americas, but few have epiphytic cacti. Of the rainforest
cacti, *Selenicereus* seems among the most hardy, some plants surviving even
mild freezing conditions in cultivation.

The number of cacti adapted to cold, high alpine conditions is surprisingly large. Genera with species that live routinely above 8000 feet (about
2500 meters) altitude include *Arequipa*, *Austrocylindropuntia*, *Corryocactus*,
Lobivia, *Maihueniopsis*, *Matucana*, *Mila*, *Neowerdermannia*, *Oreocereus*, *Oroya*,
Soehrensia, *Submatucana*, and *Trichocereus*. The very highest dwellers, *Oroya*
and *Maihueniopsis*, are common above 12,000 feet (3700 meters), where they
form low cushions. Their stems branch profusely, but each branch is short
and stubby. Every branch ramifies until the plant is a solid mass of branches,

Deamia testudo is adapted to rainforests—its ribs are too thin to store much water,
but they are large enough to photosynthesize. Plants of *D. testudo* climb trees
by clinging to them with their roots, growing upward until they reach bright sunlight.
Cultivation of rainforest cacti often requires mist systems to keep the humidity high,
which is not something you would expect a cactus to need.

each packed tightly against neighboring branches. The cushions usually are
less than 1 foot (30 cm) tall, even in very old plants, and are solid enough
that you could walk on them without causing damage. This compact shape
helps the plants retain what little heat and moisture they have, and it also
keeps the wind at bay on its surface rather than permitting it to swirl around
the trunk. Snow covers these plants during parts of winter, but water in snow
is frozen and cannot be absorbed by the cacti. Much of the time the ceaseless
wind is dry and desiccating. These are cold deserts of the severest kind, and
yet this is home for these cacti: to portray them as struggling for existence
would be misleading. If a cushion of *Oroya* were transplanted to the nice
warm, moist conditions of some lowland habitat, it would die within days.
Just like polar bears, they are adapted to their habitat.

Cacti in the less extreme high altitudes are a mix of small, low, hidden
plants like *Neowerdermannia* and tall, big, columnar cacti such as *Oreocereus*

Many cacti of high altitudes, such as this *Maihueniopsis boliviana* in Parque Lauca in northeastern Chile, grow as low, compact cushions. It is likely that many never experience truly hot days, but they have undoubtedly been covered by snow many times. The volcano is Cerro Parinacota, 19,890 feet (6120 meters).

celsianus that show no obvious adaptations to their cold climates. Looking at them in a greenhouse, you would never guess they are alpine plants. This seems to be the case with most of the high-altitude cacti: their adaptation to cold must be in their physiology not their anatomy because they simply do not look any different from cacti that die in the mildest frosty night.

GEOLOGICAL HISTORY OF SOUTH AMERICA: SETTING THE STAGE FOR CACTUS EVOLUTION

During the millions of years that the Cactaceae was coming into being and then evolving to its present condition, the continent of South America was also evolving. About 400 million years ago, all the continents (which float on the earth's hot, liquid mantle) were drifting toward the same spot and beginning to coalesce, initiating the formation of one single giant continent,

Pangaea. This was about the time that land plants originated from their ancestors, green algae. Because all land on Earth was in one mass, these earliest land plants were able to spread wherever they found suitable habitats.

After a few million years, currents in the mantle changed and began pulling Pangaea apart; the northern part (known as Laurasia and consisting of the forerunners of North America, Europe, and Asia) drifted slightly north, leaving Africa, South America, India, Australia, and Antarctica together as a continent called Gondwana (sometimes called Gondwanaland). By the time this happened, plants had evolved to the level of conifers but not yet to flowering plants. Dinosaurs were the dominant land animals. Continued drifting tore North America away from Laurasia and sent it moving rapidly (almost 1 inch [2.5 cm] per year) westward, creating a gap that filled with water that is today the northern part of the Atlantic Ocean. In the south, South America tore away from Gondwana, and that gap became the southern part of the Atlantic. The north Atlantic and south Atlantic finally came together about 100 million years ago as South America broke completely free of Africa. Later, Antarctica moved to the south, and Australia broke off and drifted east at the same time that mammals were becoming established, which is why Australia has so many primitive mammals. India separated from Africa in the Southern Hemisphere and then drifted north until it ran into Asia. It is running into Asia even now, and the collision is creating the Himalayas.

South America continued to move away from Africa, and the Atlantic Ocean became wider. Taxonomists believe that this is when the first cacti in the northeastern part of South America became distinct from the ancestors of the portulacas. If cacti had originated earlier while South America and Africa were still attached, we would expect to find cacti in Africa as well as South America. Cacti likely did not arise until after the south Atlantic was so wide that birds could not fly back and forth between South America and Africa (otherwise they would have carried cactus seeds to Africa). At this time, North America was farther to the north and separated from South America and her primitive cacti by thousands of miles of open ocean; there was no Central America at that time. Then North America began to drift south, and South America turned north. Their approach caused mountains to form on the ocean floor. Once the mountains became tall enough, they protruded above the ocean surface as a series of islands. As they grew, they coalesced and gradually formed Central America. This collision is still in progress as the numerous active volcanoes of Nicaragua, Costa Rica, and Colombia prove.

Even while Central America was nothing more than a set of widely dispersed islands, cactus seeds were carried by birds from South America to all the islands and eventually to Mexico. Central America as a continuous land mass uniting North and South America is only two million years old or less, but cacti would have arrived in Mexico millions of years before then. The question is, how many millions of years ago? We have no fossil records to give us solid dates, so only the broadest estimates are possible. Flowering plants may have arisen about 120 million years ago, and because the ancestors of cacti were sophisticated flowering plants, flowering plants must have been evolving for several tens of millions of years before cacti developed. The south Atlantic was probably wide enough to stop east-west bird flights somewhere around sixty to eighty million years ago, and that may be the time that cacti became distinct from the portulacas. Cacti must have been restricted to South America for several tens of millions of years before North America drifted close enough and became dry enough for them to migrate into Mexico. During this time (100 million years ago), the areas we think of as ideal cactus habitats—northern Mexico and the southwestern United States—were not available to cacti because they were under water. There is so much diversity in North American cacti that they must have been there for several tens of millions of years, but there are very few data to guide our estimates.

If the earliest cacti arose as far back as eighty million years ago, they would have coexisted with the last dinosaurs before they became extinct sixty-six million years ago. At the time that cacti may have been emerging, South America was home to many species of giant herbivorous dinosaurs that resembled brontosaurs. Is it possible that the last dinosaurs were eating the first cacti? Early mammals were also present and widespread in South

America, so we may never know if spines in early cacti were useful in deterring herbivory by dinosaurs or by mammals.

When South America separated from Africa, it was a very different place. The Andes did not form until South America began colliding with the plate that carries the floor of the Pacific Ocean. Initially, South America was flat, and rainstorms could sweep from one side to another without being stopped by mountains. South America was also farther south, so the desert zone that lies south of the tropic of Capricorn would have fallen across northern South America at the point where we think cacti originated. An important influence on the flow of water between North and South America was the absence of Central America. In its place was a giant ocean that allowed water to circulate in a completely different fashion than it does now. Although most big rivers drain into the Atlantic Ocean—the Mississippi, Rio Grande, Amazon, Río de la Plata, Danube, and Nile—it is the Pacific Ocean that provides most of the water that makes the clouds that produce the rain that falls into these rivers and then ends up in the Atlantic. It is as if there is a giant pump moving water from the Pacific to the Atlantic. Central America blocks an easy return of water to the Pacific, so the water must squeeze between Patagonia and Antarctica at the tip of South America, where it becomes frigidly cold. As it moves north along the coast of Chile and Peru as the Humboldt Current, the water is so icy that onshore winds pick up too little moisture to bring rain, although the fog that is formed gives rise to the exquisite cactus deserts of Peru and Chile. Before the formation of Central America there was no cold Humboldt Current, so the Peruvian and Chilean coasts must have been moist and covered with vegetation.

The drift of South America and North America toward each other had another major consequence besides their eventual connection and the formation of Central America. It brought both continents into the desert-creating influence of the tropics of Capricorn and Cancer. The sun's heating of Earth's surface is most intense at the equator, creating an equatorial zone of rising hot air. As air gains altitude, it expands and cools, causing clouds to form and produce rain. Loss of rainwater dries the air. Once the air has reached its maximum altitude, half of it flows north and half flows south, all of it losing heat by radiating it into space. By the time the air has spread from the equatorial region to the two zones of the Tropics, it is so cold it sinks. As these two masses of air descend they become compressed, which in turn heats the air masses and increases their ability to hold water. As they reach ground, rather than forming clouds and providing rainfall, they instead absorb moisture from plants and land, creating hot, dry desert zones. South of the tropic of Capricorn are the xeric regions of Peru, Chile, South Africa, and Australia, and the descending air at the tropic of Cancer gives rise

These plants of *Corryocactus brevistylus* are adapted to the desert conditions of highland Peru inland from Nazca. As continental drift carries South America northward, this region eventually will move into a wetter, milder latitude.

to the deserts of the United States, Mexico, northern Africa, and the Middle East. As South and North America slowly drifted toward each other, different parts of both continents passed through the desert zones, and the plants and animals living there must have been affected. Given that each desert zone is several hundred miles wide and that continents drift at only about $\frac{1}{2}$ to 1 inch (1.25 to 2.5 cm) per year, a particular area of habitat that was carried into a desert zone would probably stay in the zone for thirty or forty million years before emerging into the moister equatorial zone on the other side.

Unfortunately, we lack so much knowledge about when and where cacti originated and diversified, and about the topography and climate of South America that we cannot fill in the many holes in the sketchy outline we offer in this chapter. Without the Andes present, was there an Amazon River, or did multiple rivers drain the continent in various directions? If cacti really have been present for eighty million years, it is enough time for numerous mountain ranges to have formed and eroded away. But how would those ranges have affected the survival and spread of cacti and the animals they depend on to pollinate their flowers and disperse their seeds? There are still many research opportunities.

CLASSIFICATION OF THE CACTUS FAMILY

The processes of continental drift, natural selection, and evolution, together with the effects of plants, animals, climates, and geography interacting with one another, have combined to produce the cacti alive today. Between one thousand and two thousand types of cacti now exist. Botanists are trying to develop a classification of cacti that will give every species its own unique name while at the same time reflecting the evolutionary relationships that exist among them. This is a difficult task because many species have become extinct without leaving any fossil remains, so we will never know what features they had. Furthermore, there are many species that have not yet been discovered, and of the cacti that we do know about, many aspects of anatomy, physiology, reproductive biology, and DNA have not been studied. Therefore, while trying to name cacti and work out evolutionary relationships, we are working with a very incomplete set of data; mistakes are made, and disagreements exist. Because of their differing interpretations of data or their various opinions about how evolution has occurred, taxonomists sometimes give different names to the same species.

All cacti are grouped together in the family Cactaceae. There are differences of opinion, however, about the number of cactus species that exist (the singular of *species* is also *species*). Some taxonomists (referred to as splitters) are intrigued by differences between species, so whenever plants differ even slightly, splitters tend to place them in separate species. A splitter would argue that there are 2000 or 2200 species of cacti. Taxonomists who are lumpers emphasize similarities and put the number of cactus species at 1100 (certainly no more than 1300). Is there any way to know which taxonomic approach is correct?

A plant is not a separate species from another if the two plants interbreed. In other words, if two plants are cross-pollinated and produce good seed that then grows into new plants, they are members of the same species. This general rule was designed by zoologists studying animals, but it does not work too well for plants. Good, viable seed has been produced after hand pollination between two plants of different species, and there are even examples in which two species in completely different genera have been forced to interbreed. Because of these problems, the rule is slightly modified for plants: if two plants do not cross-pollinate in nature, even when growing together, then they are distinct species. It is therefore extremely important that we study plants in nature to see if they are interbreeding or not.

It is more important to know whether plants are closely related to each other than to worry about whether they are the same species. In many cases, taxonomists agree on which plants are closely related. For example, the genus *Gymnocalycium* occurs widely throughout Argentina, Paraguay, Uruguay, Brazil, and Bolivia, but plants of all *Gymnocalycium* species resemble each other so much that they are easily recognizable as gymnocalyciums. In the years since the first specimen of *Gymnocalycium* was discovered, 138 species have been named, but some of these are so closely related that they are probably just varieties of one species. In fact, *G. brevistylum*, *G. eytianum*, *G. fricianum*, *G. hamatum*, *G. matoense*, *G. megatae*, *G. michoga*, *G. onychacanthum*, *G. pseudomalacocarpus*, *G. tortuga*, and *G. tudae* are all listed by David Hunt in the CITES *Cactaceae Checklist* as being variations of one species, *G. marsoneri*. It is not particularly important if each of these is considered a species or a variety; what is important is that we realize they are a closely related group that share a common ancestor.

Closely related species are grouped together in a genus (the plural of *genus* is *genera*). As problematical as the definition of species is, the definition of a genus is more so. Each genus should contain only those species that have all descended from the same ancestral plants. It must also contain all the descendants of those ancestral plants without leaving any out. Creating a genus requires obtaining detailed information, not simply about each species, but also about its ancestors, its evolution, the other species it is related to, and even those to which it is not related. We have all this information for only very few groups of species, so for the most part, the genera we use are educated guesses. Splitters see many small genera each with a few or even a single species, whereas lumpers recognize only a few big genera, each with dozens of species. Fortunately, some genera are so distinctive everyone agrees which species should be classified into them. All adult plants in all species of *Melocactus*, for example, have a cephalium on top of a short green body. The species also resemble each other so strongly in every other feature that we have no doubt they have all descended from the same ancestor. And no other plants resemble them enough to be included in the genus *Melocactus*. If only all genera were so easy.

A group of species that poses greater classification difficulties occurs in a complex of genera such as *Echinopsis*, *Lobivia*, *Soehrensia*, *Trichocereus*, and a few others. Although the species resemble each other in many aspects, there are also differences. Members of *Echinopsis* are short and usually small, glob-ular, lowland plants; those in *Trichocereus* are columnar and often giants with habitats that range from lowlands to intermediate altitudes; plants in *Soehrensia* are very broad, massive globes up to 2 feet (60 cm) in diameter that live at altitudes above 6000 feet (2000 meters); and the species placed in *Lobivia* are mostly smaller plants adapted to high altitudes. Some taxonomists would classify them all into *Echinopsis*, making this a very large genus, while others would separate them into the four genera named above. Still others would separate them into even more, smaller genera. It is difficult to say which method is correct. Although it appears that all species are descended from the same ancestral plants, thus making a single genus *Echinopsis* techni-cally acceptable, it would obscure the great variation in body type. For exam-ple, plants of *Echinopsis klingeriana* are always small and globose, whereas plants of *Trichocereus pasacana* are small when seedlings but become giant

With its round, green base, numerous
short white spines, and white hair,
Melocactus schatzlii of Venezuela
is easy to recognize.

Echinopsis klingeriana in Bolivia always has small globose bodies.
It never becomes large or columnar.

As a seedling, *Trichocereus pasacana* in Argentina is as small as its relative, *Echinopsis klingeriana*. After a few years spent growing in full sunlight, it will be the tallest plant in its habitat.

This is an example of *Cleistocactus baumannii*, but plants like it can be found in *Borzicactus* and *Clistanthocereus*. There is no agreement whether they should all be classified into the same genus or left as they are.

columns after a few years of growth. The most important thing to realize, however, is that these species are all related whether they are in one genus or in many. Most of us who work with cacti can ignore this problem and use whatever names we want—*Trichocereus pasacana* or *Echinopsis pasacana*—depending on our own point of view of the genera.

Taxonomists are far more concerned about mistakenly creating a genus that contains species that are not all related to each other. For example, the genera *Borzicactus*, *Cleistocactus*, *Haageocereus*, and several others resemble one other because some of the plants are narrow, columnar, and have many low ribs that each bear numerous areoles with short spines. If these genera resemble each other because they are all descended from the same ancestor that had these characteristics, they could all go into one genus. But if their similarity is due to convergent but coincidental evolution, it would be a real mistake to place them in the same genus. A genus that does not reflect the natural evolutionary relationships of the species it contains is said to be unnatural.

There is, perhaps surprisingly, almost universal agreement about the subfamilies of cacti. A subfamily is a group of genera whose members are all related because they are all descended from the same set of ancestral plants. The family Cactaceae has only three subfamilies, Cactoideae, Opuntioideae, and Pereskioideae (the ending *-oideae* is pronounced oh id ee ee). The subfamily Pereskioideae contains those genera whose species have changed very little since the early days when the cactus family first arose. They all have actual, unmistakable leaves, and their stems are narrow and not succulent. They are highly branched trees or shrubs with woody trunks. Most people—including most botanists—would never guess they are cacti, but they have areoles (the modified axillary buds whose bud scales are spines), which are the critical characteristic of cacti. Pereskioideae has only two genera, *Maihuenia* and *Pereskia*.

Subfamily Opuntioideae contains prickly pears, chollas, and their relatives, often simply called the opuntias. In North America we mostly have two groups of opuntias: prickly pears, with their flat pads (which are actually flattened shoots), and chollas, which are bushy opuntias with cylindrical shoots. (Lumpers put prickly pears, chollas, and many others into a giant genus *Opuntia*; splitters put prickly pears into a genus *Platyopuntia*, chollas into *Cylindropuntia*, and so on.) Both types are easily recognized as cacti because of their spines and succulent bodies, and they are identifiable as opuntias because their leaves, although temporary (they fall off after spring), are large enough to be seen and are almost always cylindrical and sausage-shaped.

In South America, there is a much greater variety of opuntias. There are a few species of prickly pear opuntias and chollalike cacti (although not called chollas in South America), but there are also treelike *Opuntia quimilo* and *Quiabentia*, small spreading plants of *Maihueniopsis* and *Tephrocactus*, tiny, almost subterranean plants of *Pterocactus* and *Puna*, and vinelike *Tacinga*. Most of these can be recognized as cacti by their spines and succulent bodies, and many have small leaves. In some the leaves are almost invisible, and spines are sometimes so short that only if you cut the plants open are they visible. One feature that unites these many species is that they produce big, white, bony seeds that are much larger than those of subfamilies Pereskioideae and Cactoideae. And all members of Opuntioideae are further united because they produce glochids. Glochids are tiny spines produced by the dozens (sometimes by the hundreds) in each areole. Once mature, they break off at the base and remain on the plant only because there are so many they are too tightly packed to fall off. Lightly handling the opuntias, or accidentally brushing them even with clothing, is enough to dislodge scores of glochids. They are too small to be seriously painful but if you are stuck by many, they will cause irritation. Unlike the genera of Opuntioideae, those of the Pereskioideae or Cactoideae do not produce glochids.

Perhaps because of the difficulty of dealing with glochids, our knowledge of the Opuntioideae is not very complete. Most people will not collect or cultivate these plants, and few have studied these plants' anatomy or physiology in their laboratories. We therefore do not have much data on which species are related to each other, what the evolutionary lines are, and where the first opuntias arose. Some people have taken an extreme

This speciman of *Opuntia quimilo* in General Güemes, Argentina, is a good representative
of the subfamily Opuntioideae. It has the flat, padlike stems of prickly pears,
yet can grow as large as a tree; its hard woody trunk is probably a primitive feature.

lumper approach and put almost all species of the Opuntioideae into a single giant genus, *Opuntia*. Others have appreciated the morphological and lifestyle diversity in this group and recognized more than a dozen genera. Because of this uncertainty, we often refer to the group informally as the opuntias or the opuntioids. Both words have the same meaning and are meant to be vague.

The Cactoideae is by far the biggest subfamily, containing all the cacti that most people think of as cacti other than the opuntias. Here we find the big columnar cacti (for example, *Browningia*, *Neoraimondia*, and *Trichocereus* in South America, and *Carnegiea* and *Pachycereus* in North America), small globular ball cacti (*Blossfeldia*, *Eriosyce*, *Frailea*, *Gymnocalycium*, and numerous others), the epiphytic rainforest Christmas and Easter cacti, the climbing queen of the night cactus (*Selenicereus*), and many, many more. This subfamily is mostly held together by what its members lack: they never have large, true leaves like Pereskioideae, or the glochids and big, bony, white seeds like those of Opuntioideae. Members of this subfamily will feature prominently in the following chapters, and more of their story will be told there.

The cactus family is a significant, often dramatic part of the vegetation of two large continents. Not only does it dominate the extensive desert regions of the United States, Mexico, Argentina, Bolivia, and Peru, it is a key component of other ecosystems as well. Despite its importance, we still have only a rudimentary knowledge of many aspects of its biology, in particular its evolution, ecology, anatomy, physiology, and reproduction. There has been a great deal of research aimed at understanding the evolutionary patterns in such a large, diverse group, but most of these investigations have focused on cacti of the United States. In contrast, many South American cacti are a complete unknown, the only studies often being the original paper that described their discovery and gave them their name. Some of the simplest and most basic details have never been examined. For example, flowers of the genus

Calymmanthium, a Peruvian native, develop so deeply in stem tissue that they literally tear the stem open when they bloom, yet this remarkable feature is completely unstudied. Or consider that epiphytic rainforest cacti hang from trees, their roots above their shoots: these plants, unlike all others, actually conduct water and minerals downward, which must have a dramatic impact on their physiology. This too has never been investigated. Other examples of the remarkable biology of this family will be mentioned throughout the following chapters. We hope that one result of this book will be to stimulate new research on these wonderful plants.

This *Austrocylindropuntia verschaffeltii* shows several characteristic features of the Opuntioideae, in particular the cylindrical, sausage-shaped leaves that are large enough to be visible.

2

LOWLANDS OF EASTERN BOLIVIA:
Cacti in the Forest's Shade

As our pickup heads out of Santa Cruz and east toward the lowlands of Bolivia, we are sure we have made a big mistake: this green, lush forest surrounding us could not possibly be cactus country. A few days ago, as our American Airlines jet descended for a landing in Santa Cruz, giant clouds were dropping scattered downpours on all sides of us, the rain falling onto a tremendous flat plain that appeared to be a tropical jungle, not the cactus paradise that we had been promised. An immense river, the Río Guapay, meandered off into the distance where it passes through the Bañados de Izozog, an extensive marsh. It is March, the end of summer in the Southern Hemisphere when the dry season should be starting, but the vegetation here appears to never suffer from drought. Only a few miles from Santa Cruz, the pavement ends and our road turns to dirt; fortunately, we do not know that two weeks will pass before we see a paved road again. Bridges will be even rarer: rivers must be forded, so travel is only practical during the dry season. A rail line runs directly east to our destination of San José de Chiquitos, but no road makes it all the way.

The three of us—Roberto Kiesling, Jim Mauseth, and Carlos Ostolaza—have been studying the cacti of South America for longer than any of us cares to admit. Having decided to combine our efforts whenever possible, we travel and work together to obtain the greatest amount of data about our favorite plants. Our field studies have taken us to many regions of South America, and whenever we are working in an area with a university, we give lectures

The area near Santa Cruz, Bolivia, does not look like cactus habitat: too flat, too grassy,
and too forested. Most of our travels through lowland Bolivia to the southeast of Santa Cruz
pass through habitat such as this. Fortunately for us, the area harbors many unusual cacti.
In about May or June, it will be much drier than this.

about desert biology and invite faculty and students to participate in our
research. Consequently, we now find ourselves in a pickup from a natural history museum in Santa Cruz (called the Museo de Historia Natural Noel
Kempff Mercado) accompanied by one of its professors and two of its students
who all assure us that, despite the greenery, we really are surrounded by cacti.

A carload of cactologists cannot stay loaded in a car for long, so despite
the inauspicious look of the forest's shade, we stop to explore. Within minutes we come across two splendid cacti, *Brasiliopuntia brasiliensis* and *Cereus
stenogonus*. It is hard to believe cacti thrive in conditions that include trees
towering overhead capturing almost all the sunlight and letting only a little
pass through to the cacti.

The plants of *Brasiliopuntia* are exotic in their shape. As their name
indicates, brasiliopuntias are basically opuntias, so they are at least distantly
related to the prickly pears in the genus *Platyopuntia* and to chollas or
Cylindropuntia that are common in the southwestern United States. It is

The flattened pads on the sides of *Brasiliopuntia brasiliensis* reveal that it is an opuntioid species.
Notice the round trunk—even when young it is cylindrical, not flattened.
As it continues to grow, the trunk becomes stout and woody, and the lateral pad-shaped
branches elongate by adding new pads that gradually become
rounded as wood accumulates inside them.

easy to recognize prickly pears because they grow as a series of flat "pads" whereas chollas have more ordinary, cylindrical, rodlike trunks and branches. Yet this brasiliopuntia is growing like both its relatives: its main trunk is a narrow cylinder with tiny leaves like those of a cholla, but all its side branches are large, flat pads like a prickly pear's. In most plants, cacti included, the trunks and branches of a particular plant are so similar it is difficult to tell one from the other, so having a cylindrical trunk that bears flat branches is striking. Bamboos and canna lilies are slightly similar: their thick, fleshy rhizomes grow horizontally underground and have inconspicuous scalelike leaves, but their branches grow upward out of the ground and bear the ordinary, familiar big, green leaves. Every plant has two very different types of stems.

By having a narrow cylindrical trunk rather than a broad, flat, thick one, a young plant of *Brasiliopuntia* can grow upward without needing much energy. The thicker and stouter a shoot, the more materials a plant must

Brasiliopuntias flower easily in colors like this nice golden orange and bright lemon yellow.
Such bright colors are easily visible to pollinators, although the flowers may occur in forest
shade. They are attractive in a rock garden or greenhouse collection.
They can become quite large or be pruned back for smaller spaces.
Photographed at the Jardin Exotique, Monaco.

dedicate to its construction, so the slender trunks of brasiliopuntias allow
each plant to reduce its construction costs. Before long, a plant should be
tall enough to stick its head above the leaves of the surrounding trees and
receive full sunlight. But that takes a plant of *Brasiliopuntia* years to
achieve, and we wonder how it survives until then. The flattened side
branches may be efficient at catching light, but there is simply not much
light to be had. Perhaps we are getting a biased impression of its habitat by
visiting at the end of the rainy season, when all the ordinary, leafy trees are
in full health and casting a lot of shade. In a month or two, many trees will
be leafless, and much more sunlight will pass through their naked branches
and reach the young plants of *B. brasiliensis*. However, if this is so, there is
still a problem: will the cacti carry out their growth and metabolism during
a season so dry that surrounding plants become dormant? Do those same
conditions that cause most plants to shut down (to go into the plant equivalent of hibernation) cause the cacti to wake up and become active?

Cereus stenogonus is only a little less surprising than *Brasiliopuntia brasiliensis*. Because it is a tall, branching, columnar cactus, its many arms reach skyward. Tropical vines are using it as a trellis and thus hiding much of its surface, yet it somehow gets enough light to grow into the forest canopy. Cerei are ordinary cacti that are a little on the plain side; they do not have any of the special modifications present in some other cacti, but they are definitely well adapted to drought conditions. Their thick stems (about 5 inches [12.5 cm] in diameter) have enough succulent cortex tissue to store large amounts of water whenever it rains, so allowing the plant to survive during dry periods, when other plants are suffering or dying. And the ribs on this *C. stenogonus* represent a remarkable adaptation: as a cactus absorbs water during a rainy season, its stems swell and increase in thickness. During dry seasons, the stems shrivel back to a narrower diameter as the plant uses its water reserves. The skin, or epidermis, of the cactus must somehow accommodate this repeated swelling and shrinking without tearing open. The ribs are the key. As the stem swells, its ribs also fill with water, become broader at their base, and push away from each other. As water is depleted during the dry season, each rib becomes narrower, one side moving closer to the other and drawing all the ribs together. When fully hydrated, the stems are broad and covered with low, wide ribs, but when desiccated, they are narrower and have thin, sharp-angled ribs. No tearing, no wrinkles. It would be nice if this *C. stenogonus* could swell up enough to kill the vines that entwine and shade it, but that will not happen. Fortunately, the cactus is perfectly healthy despite the vines.

Success on our very first stop—two great cacti. We continue on toward Concepción in high spirits. The dirt road is so badly rutted and rough with washboard compaction that we cannot drive more than about 20 miles per hour (33 kph), but we tell ourselves the slow pace makes it easier for us to watch for cacti. The terrain has turned into rolling hills covered in a mix of grasslands and forest. Flat land, like the plains near Santa Cruz, usually has rather uniform vegetation. We might, however, find some cacti here that have adapted to valley bottoms where cool air settles at night and moisture accumulates, or we might come across other cacti that have adapted to the

Cereus stenogonus is growing near the brasiliopuntia and is also struggling for sunlight in the shade of the surrounding trees. Notice the wide leaves of a philodendron that is climbing the tree in the foreground—a good indication that this region receives ample moisture.

Cereus aethiops demonstrates how ribs allow a plant to absorb and lose water without tearing themselves apart. This plant was photographed in habitat at Puelches, Argentina, in March (late summer). Its tip has died back a little, and the shoot is shrunken from a lack of water. Ribs are narrow and draw together as the shoot loses water. After the next good rain, the ribs will swell up again.

This *Cereus aethiops* specimen was photographed in the Jardin Exotique in Monaco
and is obviously not suffering from lack of water. Its shoots are so well hydrated they are
swollen, pushing the ribs outward. The ribs too have expanded
to the point of being broad and flat.

tops of hills that dry quickly after a rainfall. The sides of hills are especially good sites for cacti. Hillsides facing the equator (those facing north in the southern hemisphere) receive stronger light, so they are warmer and drier than hillsides that face away from the equator, which are often shaded, cooler, and more moist. Finding different species on either side of the same valley is not uncommon. The area around Concepción looks promising except for the tall forest, although we have already learned that is not necessarily a problem for cacti.

The next morning we turn south toward El Cerrito ("the little hill") and San Antonio del Lomerio. Before long, we come across a *laja* (pronounced la ha), a bald area of exposed, flat rock. The visible rock in a laja is usually not extensive (only several square yards), and on its edge there is a thin film of soil covering the rock. A few feet farther away, the soil is deeper and its water-holding capacity is greater. Because trees can surround a laja but cannot grow too close where the soil is thin, parts of a laja are shady and other parts suffer the full intensity of the midday sun. This would be a good spot to find *Frailea,* but we do not have such good luck at this laja. Instead we find a snake, a long, thick, green snake. Fortunately it is slow-moving—in fact, it is not moving at all. Inspection from a prudent distance reveals it is a cactus, *Monvillea kroenleinii*.

Plants of *Monvillea* often lie on the soil. They do not lie perfectly straight, but undulate in a way that is convincingly snakelike. This similarity is not too bad when you come across them in the open desert and can see them from a distance, but when you almost step on plants of *Monvillea* in brushy undergrowth like this, yikes. As if that is not bad enough, they climb up trees and then dangle downward, another very snakelike thing to do. We are surprised to encounter a species whose plants can grow in dramatically different habitats. Individuals of *M. kroenleinii* can be found in sites ranging from full sun to heavy shade, although plants in shade often appear not to be thriving—they are narrower, paler, and have thinner, weaker spines compared to plants growing in full sun. It would not be surprising to find that plants in shade produce fewer flowers, fruits, and seeds than those lucky enough to be in sunnier microhabitats. On the other hand, cacti in the gen-

This specimen of *Monvillea cavendishii* snakes along the ground. Only if it accidentally encounters shrubs that will support it does it grow upright. Adventitious roots emerge wherever the stem touches the ground. Other species of *Monvillea* are more upright and treelike.

era *Rhipsalis* and *Epiphyllum* have become adapted to extremely dim habitats in rainforests and now would not tolerate prolonged exposure to full sunlight.

The next plants we find at the laja look and act like real, self-respecting cacti. They are small globose plants of *Echinopsis hammerschmidii*, each with many low ribs and short spines that mean business. The plants grow in clusters, some because they are the offsets of the central plant, others because several seeds germinated at the same spot. When a plant offsets, it is forming branches from its lowest, ground-level areoles. It is basically growing like a small, branching shrub. Because they lie so low, the branches are in contact with soil and typically form roots. If the central, "parental" shoot dies, each rooted branch survives as an independent individual, each being a clone of the parent. Offsetting is extremely common in the genera *Echinopsis*, *Lobivia*, and *Rebutia*, all of which have plants with small globose bodies. In stark contrast, other genera with similar bodies, such as *Matucana* and *Melocactus*, remain solitary and do not form offsets.

Monvillea cavendishii did not bloom for us in the greenhouse,
but when we transplanted it outdoors, it began to flower reliably.
Flowers open at night and do not last long past sunrise, but the burst of white petals and the
cluster of stamens are sufficient rewards to getting up early.
This plant is only two years old and is grown from seed we collected in Bolivia.

Plants of *Echinopsis* often prefer filtered light, and this open forest area with trees separated by lajas is a perfect habitat. Echinopsises grow where they receive good sunlight in the morning or afternoon but are protected from the full force of the sun during the day. Species of *Echinopsis* are widespread throughout the cactus country of South America, but they can be hard to find in desert areas where they hide under nurse plants protected by their shade and hidden by their branches. When *Echinopsis* plants bloom, their spectacular flowers are long enough to reach above the nurse plant and display themselves to pollinators, but when the plants are not flowering, they are well camouflaged. About the only time that echinopsises can be found in the open is at very high altitudes in mild areas where cloudy conditions and cool breezes keep them from overheating.

It is a marvel to see *Echinopsis hammerschmidii* here. The plants will always be small even when many years old, and will always need protection.

These plants of *Echinopsis hammerschmidii* are growing at the edge of a laja.
The exposed rock is visible in the foreground, but there is soil where there are cacti.
The echinopsises prefer the edge of the laja, where soil is not too deep.
These cacti are temporarily in the sun but will be shaded as shadows of surrounding
trees move across them. Behind the echinopsises are terrestrial bromeliads.

And yet their close relatives are in genera such as *Trichocereus* and *Soehrensia*,
massive plants that grow to be huge columnar cacti up to 20 feet (6 m) tall
or giant spheres over 1 foot (30 cm) in diameter and that thrive in full sunlight of maximum intensity. If we considered only their ecology and physiology, we would not conclude that *Echinopsis* is related to the hardy plants of
Trichocereus, but after one look at their flowers, we see that the kinship is
obvious.

El Cerrito, "the little hill," is in an area that consists of nothing but
rolling hills. One hill has a name, the others do not. Why? We suspect it will
be special somehow, and we are not disappointed. El Cerrito is a large, round,
single mass of rock protruding several hundred feet above the forest. Patches
of soil and scrubby vegetation cling precariously to areas near the top that are
not too steep, all of which indicate that this is a place with a lot of promise.
We follow a trail to its base, seeing many more individuals of *Echinopsis*,

Flowers of *Echinopsis* are always wonderful,
making them some of the most popular cacti in cultivation.
Many species and hybrids can be purchased from nurseries, and they bloom every spring,
often with many large flowers on each stem. Give them Bolivian lowland conditions:
dappled sun, rich soil, and lots of water in summer.

Monvillea, and other plants from the morning. A quick climb up the bare sides brings us to the first vegetation patch, a small "lawn" of terrestrial bromeliads. These are tough plants with coarse, cutting leaves that can slash through clothing and skin easily: they are not the delicate epiphytic rainforest bromeliads often found with orchids in tropical greenhouses. These bromeliads survive weeks of relentless sun without any rain at all, relying instead on water stored in a tangle of leaf bases and roots. Big Bend National Park, located in the Chihuahuan Desert of west Texas, has large areas covered by the ground-dwelling bromeliad *Hechtia*, but it is so coarse and tough that park visitors routinely mistake it for an agave. Extensive mats of terrestrial bromeliads are rather common in deserts, and their airy, moisture-holding leaves provide an excellent "soil" for many other species. *Parodia chrysacanthion* in Argentina thrives best in mats of *Abromeitiella brevifolia*, but here we find not a cactus but *Begonia*. The begonias look completely out of

This mass of bromeliads acts as home for these flowering begonias
that clearly are healthy even in full sun. Individuals of *Echinopsis* also grow among
the bromeliads, and several plants of *Cereus* have taken root
where clefts in the rock are wide enough.

place. They are delicate, even fragile, and because we have seen them only as
houseplants, it seems incongruous that here they are surrounded by cactus
and rock. During a sunny summer day, the heat must be incredible, yet the
plants survive. The begonias are obviously healthy and happy, and so beautiful that we do not mind that we have not found any new cacti up here. The
view is wonderful, but still it is hard to look at the forest—a sea of green
extending in all directions—and realize this is the home of many cacti. It
does not look anything like Arizona.

Returning from the top of El Cerrito, we stop for lunch at the only house
in the area. We had talked to the folks in the house when we arrived, and
they showed us the path we needed to take to get to the top of El Cerrito.
Then they insisted on preparing a nice hot lunch for us of rice and chicken,
the chicken being very, very fresh. As is so common in rural areas, people are
generous and helpful. They also gave us directions to Piedras Marcadas, a

locality where *Frailea* has been collected by other plant explorers. The location is not too far away, but the road is nothing but rock and dirt—arduous, in other words—and will delay us greatly. None of that matters, however, when it comes to a genus like *Frailea*.

Most plants of *Frailea* are fully grown while still less than 1 inch (2.5 cm) in diameter, and a plant 2 inches (5 cm) across is definitely large. When they bloom, the plant's body is dwarfed by a flower whose petals spread much wider than the stem. Even though the plants are almost solely water-storage tissue, there is simply not much volume in which water can be held, and fraileas are not capable of withstanding severe desiccation. They are definitely not desert plants, and their microhabitats must be moist most of the time. The laja at Piedras Marcadas should be perfect, and sure enough, little plants of *Frailea chiquitana* are abundant. They survive only in a narrow zone of thin soil around the edges of the laja. Closer to the rock there is no soil at all. A little farther from the rock and the soil is thick enough to support grasses that grow over the fraileas, cutting off their sunlight. Only a narrow band is just right. During a rain, water runs off the gently sloping rock and accumulates in the *Frailea* zone, giving the cacti enough time to absorb some before it evaporates. Other fraileas must grow in similar microhabitats because photos of these plants in nature often show them surrounded by mats of *Selaginella*, mosslike plants that prefer areas such as this laja. And *Frailea* seeds have adaptations that allow them to float and be swept to new lajas during heavy rains and occasional floods.

In cultivation, fraileas are a delight because they grow quickly and achieve flowering size in just two years or so. You may notice flower buds developing on your cultivated plants, and although you watch them patiently, you are disappointed to find the buds dry and dead one day, no beautiful flower ever having shown itself. A closer inspection will reveal the dead object to be a fruit full of seeds, not a withered flower bud. How can a flower bud produce a fruit without ever opening and carrying out cross-pollination? Fraileas are self-fertile, and the pollen from a flower can fertilize the stigmas of the same flower even though the flower never opens.

These plants of *Frailea chiquitana* are growing on the edge of a laja, where the soil
is only 1 inch (2.5 cm) or less deep. Look closely for the many tiny *Frailea* seedlings.
Most of the vivid green plants are *Selaginella*, very primitive plants that reproduce by spores,
not with seeds. These selaginellas are similar to some of the earliest land plants
that originated in Pangaea about 400 million years ago.

Such tiny cacti are a delight, and to see so many thriving is wonderful.
We want to look at all of them but are afraid that a single false step will
squash two or three if we are not careful. By staying only on the rock, we
can walk safely and see all the plants. Because the suitable zone is so narrow, we can jump across it to get on or off the rock without ever putting any
fraileas in danger. Because the adult plants are so small, seedlings are almost
microscopic, often hidden under fragments of fallen leaves. The soil is still
moist from the last rain, but we are at the end of the rainy season for this
year and wonder how long the dry season will last. How many of these
plants will survive until next year? Although abundant here, we had
checked almost every laja we encountered, and none but this one had
fraileas. They seem so vulnerable.

By the time we finish with *Frailea chiquitana* at Piedras Marcadas, the sun
is low, daylight is fading, and we still have a long drive back to Concepción

This is usually all you see of your frailea flowers. Flowers of *Frailea magnifica* look like this
while developing and also while they are fruits because they have no intervening open phase.
But the fruits are always full of seeds that germinate well,
and a potted plant is usually surrounded by seedlings before long.

for the night. We do not know it at the time, but throughout all our weeks of
travel in Bolivia, Peru, and Argentina, we will never learn to budget our
time. We will never arrive at a hotel until well after dark, and we will never
eat dinner before 8:00 or 9:00 P.M. Field work is always a matter of balancing
resources: to arrive at a hotel early means that we have wasted daylight that
could have been used for exploring, but to drive after dark is to run the risk
of passing by an important plant without seeing it. Our aim is to arrive at
dusk, shower, have dinner and some relaxation, then begin to press plants for
herbarium specimens, dissect samples for anatomical studies, make notes,
measure, photograph, and generally produce a great deal of spiny trash that
has undoubtedly caused many hotel maids to be unhappy with us the next

Frailea flowers do open sometimes, such as this flower of *F. pygmaea.*
Anecdotal reports indicate that opening may be triggered when there is
plenty of sunlight on the day the flower is capable of opening. Our experience,
however, suggests that conditions during flower development may be more important:
under some conditions flowers develop such that they can open;
under other conditions they develop in such a way that they cannot possibly open.
This aspect of *Frailea* biology needs to be investigated.

morning. With luck, we can be finished as early as midnight or 1:00 A.M., but finishing at 2:00 or 3:00 A.M. is not unusual. That still leaves three or four hours for sleeping before we get up and start all over again at 6:00 A.M.

It is already dusk when we begin the drive back to Concepción, but a tangled mass hanging from a low tree branch next to the road stops us in our tracks: *Epiphyllum.* Even though we can barely see in the dark, this tangle has to be the famous epiphytic cactus that never grows on the ground. Its seeds are carried by birds to tree branches where they germinate. The rest of its life is spent as an epiphyte, its roots clinging to the tree bark, its stems able to project in all directions because there will be equal amounts of air and sunlight on all sides. Although this part of Bolivia had seemed too wet for cacti, it now seems too dry for this one, especially since tree trunks here must be dry much of the time. All epiphytes, including plants of *Epiphyllum*, must use the tree's bark as their "soil," and of course tree bark does not hold water for long. After a light rain, only the tree's leaves get wet; the bark stays dry. In a heavier rain, however, water may run down the bark and the epiphyllum's roots may capture some of it, but they must be quick because the bark will dry out just hours after the rain stops. Even the sandiest, rockiest soil is better at retaining moisture. Although bark is organic, which we tend to think of as healthful, it contains cork and is thus virtually inert. The rainwater that *Epiphyllum* absorbs has been able to extract very few minerals from the bark as it trickles down the tree's branches.

Even in the dark we have no difficulty confirming this plant as *Epiphyllum*, one of the few cacti that are spineless. To be more precise, the very young seedlings have a few delicate spines, and the older plants have spines that are so short they do not protrude above the stem's surface. We cannot even feel the spines and must use a microscope to see them. Epiphyllums have only two ribs, so the stems appear flat and leaflike. As soon as we touch the plants, we know we have *Epiphyllum*, and in this area it can only be *Epiphyllum phyllanthus*.

Our surprise at finding an epiphytic cactus in this dry habitat is justified because the plant has many dead branches. It grew well when rain was available, but then had to let parts of itself die when drought set in. Although this produces a ratty-looking plant, it is actually a sophisticated adaptation. Rather than trying to maintain all of itself alive and hydrated, it lets certain branches die and redirects the little water it has to only one or two branches. It is better for only a fragment of the plant to survive than for all of it to die. This phenomenon occurs in another epiphytic cactus, *Lepismium*, which often looks awful in cultivation (betraying, no doubt, our occasional failure to water it). In contrast, the Brazilian epiphytic cactus *Hatiora* is much more discreet: if it must let a branch die, it cuts the branch off (it abscises the branch) and lets it fall. This self-pruning keeps rotting parts away from healthy ones, and cultivated plants always look good, regardless of their caretaker's forgetful ways.

Epiphyllums have spectacular night-blooming flowers, but we have even better luck—this plant has a fully mature, ripe fruit that is the size of a small egg (almost 2½ inches [about 6 cm]) long and full of black seeds. A sticky pulp envelops the seeds, but we will be able to clean the seeds and use them for cultivation. Little do we know that every seed will germinate and quickly produce hundreds of vigorous seedlings. The plants can bloom when only about a year old, after which they flower prolifically. Because they are self-fertile, almost every open flower results in a brilliant red-pink fruit that lasts for weeks, giving a plant

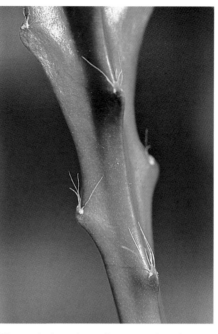

The newly formed, rapidly growing branch of an *Epiphyllum* hybrid starts from a bud and grows with four ribs. The bristlelike spines are true spines, but are sometimes called bristles. All cacti produce leaves, and although most are microscopic, you may be able to see a real cactus leaf just below each of this plant's areoles.

as much or more color than do the short-lived flowers. We feel very lucky to have found *Epiphyllum*, especially as nice a species as *E. phyllanthus*.

Our first few days have brought surprising rewards: cacti where it seemed too wet, still more where it seemed too dry. We may have timed our trip perfectly because we have had only beautiful blue sky. Bolivia, like Montana, is big sky country. Looking at the clear blue above us, we wonder if perhaps we have never before experienced truly clean air—no dust, no pollution, no imperfections at all.

As we continue from Concepción to San Ignacio de Velasco, the vegetation around us remains thick and green. Obviously this is not cactus coun-

Flowers of *Epiphyllum oxypetalum* are spectacular,
and although the genus *Epiphyllum* has only a
few species, they have been used extensively
for crosses to produce beautiful hybrids.
In nursery catalogs, plants of *Epiphyllum* and
their hybrids are often listed as "orchid cacti."

try, and yet the occasional protrusions of *Cereus stenogonus* remind us that many cacti actually do call this area home. When we stop to botanize, we do not come across any new cacti, only the familiar friends from the last few days. Yet we are not disappointed because we are in plant heaven, with lakes and marshes further contributing to the abundance of plant life. Giant cassias are covered in sprays of yellow flowers, and in low areas with standing water, there is a morning glory (*Ipomoea carnea*). They are not the vines we are accustomed to but are woody bushes. Species of *Bauhinia* abound. These shrubs and small trees of the legume family are easily recognizable because each leaf has two identical lobes. Every variety of *Bauhinia* leaf is somehow more beautiful than the last. These would certainly make superb plants for landscaping, and a plant collector could quickly gather numerous species for introduction to the horticultural trade. He would, however, have to avoid being distracted by the dozens of mallows.

At San Ignacio, we stop for lunch and check the map. We had planned on heading south toward San José de Chiquitos, where the vegetation, called the *chaco*, becomes much drier, more brushy than forested, and boasts an abundance of cacti. Because the restaurant we choose is Brazilian, we are tempted to drive north to Mato Grosso in Brazil, another area rich in cacti. However, we are advised that the road northward is barely a trail, has no towns alongside it for hundreds of miles, is almost devoid of traffic, and is sus-

All species in *Bauhinia* have leaves with twin lobes.
This species and many others would be good as landscaping and accent plants in the garden.

ceptible to robbers who prey on those who travel without an army escort. Our original plan of driving south to San José looks very appealing again!

After spending the night in San José de Chiquitos, we cross the *serranía*, the small mountain range to the south of the city, and enter chaco vegetation. The vegetation looks slightly drier; it is shorter and shrubbier, and not easy to walk through. Few plants are big trees; most are only 10 to 12 feet (3 to 4 m) tall and grow so close together that branches are always in our way when we try to search for cacti. Many plants have spines, not only the cacti. The temperature is high and so is the humidity, giving the place the feeling of south Texas in summer. This area is much richer in cacti than the region around Concepción. The presence of species of *Castellanosia*, *Cleistocactus*, *Echinopsis*, *Gymnocalycium*, *Harrisia*, *Monvillea*, and *Stetsonia* all growing within sight of each other keeps us excited and enthusiastic. With such an abundance of cacti beside the road, we do not have to torture ourselves by exploring deep into the brush. We have a great time photographing, collecting, measuring, and obtaining fruits and seeds, and we are lucky enough to come across a ranch house where we get some shade, water, and rest. We also

Tall plants of *Stetsonia coryne* and clear blue skies indicate that we are in the chaco region where the soil is thick but not rocky, and where humid, wet seasons alternate with those that are hot and dry. The area resembles southern Texas, where humidity from the Gulf of Mexico helps create dense vegetation of small trees and shrubs that are difficult to walk through.

The genus *Castellanosia* was created by the Bolivian botanist M. Cárdenas in 1951
for just one species, *C. caineana*. Unlike the species of *Browningia*, *C. caineana*
begins to produce longer spines once it is old enough to flower.
Castellanosia caineana is fairly widespread; this one was photographed in western Paraguay.

receive a nasty surprise—the owner of the house is drying the skin of a *tigre*
he has just killed, and the meat is being dried to make *charqui*, or jaguar jerky.
There are many jaguars in the area attacking the cattle, including where we
had been collecting and paying attention only to plants. That afternoon's
botanizing is done from inside the pickup with the windows half rolled up.

Of the many new species and genera that we come across, *Cleistocactus*
merits special attention. It is a popular genus among hobbyists and horticul-
turists for several reasons. First, cleistocacti thrive on conditions ranging from
too dry to too wet, from very sunny to completely shaded; in other words,
almost any condition is just right. Jujuy in Argentina is almost completely
surrounded by rainforest and does not appear to be cactus habitat at all, yet
cleistocacti grow well there. *Cleistocactus hyalacanthus* will even thrive on
rocky outcrops that receive pouring rain, and in southern Bolivia, *C. baumannii* grows in full sun and drought.

A second reason for the popularity of cleistocacti must be their flowers.
The plants flower readily in cultivation and produce an abundance of bright

This fresh jaguar skin gave us pause.
The rancher had killed it in the same area where we had been collecting that morning,
and it was just one of many.

red or yellow tubular flowers (those of *Cleistocactus smaragdiflorus* are green-tipped) that frequently develop into fruits through self-pollination. The term "cleisto" in the genus name *Cleistocactus* means "hidden" or "closed," and although the flowers are rather large, they never open wide. Instead of bending outward, *Cleistocactus* petals tend to remain tightly clustered; many of the species' flowers are almost completely closed. They are easy to recognize with their slender, tallish stems and numerous low ribs.

A final point of interest about *Cleistocactus* is the variability of its spines. For example, *C. strausii* has so many long white spines that the green stem is almost completely hidden, whereas stems of *C. horstii* are nearly naked. And yet both are in the genus *Cleistocactus*. This variability of spines often raises doubts about whether a particular plant belongs to *Cleistocactus* or not.

We decide to set out to the east from San José de Chiquitos. We could not have continued farther south because the road beyond the ranch house had become an overgrown trail and there were no towns in that direction

Petals of *Cleistocactus baumannii* are typical of *Cleistocactus* flowers in that they project forward such that the flower barely opens. The flower tube is also bent twice, near the base and the tip. This seed-grown plant bloomed when less than two years old and now produces dozens of flowers all summer long every year. If cross-pollinated, it produces red fruits the size of a cherry in only a few weeks.

where we could spend the night. We soon discover that we cannot go as far to the east as we would like because of flooding near the Paraguayan border, even though the road is good (it is a dirt road—we will not see pavement again until we return to Santa Cruz) and the area worth observing. Because we do not cross the serranía south of San José de Chiquitos, we find ourselves not in chaco but in a taller, more damp forest similar to the one nearer Santa Cruz. The plants here should be similar to those we have seen earlier, but there is still a particularly important cactus that we have not yet encountered, *Pereskia*.

Why is it that people who spend their lives studying cacti should be so desperate to see plants of the one cactus genus that is the least cactuslike? Pereskias do not look anything like cacti. They are medium-sized trees with a good, hard, woody trunk and big, slightly fleshy leaves. They have virtually no succulence. The ferocious spines on their trunk and branches are a sign that something is amiss with these trees, but no one would look at a pereskia

Plants of *Cleistocactus*, like these *C. strausii*, almost always appear healthy and beautiful, whether growing in nature or, as here, in the ideal conditions of Huntington Botanical Gardens in San Marino, California. The abundant long spines have remained a pristine white although most are many years old. The numerous small white bumps on the stems are flower buds that are still a few weeks away from opening.

and think *cactus*. The plants that were the ancestors of cacti and that began evolving into cacti millions of years ago were, of course, not themselves cacti. We think they were trees similar to pereskias but that they lacked spines and had thinner, more ordinary leaves. After only a few evolutionary changes they developed spines and fleshy leaves, and had there been any plant taxonomists back then, those plants might have been classified as *Pereskia*. Further evolutionary changes occurred within most of those plants, perhaps producing more succulent stems and smaller leaves until the plants looked more like cacti. Further diversification saw some plants evolving into opuntias, others into cerei, echinopsises, fraileas, stetsonias, and so forth.

Some plants, however, changed very little and continued to strongly resemble the ancestral plants. These relatively unchanged plants are the pereskias. Perhaps their treelike form and large leaves made them well adapted to conditions (such as those here in southeast Bolivia) that are not too dry. Everywhere around us are real trees with real leaves, and if they are

Pereskias are not desert plants by any means and would probably die quickly if planted
in even the wettest part of Arizona. This is the habitat of *Pereskia sacharosa*
(many trees here, except the tallest tree on the left, are pereskias),
and although it is moist enough to be this green, it does have a seasonal drought
during which *Pereskia* survives by dropping its leaves.

able to thrive here, why should treelike, leafy cacti not also thrive? Pereskias
have not remained static or arrived at an evolutionary dead end: there are
seventeen species of *Pereskia*, some with smaller, bushlike bodies, others with
tiny leaves that fall off during droughts, and still others that have a small
amount of water-storage tissues in their stems. The genus is widespread,
occurring in Florida, throughout the Caribbean, along the north coast of
South America, on the eastern Andes in Brazil, and in Paraguay, Uruguay,
Bolivia, and Argentina.

A group of plants that appears to have changed so little over the years is
a great resource for studying the family. *Pereskia*'s wood was studied extensively in the 1950s and '60s by I. W. Bailey of Harvard. He discovered that
Pereskia wood, like that of many other trees, has few modifications that are
useful in really dry habitats. Its epidermis, cortex (the soft tissue just beneath
the epidermis), and pith differ from those of more typical cacti, and by studying these tissues in *Pereskia*, we can reconstruct the evolutionary changes

Flowers of *Pereskia grandifolia* are large and resemble roses.
They are good ornamental plants for areas that receive only a few moderate frosts.
Although they do not seem to bloom abundantly, each flower is very nice.
Like most cactus flowers, however, each is open for only one day.

that must have occurred as members of the cactus family gradually adapted to deserts.

At San José de Chiquitos we find *Pereskia sacharosa*, the species with the largest plants. These are full-size trees up to 20 feet (6 m) tall with spreading branches. The branches are ungainly, forking infrequently and at odd angles, one branch extending through the crown of a neighboring tree, another branch jutting into open air. Trees of *P. sacharosa* must produce only one flower per week over many months because the plants here have open flowers as well as ripe fruits full of shiny, black seeds. We harvest fruits and seeds, and it is not long before we have a mini-plantation of *P. sacharosa* plants growing in central Texas. Rather surprisingly, the plants easily survive heavy frosts, including a good freeze lasting several days (down to 22°F [-6°C]). For some reason, pereskias are not often included in the hobbyists' cactus collec-

Flowers of most cacti have inferior ovaries, meaning that stem tissue grows around
the base of the flower. Consequently, the flower appears to bear leaves with buds.
In pereskias and opuntias, such as the chain-fruit cholla (*Opuntia fulgida*),
the buds can flower, and there are flowers emerging from fruits,
which results in young fruits hanging from older fruits.
No plants other than cacti have this growth form.
These are ripe fruits of *P. sacharosa*.

tions or used for landscaping, but their flowers are wonderful in their similarity to wild roses, and their leaves are also attractive.

Farther east beyond the pereskias, the terrain becomes more hilly and the forest denser. We explore the woods where the soil is moist and cool, and the air dark. It is difficult to understand how cacti could survive here where their companions are orchids, philodendrons, and ferns. There are snakelike shoots of *Monvillea* and *Harrisia* everywhere around us—on the ground, climbing up trees, hanging from branches. They are a sorry sight, thin and scraggly, broken in two or rotting apart, small bits and pieces scattered everywhere. We are almost unable to tell plants of *Monvillea* apart from those of *Harrisia* because they are completely without flowers and fruits in this heavy shade. Both plants consist of anemic narrow stems with a few puny ribs and unremarkable spines. During the dry season when the trees lose their leaves, the forest floor will be much sunnier, and the cacti will have to take advantage of their brief opportunity for photosynthesis. When they grow in full sunlight, plants of each species develop stronger, more robust ribs and spines on thicker stems. They become easily distinguishable from one another when they bear fruit: those of *Monvillea* are smooth, while *Harrisia* fruits have scales. In Peru we will have similar trouble distinguishing non-flowering stems of *Monvillea* from those of *Rauhocereus*.

We climb to the top of a hill from where we can see extensive woodlands stretching in all directions. When we look closely, we can detect the tops of columnar *Cereus stenogonus*. Oddly angled branches with pink flowers betray the scattered presence of *Pereskia sacharosa*. As the sun lowers and dusk sets in, we find a broad laja covered with *Frailea uhligiana*. Once again we will not get to the hotel before dark.

The drive back from San José de Chiquitos to Santa Cruz is satisfying. We have had such great luck collecting so many species in so many genera. We stop to botanize occasionally but we know that we have found most of the cacti reported to be in this area, so we pay some attention to other things. Near Concepción we notice an *Obrignia* palm, a plant that indicates we are in a type of vegetation that is transitional to that of the Amazon basin. Although we have seen rain in many places almost every day, we have had the good fortune never to be rained on while out collecting. Storms mostly form in the afternoon, and rainfall is either brief and light, or brief and heavy. Surprisingly, the rain does not penetrate the soil deeply enough to stop the road from sending up clouds of dust as we drive along, but it does cleanse both the plants and the air. An afternoon shower temporarily replaces the hot, muggy air with a fresh, cool breeze. Puddles form and butterflies congregate at their edges, examining the mud with their proboscises and transforming the scene into a landscape of yellow and white polka dots. As we approach Santa Cruz from the northeast, mountains begin to loom in the west beyond the city. They are our next destination.

3

HIGHLANDS OF CENTRAL BOLIVIA:
Rain, Desert, and More Rain

O ur destination is the region of dry valleys in the mountains of central Bolivia. Santa Cruz is much like Denver. To its west the land rises and becomes a tremendous mountain range, while to the east of the city lies an extensive plain. Moist air from the Atlantic sweeps in from the east, rises, and drops rain on the mountain's lower slopes, but as the air descends into the mountain valleys, it compresses, warms, and retains its moisture. Wet and dry areas are separated by narrow mountain ridges that keep the floras distinct.

After a few days spent in Santa Cruz getting organized, consulting maps, and restocking supplies, we head out toward the southwest. The description we had read of the area is coming to life immediately. Only a few miles west of the city, the road begins climbing dramatically, and deep ravines drop away on either side of us as we climb through the valley of the Río Piray. Before long we are looking out across a broad valley at mountains, not yet the full Andes range, but mountains nonetheless. They are much bigger than the serranías of San José de Chiquitos and are the Serranía de Parabanon. Santa Cruz lies at about 1200 feet (370 m) above sea level, and after we have driven barely 50 miles (80 km), we are above 3600 feet (1100 m).

We arrive at the town of Samaipata hoping to find a very rare cactus, *Samaipaticereus*, but the information we have about its location—by the bridge in town—worries us. An urban location is risky because plants can be endangered by urban sprawl, development, flood control, or the sheer bad luck of being viewed as weeds in need of eradication. Samaipata is a small town with only one bridge, which makes our hunt much easier. But this one and only bridge does not have any *Samaipaticereus* near it. The area has been cleared and used for a variety of purposes, and no natural vegetation remains. We also have reports that *Acanthorhipsalis* has been collected here, but we conclude that must certainly be an error because this area is much too dry for delicate rainforest plants like acanthorhipsalises, which need even more moisture than the *Epiphyllum phyllanthus* from Concepción. We will find *Acanthorhipsalis* later, hundreds of miles to the south in an area that never dries out, but there is no chance that it was ever at home in Samaipata.

We leave Samaipata empty-handed and continue driving higher into the mountains toward the town of Pampa Grande. There are cleistocacti everywhere, as well as *Roseocereus*. *Roseocereus* has only a single species, *R. tephracantha*, and most people consider it to be more appropriately classified as *Harrisia tetracantha*. (All species of *Eriocereus* are often similarly placed into *Harrisia*.) These three genera certainly do resemble each other, but their differences cannot be dismissed lightly. Plants of *Roseocereus* are trees of medium height, whereas those of *Harrisia* and *Eriocereus* are smaller, shorter, and sprawling rather than upright. Additionally, harrisias grow in the Caribbean, while eriocerei grow in the central part of South America. There are hundreds of miles of Amazon rainforest separating the two.

We soon forget about taxonomy because we come across a house that is surrounded by an entire orchard of *Roseocereus* trees. The woman who lives here cultivates the trees for their large fruits, each about the size of a lemon and full of sweet pulp and crunchy black seeds. Fruits are abundant on the trees, though their dark, red skin is barely visible in the weak light of dusk. The fruit is called ulala, the woman tells us, and she generously gives us an entire bagfull and lets us take pieces of stem and wood for anatomical specimens. The fruit is indeed delicious, but we manage to save some seed for later cultivation. Although they have grown very well for us in the few years that we have cultivated them, they have developed into sprawling plants like

Flowers of *Roseocereus tephracantha* are large and have a long, thick tube, and long,
white petals. A plant can be covered in hundreds of flowers at one time,
which must look wonderful.

Harrisia guelichii rather than into upright trees. It could be because greenhouses do not provide the right conditions for normal growth. The plants
have giant, white, night-blooming flowers; an orchard of *Roseocereus* in full
bloom must be an astounding sight.

Our destination tonight is Pampa Grande, and we arrive, as is our cus-
tom, later than we had planned and well after dark. Pampa Grande is a small
village that is rather isolated high in the mountains. The arrival of strangers
provides the local folks with some entertainment, and we soon have a large
crowd watching us attentively. They seem baffled that anyone would come so
far just to look at plants, cacti especially, but they courteously give us room
and try not to interrupt us with questions. We can hear quiet conversations
within the crowd. The talk is in Quechua rather than Spanish so we do not
understand what they are saying, but the tone of the voices seems inquisitive,
not incredulous.

A small, nearby building serves many purposes, mostly as a meeting area,
but also as a restaurant. A hot meal is prepared for us—a stew of chicken and

These ripe, red fruits of *Roseocereus tephracantha*
will open when a hole along one side of the fruit
is formed, thus allowing birds and ants
to remove the sweet, white pulp
from the black seeds.

rice—with beer to drink. Food is always something to be careful about, but anything that has been boiled and served hot should be sterile; beer drunk directly from the bottle is safe. Of course, water, ice, and wet plates or silverware must be avoided by all visitors whose immune systems have not made peace with the local microbes. The meal here, served by lantern light, is excellent, and the next morning none of us has any problems.

After dinner we must do our evening work as always. Plants must be prepared, labeled, dissected, and photographed. We open *Roseocereus* fruits to begin gathering and cleaning the seeds.

Cleaning seeds from dry cactus fruits is simple: the fruits are broken open and the seeds picked out. Juicy, pulpy fruits, on the other hand, like those of *Roseocereus*, are more difficult—unless one knows the special technique. We scoop the seeds and pulp out of the fruit rind and place them into a cloth bag made either of fine mesh or taffeta paint-strainer bags, and then we massage, knead, and squeeze the bag using plenty of water. The pulp typically releases slimy mucilage, often in copious amounts and of a disgusting texture, but before long both mucilage and pulp will be washed away leaving the seeds clean. The seeds must be dried, and we typically tie the bag to the outside of the pickup and drive around South America for an hour or so to dry them. The clear, hot weather dries the *Roseocereus* seeds in minutes.

The plaza of Pampa Grande provides ample flat spaces where we spread out all our equipment and supplies. There is a water faucet we can use to wash seeds, but there is no electricity at this hour. The generator has been turned off to save costly fuel, so we bring the kerosene lanterns from the restaurant with us to the plaza. The entire crowd comes too. They are fascinated with our work, and this allows our professorial sides to come forward. We describe what we are doing and why, and volunteers generously help with various tasks. Even though we must concentrate and keep busy to get all our work done, the magic of the evening is palpable. We are high in the mountains, the night air is cold, the faces that surround us are purely Inca (but the clothing worn is modern), the language spoken is Quechua, and the buildings around us evoke colonial times.

The priest of Pampa Grande, Fray Andres Langer, knows the local plants well. He is familiar with the cacti we are looking for, even with *Samaipaticereus*, and he volunteers to guide us to the various sites in the morning. His assistance turns out to be vital because many plants occur only in a few localities, and it would be almost impossible to find them on our own. For example, Fray Langer leads us to a ravine beside a narrow road and signals us to stop at a particular point. The ravine is almost completely overgrown with trees, and there is no real sign of cacti. Beside the road is a tall plant of *Cleistocactus*, and although it is impressively large, it is not the specimen of *Samaipaticereus* we are seeking. Fray Langer next leads us to a path that descends into the ravine, veers a little to the right, a little to the left, then continues slightly farther until—there it is, a lone plant of *Samaipaticereus*.

Why go through so much trouble for this particular cactus? Even if you are familiar with cacti and succulents, there is a good chance you have never heard of this genus. It has only two species, *Samaipaticereus corroanus* and *S. inquisivensis*, neither of which is commonly cultivated (it has been suggested that the second species be placed in its own genus as *Yungasocereus inquisivensis*). Certainly all cacti are beautiful, but in some, the beauty is an inner rather than an exterior one. The specimen of *S. corroanus* here would probably not win any "Best of Show" awards; it is an awkward tangle of slender shoots sprawling through the branches of the surrounding trees. Because its shoots go in all directions, it takes us a while to be certain that it is a single

These branches of *Samaipaticereus corroanus*
support themselves only initially; they will soon
become tangled in tree branches,
and afterward will produce very weak wood.

plant. Surprisingly, all these branches of *Samaipaticereus* converge at the cactus' single trunk. The trunk is a real one in that it is several feet tall, about 5 inches (12.5 cm) in diameter, hard, woody, and covered in bark. In contrast, the branches are narrow, green, and flexible, not at all hard or woody, and their low ribs bear short spines. The trunk and branches do not seem to belong to the same plant.

By cutting a branch in two, we confirm our suspicions that *Samaipaticereus corroanus* has dimorphic wood, and we confirm that our efforts to find the plant were worth the trouble. By *dimorphic wood* we mean that a plant produces two types of wood. Whether growing upright as a trunk or at an angle as a young branch, every shoot must be strong enough to support its own weight. Each shoot produces a type of wood composed mostly of fibers that make the shoot strong enough to hold itself up as long as it is not too heavy. This type of wood is similar to that found in *Pachycereus*, *Pereskia*, *Trichocereus*, and other large cacti. As a branch of *Samaipaticereus* continues to grow, its weight becomes too much for even this wood, and the branch sags until it rests on the branch of a tree. When that happens, the tree is forced to do all the work of supporting the branch of *Samaipaticereus*, thus allowing the cactus to produce a much weaker wood that lacks fibers. It requires a great deal of energy to make strong wood and only a little to make weak wood. By leaning on a tree, *Samaipaticereus* can get by with producing weak wood, and the energy it saves can be used for other activities, such as further growth,

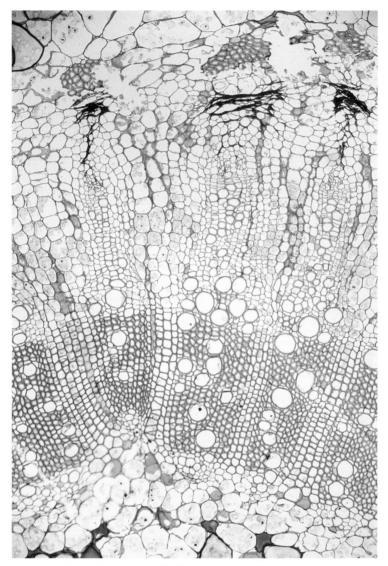

This is dimorphic wood of the type found in *Samaipaticereus*.
When the stem was young, it produced the wood at its center
(the dark red-purple band). The color is dark because of the many thick-walled
fiber cells that give the wood its strength. The white circles are
the water-conducting cells called vessels. When the stem was older and wider,
it produced the bluish wood. It is blue because the cells have only thin,
weak walls, and there are only a few vessels (the small red circles).
Most trees or shrubs produce only strong, fibrous wood.

flowering, and fruit production. This arrangement is clearly advantageous for *Samaipaticereus*, but what about the tree? It now has to spend more energy making wood strong enough to hold up not only its own branches but also those of the cactus, so it has less energy left to make its own leaves, flowers, and fruits. Perhaps in return the tree gains some protection from hungry animals who are deterred by the spiny cactus growing in it.

It is unfortunate that this plant of *Samaipaticereus* has no flowers or fruits, particularly since it would have been good to find seeds for propagation. Both species of *Samaipaticereus* are rare in cultivation and can be found only at a few specialist cactus gardens. This is true also for several other cacti that are not pretty enough to be popular with us enthusiasts. The plants in one garden are often cuttings from plants of another garden, and those in turn were cuttings from a third garden. While it may appear that there are at least three plants in cultivation, in fact there is really only one plant with pieces of itself growing in three different places. It is like trying to understand human biology by studying only one or two individuals—we can learn something valuable, but our understanding would be so much greater if we could study ten or twenty people. Trying to maintain a healthy population of plants in botanical gardens by starting with only two individuals is almost impossible—the offspring would need to breed with each other or with the parents, and the next generation of offspring would also need to interbreed. Before long genetic problems would appear. Even if we had found only ten or twenty seeds, we could have greatly increased the genetic resources for cultivation of *S. corroanus*. The lack of fruits on this specimen is a real disappointment.

Fray Langer also keeps us from missing the location of *Gymnocalycium pflanzii* and *Weingartia neocumingii*. He directs us to a field that ends in an uncultivated natural area, and about a quarter mile (less than half a kilometer) beyond that, a rocky hill protrudes above the shrubby vegetation. The cacti are on the hill. We set out while Fray Langer attends to some other business with a promise that he will soon return and check on us. Getting through the field is easy enough, even for a bunch of city slickers, but the brushy area beyond can only be described as a spine forest. Not a single plant is without spines. Much of the ground is covered with a bromeliad whose tough, leathery leaves all point upward and all end in fierce needles. The shrubs are acacias, nasty members of the legume family, and spines adorn every part of the branches and twigs. Every few yards we come to a clearing and think our troubles are over, but once inside the clearing, we see no way out, not even where we just entered. It probably takes only about forty-five minutes to fight our way to the hill, but it seems much, much longer.

At the base of the hill where soil gives way to rock, huge plants of *Gymnocalycium pflanzii* grow in profusion. Their site is very restricted; they are neither in the deep soil in the flat shrubby area, where water held too long after a rain encourages fungal infections, nor are they on the hill itself, where it is so rocky and porous that rain drains away too quickly for roots to capture any moisture. The gymnocalyciums grow where the soil and rock mix together. Rain running off the big rocks drains toward the gymnocalyciums (even a light rain will give them some moisture), but the combination of rocks and soil provides good drainage. As with the fraileas at the lajas, only a very narrow region is suitable for these cacti.

The gymnocalyciums are clearly happy in this narrow region. They are huge balls up to 6 inches (15 cm) in diameter and 7½ inches (19 cm) tall. The plants are the picture of health, yet when we cut them open later, we find large tubular holes inside that reveal what appear to be rotten areas. These rotten-looking parts are common in large gymnocalyciums, both those in nature and in cultivation. The holes look as if a grub has burrowed through the plants, and often there is crumbly, dark material in the tube. The tubes themselves are lined with bark because the plant detects the damage and activates its cells to put down a layer of wound bark that protects the rest of the plant. Although we have seen these tubes in many gymnocalyciums, we have never seen grubs or any other insects inside the plants. It may be that this is some sort of natural process that the plant goes through even though it is healthy. But the tubes look so odd it is difficult to believe this hypothesis.

Weingartia neocumingii compete with terrestrial bromeliads for space.
The weingartias occur mostly in the shade of large acacia trees in a heavily forested area.
There is soil where large numbers of *Gymnocalycium pflanzii* grow,
but the weingartias are found only on rocky areas.

We continue up the hill and soon find the weingartias. These occur in areas that are nothing more than cracks in solid rock, and like the gymnocalyciums, they love the shade and do not grow where the sun shines on them for long. Although the weingartias are also big, globose plants up to 8 inches (20 cm) long, their root system is too weak to support them, and they soon fall over. Yet that does not hurt the plants; it simply stabilizes them, and they continue to grow with their tip gradually turning upward. Some of the weingartias are too close to the edge of a rock ledge and have fallen off, and there they dangle by their roots with their upturned tips.

The gymnocalyciums and weingartias—and admittedly the shade—are so pleasant that we stay on the hill for a while, but we have to face recrossing the sharp, spiny, shrubby area to reach the road. We set off in a slightly different direction because anything has to be easier than the way we came. It is still a struggle, and when we reach the road, we console ourselves that all our puncture wounds, scratches, and blood prove that we are pretty darn

Weingartias flower easily and profusely in cultivation. Individuals of *Weingartia lanata*
(lanata means "wool") grow quickly and with no fuss,
yet reward you with these beautiful flowers.

tough not to let anything stand in our way. Then we see Fray Langer and the
two students who have been traveling with us. They are clean, cool, and free
of scratches or wounds; not a hair is out of place as they carry a bag of cacti
they had just collected. Why, Fray Langer wants to know, had we not taken
the nice wide path that leads directly to the hill?

Fray Langer shows us the road toward Saipina and then bids us farewell.
After a few miles we reach the town of Mataral (it consists of three or four
houses, one restaurant, and a couple of fifty-gallon drums of gasoline) where
we find three more species that are a real delight. The first is an old friend by
now, *Pereskia sacharosa*. We had seen these plants east of San José de
Chiquitos growing among large trees in an area that was still receiving rain.
Those pereskias were large leafy plants that were difficult to see clearly
because of all the surrounding vegetation. Here, however, the rainy season
has long since ended, and although this region does not look like a stereo-
typical desert from a cowboy movie, it is definitely drier and hotter than in

the lowlands with few trees to hide the pereskias from view. The plants of *P. sacharosa* have mostly let their leaves fall and their branches are nearly naked. Their sparse, angular branching pattern is evident, as are their businesslike spines, and in this leafless condition it is much easier to accept the idea that these plants are indeed cacti. At San José the forest was so dense we could not be certain if the plants of *P. sacharosa* were abundant or rare because we could see nothing other than the few pereskias growing immediately beside the road. Here at Mataral there are few other trees to obscure our view, and we see that pereskias are plentiful; we have the impression that we are in a leafless orchard.

The capacity of *Pereskia sacharosa* to abscise its leaves during dry seasons (technically known as drought deciduousness) may warrant investigation. The plants of this species grown from the seed we collected on this trip have thrived in Austin, Texas, and during the worst of our summers, the plants have kept their leaves and appeared healthy. So far, they have lost their foliage only after autumn frosts. Apparently the leaves are not such a water loss liability that the plants will sacrifice them during mild, ordinary summer dry spells.

The second species in Mataral is *Pereskia diaz-romeroana*, a close relative of *P. sacharosa*, but it is a species whose plants are small, its leaves shorter than its name. These cacti rarely grow larger than a small shrub and can be easily cultivated as potted plants. They do not require perfect conditions to grow and can wait until they are almost dead before needing a good watering. Their flowers are only about ½ inch (1.25 cm) across but they are bright purple and abundant. It seems that the plants use any excuse to flower. The flowers are self-fertile and do not need to be cross-pollinated—flowering is soon followed by the appearance of many pea-sized black berries, each containing one or two seeds that germinate easily and grow quickly. Plants of *P. diaz-romeroana* are not common in cactus collections but are highly recommended since they can be pruned to grow as small plants suitable for 8-inch pots.

Here at Mataral, *Pereskia diaz-romeroana* plants grow to about 3 feet (1 m) tall and their slender branches arch gracefully. They are too short to cre-

The arching branches with small leaves
in the center of the photograph
belong to plants of *Pereskia diaz-romeroana*
growing near Saipina, Bolivia.
Even though it has virtually no
water-storing succulent tissue, it survives
droughts by letting its leaves fall when
there is not enough water. Because it
blooms quickly, it is the ideal pereskia
for newcomers to the species.

Flowers of *Pereskia diaz-romeroana* are small but striking. Without any encouragement,
these plants will bloom often, not with masses of flowers, but with a few every
couple of weeks. And they almost invariably produce small black fruits about the size of a
blueberry, each containing a few seeds that will grow if given a little care.

ate a thicket and too sparse to create a tangle that is difficult to walk through. Our clothing protects us from their short spines as we brush by. Their short, thick trunks are out of proportion with the rest of the plant because when branches die back in really severe droughts, the plants resprout from the base after a rain. Such dieback and resprouting corresponds with our experience with cultivated plants of *P. diaz-romeroana*, whose stems are always slender and who, unlike *P. sacharosa*, quickly lose their leaves if unwatered for just two or three weeks. After longer dry periods, whole stems die back to the base, but a good watering will bring hidden buds to life. Unfortunately, there are no fruits or seeds on the plants here. Again, it would be nice to bring back more seeds for genetic diversity, particularly since taking cuttings is out of the question. While cuttings of most cacti can survive for months rolled up in newspapers and packed in the back of a pickup, those of *Pereskia* dry out and die very quickly.

The third species we come across in Mataral is a real treasure, *Neoraimondia herzogiana*, often called *Neocardenasia herzogiana*. These are giant columnar cacti that at first glance look like the big saguaros (*Carnegiea gigantea*) of Arizona. They have a broad trunk about 3 feet (1 m) tall and many thick arms that arch upward. All stems are bright green and covered with prominent ribs that bear spine clusters. The spine clusters are huge, much larger than ordinary areoles. A key feature of neocardenasias is that their spine clusters produce new spines and flowers every year, each spine cluster therefore growing longer every year. This is really an amazing sight because it is an unusual type of growth in the cactus family. Morphologists have concluded that areoles are axillary buds that, rather than growing out as a long, ordinary branch, grow only slightly to form an organ called a short shoot. Areoles of most cacti, however, are so tiny that there is no obvious shootlike organization to the areole. Yet when we cut open a long areole of *N. herzogiana*, its anatomy is that of a real stem. It even has a small amount of wood, pith, and cortex.

Far to the west, plants of *Neoraimondia* in Peru also have elongate areoles like this. It is such an unusual feature that most cactus taxonomists have concluded that *Neocardenasia* is so closely related to *Neoraimondia* that its single

This stand of *Neoraimondia* (*Neocardenasia*) *herzogiana* near Mataral, Bolivia, highlights an important feature: unlike other neoraimondias, plants of *N. herzogiana* have a trunk. They do not branch from the base but from several feet above ground. There was a little burro with us, and anything without spines would not have lasted long.

This close-up of an elongate areole of *Neoraimondia herzogiana* shows the long, stout spines that were produced in the first year at the bottom of the areole. In subsequent years, the areole produces flowers, hairs, and bristlelike spines that are not strong. The little bits of areole stem produced each year finally build up until the areole becomes this prominent and no longer level with the stem surface.

species, *Neocardenasia herzogiana*, would be more accurately classified as *Neoraimondia herzogiana*. Curt Backeberg, the prolific German cactus specialist who has written a six-volume magnum opus *Die Cactaceae*, created the genus *Neocardenasia* for just this one species primarily because plants of *Neocardenasia herzogiana* occur in Bolivia, whereas the neoraimondias are confined to Peru. While this reasoning is adequate for declaring a population to be a distinct species, it is not sufficient for declaring a distinct genus. The samples we collect here will be used in a study that supports the hypothesis that a separate genus is not needed for this species.

Two biological explanations exist for the geographical separation of *Neocardenasia herzogiana* on the east side of the Andes from *Neoraimondia* on the west side. One possibility is that recently (within the last several hundred thousand years), a bird carried seeds from plants of *Neoraimondia* in Peru to Bolivia where they germinated and became established. If this hypothesis is accurate, however, plants of *Neocardenasia herzogiana* should strongly resemble those of the Peruvian species of *Neoraimondia*, but they do not.

A second theory for this geographical separation is that very long ago (up to a few million years), the genus *Neoraimondia* was much more widespread than it presently is, occurring throughout Peru and Bolivia and perhaps also in Chile. Its wide dispersion would have been possible because the Andes were once considerably lower and not as inhospitable. Although numerous small mountains may have existed in the area, there could have been many low, dry valleys populated by neoraimondias. But as the Andes continued to rise (they are still rising today), these habitats were elevated, they grew colder, and their populations of *Neoraimondia* became extinct. *Neocardenasia herzogiana* would have become the only eastern survivor of the genus, separated from its closest relatives by thousands of miles.

At this point in our journey, it is worth pausing to compare the spine clusters of these two genera in order to learn more about the relationship between the neocardenasias in Bolivia and the neoraimondias in Peru, and indeed, about the cactus family as a whole.

SPINE CLUSTERS

A reoles not only provide insight into the relationship between the neocardenasias in Bolivia and the neoraimondias in Peru, but as they are the defining characteristic of the cactus, they are also fundamental to our understanding of the family. All cacti have spine clusters, but no species of any other plant family does. Moreover, the biology of areoles provides a clearer picture of the wide-ranging modifications that can occur when plants are evolving in extreme environmental conditions.

The shoots of cacti—the body we see when we look at a cactus—correspond to the shoots of other plants, and although we often say cactus shoots are leafless, that is not completely accurate. Cactus stems do make leaves, but most are so small that you would need a microscope to see them. You do not, however, need a microscope to see leaves of *Matucana aureiflora*, *Opuntia*, or *Pereskia*. In most seed plants (as opposed to plants like ferns), there is a bud slightly above every leaf, some of which are quite large and easily visible. In most plants with buds, the buds are dormant for months or years at a time and are protected by bud scales. When the buds burst open, they develop into flowers or branches. The new branches usually look like the trunk and the other branches on the plant.

Cacti are different because their axillary buds do not go through a dormant period. They instead begin developing as soon as they are initiated. The buds also make leaves, but the leaves develop in a highly modified form as spines. While only a few buds ever grow out as branches in a non-cactus plant, every bud of a cactus grows as a leafy branch, but because it is a cactus, the branches are very, very short and the leaves are spines. Cacti therefore have two types of shoots and leaves: the ordinary body (called a long shoot) with microscopic leaves, and the buds

This plant of *Austrocylindropuntia subulata* is being cultivated outdoors in Austin, Texas.
The deer have eaten the long leaves as far as they can, exactly to the point where their noses
touch the spines. The green leaves are the leaves of the long shoots,
and the spines just above each leaf are the modified leaves of the short shoots.

This young pad (or flattened long shoot)
of *Opuntia violacea* shows the full sequence
of shoot development. The original pad
(bottom of the photograph) contains
several spine clusters (short shoots) that
produced leaves (modified as spines) the
previous year. The spine clusters then
became dormant and remained clusters
of one-year-old spines. Only the spine
cluster at the top reactivated; it grows
out as a branch, changing from a short
to a long shoot, and makes ordinary
green leaves rather than spines.
Slightly above each new leaf
is a little bud — a short shoot—
and each of those is making spine-leaves.
A few new buds will grow out the
following year as more branches; others
will develop into flowers. Most, however,
will remain dormant forever.

Species of *Matucana* have some of the most prominent leaves on cactus bodies,
though they do not equal those of pereskias and opuntias. The leaf at the base of each areole
is clearly visible on this shoot apex. As the body grows,
the leaf may be stretched so much that it will be difficult to see.
This plant of *Matucana aureiflora* was photographed at the Jardin Exotique, Monaco.

Each of these gigantic areoles of
Neoraimondia roseiflora is about 4 inches
(10 cm) long and almost 1 inch (2.5 cm)
in diameter. They still bear hairs and a
spine or two at the tip, but the hairs have
fallen off the older parts at the base,
and most of their surface is covered with
bark. Areoles are called short shoots
because each areole will produce several
flowers during the next blooming season,
growing longer in the process.
Areoles of *N. herzogiana* are similar,
though usually not as long.

(called short shoots) with spines for leaves. Quite a few species outside the cactus family have both long and short shoots (for example, the spur shoots on apple trees, larches, and ginkgoes are short shoots). Early botanists did not realize the spine clusters in cacti are simply short shoots, so the name "areole" was given to them. It is still used today.

Areoles of most cacti produce only a few spines (some produce just a single spine because they are short shoots with only one leaf) before becoming dormant. When they are reactivated, they bloom as flowers, which, if pollinated become a fruit. Some areoles then die, but in *Opuntia*, for example, some areoles on old trunks and branches remain alive and produce one or two new spines every year. Young areoles of *Opuntia* have a few spines, while the older ones have many.

The short shoots, or areoles, of the neoraimondias (including *Neoraimondia herzogiana*) produce both new spines and flowers every year. They somehow have enough vigor to make shoot tissue, spines, and flower buds repeatedly. Each time they make only a tiny bit of shoot—they are short shoots, after all—but after a few years the areole is not so tiny anymore. The areole becomes longer and, atypically for areoles, protrudes above the surface of the green long shoot. After many years, the areole may be 1 inch (2.5 cm) long; even from a distance, the stems look lumpy. The areoles of the Peruvian neoraimondias are especially vigorous and may become several inches long; some may even branch. The anatomy of an areole is that of a shoot: an outer cortex, a ring of vascular bundles with wood, and a central pith.

The plants of *Neocardenasia*—and their areoles—contribute so much to our knowledge of cacti that we would like to stay in Mataral for as long as possible. Once we leave this area, we may never again see a mature, full-grown specimen of *Neocardenasia*; as far as we know, there are none in any botanical garden. We must make do, however, with collecting all the necessary samples and taking as many photographs as possible before we continue traveling to Saipina as planned. We have a quick lunch before buying gasoline that is hand-pumped out of a fifty-gallon drum—always a good way to mess up a carburetor—that serves as the only gas station. As we drive toward Saipina, we cross a pass that provides a stunning view of the beautiful valley of the Río Mizque. There are occasional cacti, more *Pereskia diaz-romeroana*, a parodia, and a corryocactus, but nothing too noteworthy. Because we are not encountering any showstoppers, we decide to turn around before Saipina and head to our next destination, Vallegrande, a town high in the mountains. The Río Mizque valley is very hot and dry, and if we slow down even a bit, we are enveloped in billowing clouds of dust stirred up by our pickup. It is too dusty to keep the windows down, but too hot to keep them up. Plant collecting really is one glamorous adventure after another.

We have to backtrack through Mataral, retracing our entire route of the afternoon. Retracing a route is not an efficient use of time because we have already seen the area. Returning by a different road would allow us to explore more territory, but there is no other road within several hundred miles. This point may be difficult for a North American or European to truly comprehend; by "no other road" we mean there are not even trails (we are on a dirt road already) or paths. There are no cities or individual houses. Vast areas that stretch for hundreds of square miles (imagine areas the size of Connecticut or New Hampshire) are completely inaccessible except on foot or by horse. A plant explorer would need to carry all food, water, and other supplies necessary for several months to trek through this rough country. Most parts of Mexico have been traversed dozens of times by professional and amateur cactus collectors, yet new species, including the new genus

Geohintonia, are being discovered even in areas where we were confident that the flora was well cataloged. When we look out from horizon to horizon, we doubt that any cactus explorer—perhaps any biologist—has ever searched the myriad valleys and mountains that we are now seeing. The number of undiscovered cactus species in South America must be staggering.

We will, as usual, be late arriving at Vallegrande, and as the sun sets, the sky fills with clouds. Before long, lightning is flashing everywhere, but no rain falls. There is nothing to either cool us down or settle the dust. We remind ourselves of the assurances that Vallegrande has a very nice hotel, Hotel Ganaderos (it is among the best we will find outside Santa Cruz). The road between Mataral and Vallegrande traverses steep mountains, and by now the night is completely black and illuminated only by lightning. We have not seen pavement since we left Santa Cruz, and this road is nothing but a strip of dirt and rock through the mountains. There are no guardrails, no lights, no reflectors, and as we peer into the darkness, we realize there is vegetation on one side of us and nothing at all on the other side. We drive even more slowly, intent on not missing a sudden turn in the road.

At last the lights of Vallegrande appear far below. We had not realized how high we'd climbed, about 6000 feet (1840 m) above sea level. An hour later at a little before midnight we are in the town. Hotel Ganaderos is full. We drive around and find a hotel that, as we learn the next morning, is best seen in the dark. Now we want a shower and dinner. Unfortunately for us, the city's water pumps are turned off every night after 10:00 P.M. to save fuel, so showers are not possible. At this hour, the only open restaurant is the SuperPollo #2—a very bright, plastic-filled, fast-food place. There are two good things about being dirty, tired, and hungry: the fried chicken is always delicious, and you can fall asleep almost anywhere.

At 5:00 A.M. it is time to work on the plants again. We were too tired the night before, so the work must be done in the morning. We spread our equipment out on the sidewalk under a streetlight. Before long, our strange activities attract the attention of patrolling police, but they are courteous and helpful. No one has ever given us a hard time on any of our plant-collecting trips in South America. Just as we are ready to begin working, the lightning, which had not let up throughout the night, is joined by rain. Lots of rain. We move our material into the hotel's courtyard where there is enough light for us to do our work, but now we are worried about driving again on the narrow dirt road that is already barely clinging to the side of a mountain. Rain is not good news.

We finish our work by the time the sun comes up and the city's water is turned back on. We shower and eat breakfast. It is remarkable how wonderful it feels to be clean and well fed. We load the pickup and set out, stopping by a *mercado* (market) to buy bottled water and food for lunch as there will be no towns for hundreds of miles. South America's mercados are excellent, and some vendors are no different from those of the earliest inhabitants, their corn, beans, herbs, spices, and cheeses set out for sale on blankets. Meat is very fresh (having been on the hoof only minutes before), and every part of the carcass is for sale. In the neighboring stall, someone may be selling electronic appliances, tape players, CDs, and the latest in fashionable blue jeans and T-shirts.

As we leave the city, we see the terrain we had missed the night before. Mountainsides, green and sodden from the rain, are little more than sheer drops all around us. The sky is hidden by diffuse gray clouds that rapidly envelop us in fog as they pass. We are astounded at the immensity of the mountains that suddenly become visible during a break in the clouds. Another mass of soft, swirling mist quickly obscures the view, however. Soon we are covered in dew, a reminder that only the day before we were coated in dust. The heavy forest is interrupted in many places by fields that have been cleared and cultivated. As with the terraced farmlands that climb mountainsides in southeast Asia, the natural vegetation here must take refuge in areas too steep or rocky for farmers to bother cultivating.

Our shoes quickly become soaked as we walk through grassy areas. We do not expect to find a single cactus, and we find none in any of these grasslands. But this too is cactus country. A small rocky outcrop shows itself, which means there must be some dryness. The clouds must part and the sun must shine sometime; when that happens, rock dries quickly and soon the thin soil beside it dries too. In the midst of all this moisture, there are islands

Rebutias are high altitude plants. They like cool temperatures where the ground stays moist,
but because there is so much rain and mist, they are confined to small rock outcrops
where the drainage is slightly better. These plants of *Rebutia donaldiana*
are growing among mosses and lichens.

of dryness, oases in reverse where we will find cacti: rebutias and aylosteras.
These little rock patches are scattered across the landscape, black dots in a
sea of green, each probably harboring a specimen or two of *Aylostera* or
Rebutia. Plants of both genera grow as small, round cacti no larger than a
golf ball, often producing many branches from near their base that are called
offsets because they can be cut off and planted to produce a new individual.
In nature, the offsets cluster around the base of the original plant and then
make their own offsets, resulting in large masses of diminutive pincushions.
The flowers, although also small, are big for the plants. They are produced
in such profusion that they completely hide the little green body below.
These are good cacti for places where little light is available, but they must
have bright shade and cool conditions or they will suffer terribly. Growing
them in a place like Arizona is almost impossible—you need shade cloth and
air conditioning rather than a greenhouse. Alpine cacti such as these also
need a nice breeze (like the one blowing the clouds across us here) because
they hate stagnant air. Not surprisingly, they thrive in San Francisco.

We come across a rebutia, probably *Rebutia donaldiana*, but without flowers it is difficult to be certain. It is a strange sensation to be wet while looking for cacti, to kneel down and feel the knees of your pants become soaked through, and to clear away the mosses that are hiding the cactus. Equally as disconcerting is having to use a two-second exposure despite the fast film, and then finding that it is impossible to record the photograph anyway because the notebook's pages are too damp. Strange, but also too wonderful for words.

As we continue driving, the clouds grow darker and the mist turns to rain more frequently. The road becomes wet, then muddy. Water runs off the mountainsides above us, flows across the road, then cascades down the other side of the mountain. The water has started to eat away at the roadbed, deeply in places. The Bolivian government built a new bridge across the Río Grande, so this is a newly built road through the mountains (though it was apparently constructed by bulldozers simply scraping away a little soil about a car and a half wide). When we meet the rare on-coming vehicle, one of us finds a wide spot and waits for the other to pass. This involves placing one set of wheels on the very edge of the precipice. Grasses and shrubs will, in time, grow on the side of the road, stabilizing and holding it to the side of the mountain, but right now it is still bare, crumbly dirt, and the rainwater runoff is eating into it. At more than one point, there is so little road left that even with the pickup crowding against the cliff face on one side, the wheels on the other side are not completely on the road. One of us decides to walk around these washed out parts of the road. We worry that the road ahead of us could be completely gone. We also worry that by the time we turn around, the road could be washed out behind us too. We would be trapped, and there would be no AAA to rescue us. We have seen no town for hours, although being forced to travel less than 15 miles per hour (25 kph) means we have gone only a few miles. Although we had to stack rocks in areas of washout to reconstruct the road in places, our luck holds and we make it through.

The road runs along a high ridge, a knife-edge really, between valleys. On our right are the valley we had such difficulty crossing and the green

Although small, rebutias are splendid when in bloom. Their flowers must be visible
to pollinators despite the tiny size of the plant and the abundance of grasses and herbs that
hide the cacti. This is *Rebutia glomeriseta* in cultivation at the Jardin Exotique
and photographed by Jean-Marie Solichon, director of the gardens.

mountain, still capped by a low gray sky just as it was when we collected
Rebutia earlier in the morning. On our left is our destination, a deep, broad
valley, brown and arid under a brilliant blue sky. From this altitude, the Río
Grande, at a point slightly south of its confluence with the Río Mizque, is a
barely visible, muddy-blue streak. How can two valleys so close to each other
be so different? The rain shadow effect is stark: green vegetation versus
brown; alpine versus low habitat; and meadowland versus desert. These differences extend up the two sides of the ridge we are driving along: one side is
wet, the other dry. Beside the road on the wet side is one of the few trees we
have seen all day, and in that tree is an epiphytic cactus, *Pfeiffera ianthothele*.
And it contains a ripe, seed-filled fruit.

Pfeiffera is one of many epiphytic cacti found growing in trees in wet
areas. It is closely related to several other epiphytic cacti such as *Lepismium*
and *Rhipsalis*, and they all have slender stems that are sometimes delicate.

This is a very healthy plant of *Pfeiffera ianthothele* hanging from a tree it shares with a bromeliad. With pendent stems, the plant's roots are above the branches and water is conducted downward. Epiphytic plants do not need to hold themselves up and so do not need to produce very much wood; it is surprising that more plants have not become epiphytic. These individuals of *P. ianthothele*, if propped up by being tied to a stake, would probably grow only poorly or not at all.

Pfeifferas generally have small flowers and fruits that are very different from those of *Epiphyllum*. Although they have spines, they are sometimes so short that they scarcely emerge above the hairs that surround them in the areoles. The short spines in these epiphytes must be an advanced feature because the ancestral cacti must have had good, strong spines like those of *Pereskia*. The spines are what makes this find of *Pfeiffera ianthothele* so exciting—they are real, observable, very sharp spines up to 1 inch (2.5 cm) long, and they project in all directions to give the plant real protection. Three features of this specimen of *Pfeiffera ianthothele* suggest a link between terrestrial spiny cacti and epiphytic "spineless" species. First, although this particular specimen is slightly more robust than many other epiphytes, it is not as robust as most terrestrial cacti. Second, although its wood is hard and tough to dissect, it does not produce as much wood as ground-dwelling cacti. And finally, of course, it has spines.

Fruits of *Pfeiffera ianthothele* are berries, meaning that all parts are juicy and without a rind
or pit. The fruit has areoles with spines, and the fruit wall is so thin
that vascular bundles are visible as a network of fine lines, a distinctive feature.

By studying *Pfeiffera ianthothele* closely, we are able to understand some
evolutionary steps taken by epiphytic cacti. At some point, the nature of the
fruits and seeds eaten by birds must have changed because birds began
depositing seeds from the fruit in trees rather than on the ground. Many epiphytic species have sticky seeds that adhere to a bird's beak, and when the
bird cleans itself by wiping its beak on a branch, it leaves seeds clinging there.
It is possible for seeds to be eaten and then pass through the birds, but many
birds are neat enough not to go to the bathroom where they are sitting, so
those seeds land to the side of the branch on the ground. While the seeds of
P. ianthothele seem ordinary, the fruits are wonderful. When mature, these
fruits are glassy and transparent, and we can see their veins and the seeds
inside. We gather this specimen's single fruit carefully; later, the seeds will
germinate well and produce several vigorous plants for distribution to botanical gardens. Unlike the roots of many cactus species that need darkness to
grow well, an epiphyte's roots must be able to grow and flourish in bright sun-

light. And just as the plant of *Epiphyllum phyllanthus* near Concepción had to obtain its nutrients from rainwater running down the bark of a host tree, so too must the roots of *P. ianthothele*.

Another important evolutionary step for the epiphytes is the ability of their stems to catch enough sunlight for photosynthesis by dangling over the edge of a tree branch that is in a sunny spot. If a terrestrial plant's stems do not grow upward, they will probably be surrounded by the branches and leaves of other vegetation and become too shaded to photosynthesize. Flowers and fruits of epiphytic plants have evolved in such a way that they are produced and displayed high in the host tree where they are easily visible to birds and butterflies. The fruits and flowers of terrestrial plants, on the other hand, are hidden near the soil unless the plant grows upward and elevates the flowers on its own.

Becoming epiphytic and changing the direction of stem growth must have been two major modifications for *Pfeiffera ianthothele*, and they might not have been easy evolutionary steps despite the obvious benefits. Once again, we are so lucky that certain genera are still alive and flourishing because they teach us about important stages in cactus evolution. Like *Pereskia*, *Pfeiffera* is a real treasure.

We begin our descent into the dry valley wishing we could somehow bring a little of the coolness from the high wet valley with us. The region is arid, and the road here is not in any danger of washing away. The road drops rapidly toward the river, and cacti begin to appear all around us. There is a tall specimen of *Cleistocactus* and many plants of *Pereskia sacharosa*. It is nice to see that this latter species is so widespread and healthy. As we reach the bottom of the valley, we find our first *Vatricania guentheri*. Its tall, emerald green columns each have a long, lateral cephalium running down the side. So many cacti have a story worth telling, and vatricanias are no exception. The cephalium that each stem bears is a flowering zone, a set of ribs that produces flowers from their areoles. By contrast, all the areoles on the ordinary green ribs—the vast majority of the areoles—cannot flower but instead remain vegetative their whole life, producing spines when young and never again becoming active. We discuss cephalia in greater detail in chapter 4.

The vatricanias here are tall and fresh, and their stems are a bright green as if they were growing in a well-watered garden and not a hot, dry valley. The russet red spines that spill out of their lateral cephalia glisten in the sun, and although the lowest parts of the cephalia must be many years old, the spines retain their vibrant color. Each plant branches several times, each branch growing straight up to a height of 10 to 18 feet (3 to 5 m) and parallel to one another. There are only a few plants here, but on the other side of the newly built bridge we will see thousands. Although we search the cephalia diligently, we find neither flowers nor fruits, so we are not able to collect seeds. Vatricanias are only occasionally available from cactus nurseries, and unfortunately, they are almost never seen in cactus gardens. We have been told that they grow very well outdoors in Tucson, Arizona, surviving the winters with no trouble. Seedlings we have obtained from nurseries have grown well for us, quickly reaching heights of 4 feet (1.2 m), and they have begun their cephalium after only about four years in cultivation. Vatricanias do not produce massive displays of flowers, but the individual flowers are each attractively large with pink petals that open wide. This plant would be a stunning addition to gardens in warm climates.

Although plants of *Vatricania* could never be confused with those of *Neocardenasia*, the two genera resemble each other in several ways: both have only one species (which makes each a monotypic genus), their closest relatives are thousands of miles to the west across the Andes in Peru, and both genera were created by Backeberg. And just as *Neocardenasia herzogiana* is now considered more properly classified as *Neoraimondia herzogiana*, so is *Vatricania guentheri* now believed to be a member of *Espostoa, E. guentheri*. Backeberg created many small genera because he emphasized differences between species rather than their common features. He was an extreme splitter. Some of his genera are accepted by other taxonomists, but many have been rejected. Not only did Backeberg separate one species of *Espostoa* to create *Vatricania*, but he also separated other espostoas to make the genera *Pseudoespostoa* and *Thrixanthocereus*. Few people accept this classification, however, and instead accept the concept of one large genus.

Plants of *Espostoa* (*Vatricania*) *guentheri* are tall and have as many as fifteen branches.
Each branch grows to be about 5 to 10 feet (1.5 to 3 m) long before beginning
to produce the long, roan-colored spines of their lateral cephalium.
Notice the abundance of green vegetation in the background;
the area is dry and hot at times, but wet enough to support leafy trees and shrubs.

As with *Neoraimondia*, we again face the strange situation of having one species that is very distant geographically from all its close relatives. In addition, that lone species is to the east of the Andes whereas the multitude of species is to the west in Peru. In the past, *Espostoa*, like *Neoraimondia*, may have been a large, widespread genus inhabiting much of central South America that was later physically divided by the rising of the Andes. If this is what happened, think of the large number of species of *Espostoa* and *Neoraimondia* (and no doubt many other genera) that must have grown where the Andes are now, and imagine how many became extinct as their habitats gained altitude and became too cold.

As we are preparing to leave the vatricanias and head toward Villa Serrano, we see an almost unbelievable sight. Not another exotic cactus or a breathtaking mountain range, but an American, Marty Daignault, on a bicycle. Here, on a dirt road in the middle of the Andes, miles from anywhere. Alone. He is scouting a route for adventure cyclists to mountain bike from Patagonia to La Paz. He has already covered thousands of miles, climbed and descended tens of thousands of feet, camped almost every night, purified his water with chemicals, and carried enough food for long journeys between isolated villages. He has only "a few" mountains left to cross before La Paz, "a few" thousand more feet to climb, "a few" more cold nights to sleep through. When he has the route mapped out, it will definitely be an adventure for any cyclist. We wish him well and promise to call home to let everyone know he is all right and on schedule. As he rides off, we watch him in our rearview mirror. The pickup suddenly seems much more comfortable.

High mountains, sheer cliffs, cool, wet weather. That is our environment most of the day. The road south from Vallegrande to the new bridge near the vatricanias is narrow and precarious, running mostly through moist green grasslands. As we climb out of the valley on our way toward Villa Serrano, we must enter an equally treacherous stretch. It was sunset when we left the vatricanias; now it is pitch-black. Our headlights sometimes pick out the dirt road running ahead of us or curving to the right or left, but too often they show nothing but blackness. The only thing we can do is get out and peer

Plants of *Espostoa* (*Vatricania*) *guentheri* bloomed well in May 1998
at the Jardin Exotique in Monaco. Large plants are rare in cultivation,
and cephalium-bearing, blooming plants are a real treat. Because most stems
do not even start to make a cephalium until they are very tall, all flowers are at least
10 to 12 feet (3 to 4 m) above the ground. However, plants in cultivation in
Austin initiated their cephalia while only 4 feet (1.2 m) tall.

into the darkness, trying to see where the road goes. For much of the night
we proceed at a walking pace, slowly but safely.

After spending the night in Villa Serrano, we proceed quickly the next
morning, the combination of daylight and a good road allowing us to pick up
the pace. We are not high enough to be above the tree line, and although
small areas of forest still grow in the occasional narrow ravines, in general
there are no trees here and the mountainsides are covered in grass. This is
almost certainly not natural grassland but rather the result of thousands of
years of farming and pasturing. Humans have lived in this region for centuries, clearing land, tilling fields, planting potatoes, herding animals. There
are not many cacti at these altitudes, but we find a beautiful *Echinopsis
obrepanda* growing out in the open instead of hiding in semi-shade as the *E.
hammerschmidii* near San José de Chiquitos had done. Even full sunlight cannot overheat these plants because of the cool mountain breezes blowing

across them. A massive thunderstorm drops sheets of rain to our west, and although the storm appears headed our way, the clouds dissipate as they approach. New clouds form even farther to the west, but they also rain themselves out before reaching us. It seems as if the clouds are moving while the rainfall stays where it is. We have wonderful views of mountain ranges, the Cordillera de Mandinga extending seemingly forever to the southwest. We had hoped to continue on in that direction toward Sucre to study *Oreocereus celsianus*, but the rains make the roads too risky to drive on. We decide to turn southeast and descend to Monteagudo. No matter which direction we choose, we will find cacti that are new to us. *Oreocereus celsianus* will have to wait until 1996 when we can reach it in northern Argentina.

As we leave the mountains, the broad valley of the Río Mojotorillo lies before us, its dense forest blanketing both sides. The forest is so moist it is almost a rainforest, with epiphytic ferns and mosses hanging from the trees, and an undergrowth so thick that walking through it would be difficult. This is not the spiny undergrowth of the chaco south of San José de Chiquitos; here, the low plants are soft, wet, and covered with lichens. At our first stop we find a whole colony of *Acanthorhipsalis monacantha*. This is a close relative of the plant of *Pfeiffera* we had collected the day before, a species that always requires moisture and cool, dark conditions. This species is very rare in cultivation and is almost never available from nurseries. We collect a ripe, seed-filled fruit. The plants themselves are not actually hanging down from a tree but are likely rooted in soil at the top of the road bank, cascading down with long, rambling stems all tangled together. Even though this mass covers a patch of soil about 15 feet (4.5 m) wide and 6 to 7 feet (2 to 2.25 m) tall, we are not certain if we are dealing with a single plant or with many.

At their base, stems of *Acanthorhipsalis monacantha* are narrow, ribless, and round, only about ¼ inch (0.6 cm) or less in diameter but at their tips they are flattened and have two tall ribs (a few stems have three ribs all the way to their tips). The round portions of the stems are up to several feet long, and the plants have a decidedly ratty appearance, their decayed parts and dead pieces mingling together with beautifully healthy stems. Because we are

This is the rainforest near Puente Azero, a frost-free area with sufficient moisture to support epiphytic cacti in south central Bolivia where we found our specimen of *Acanthorhipsalis monacantha*. This species is abundant farther north and extends as far south as Salta and Jujuy in Argentina. Acanthorhipsalises grow in a tangle of trees and shrubs, many of which hang over cliffs.

accustomed to cacti of sunny deserts, it is hard for us to imagine that this cactus can live in such dark, dank conditions and not immediately rot away. When the seeds we collect later germinated, we had to cultivate them in special conditions instead of in an ordinary cactus greenhouse. The seedlings grew to be vigorous, healthy plants in a shady corner of the greenhouse, but they did not bloom until we moved them into an air-conditioned office where there was no direct sunlight. Since then they have been blooming almost continuously, each of the self-fertile, orange flowers developing into a pink, four-ribbed fruit full of seeds.

Before leaving this area, we find another plant of *Epiphyllum phyllanthus*, some cleistocacti, and various large cerei. We follow the road that runs along the Río Mojotorillo to Puente Azero, where we join the Río Azero and follow it toward Monteagudo. The terrain becomes drier and hotter, the sky less cloudy and overcast. Monteagudo is a pleasant town with a brand new hotel

Plants of *Acanthorhipsalis monacantha* are unusual among epiphytic cacti because they have spines. This plant obviously had a very good reproductive season with many of its areoles bearing ripe fruits. Plants of *Acanthorhipsalis* can be difficult to find because they grow in such shady, overgrown areas among ferns and mosses, but the bright pink or red fruits make them easier to see.

and good places to eat. Because it is Saturday night, we decide to clean up, have a nice dinner, and go to bed before midnight. Our work with the plants can wait until morning, and since it will be a Sunday, we will be able to work at a more relaxed pace, leisurely eat our breakfast, and depart for Camiri whenever we feel like it. We are in the lowlands now where there is no chance of rain washing the road off the side of a mountain; the short drive to Camiri should be a pleasant Sunday drive through cactus country. Or so we think.

The road from Monteagudo is of red dirt as it meanders through brushy territory that looks much like the mesquite scrub of south Texas. The land is flat, and the sky has puffy white clouds interrupting its blue expanse. It is a beautiful Sunday morning as we approach chaco vegetation again. Our progress is good and our spirits high; we are not at all daunted by the darkening of the clouds. A little after noon, a scattering of fat raindrops suddenly turns into a hard downpour, a real gully-washer. We can barely see even though the windshield wipers are working as fast as possible, and what little we do see is not good. After only a few minutes, puddles quickly develop, then coalesce into a sheet of water that becomes trapped between the tall edges of the road. Within ten minutes, water starts running down the road, then becomes a stream that flows faster than we can drive.

We continue on for only a few hundred yards before concluding that the better part of valor is to get off the road. We turn into the first driveway we find, which, fortunately, is a little higher than the road. We watch the road turn into a flash flood deep enough to have washed the pickup away. Water is moving over everything in such a tremendously thick sheet that we cannot identify where the road is. The rain stops after about thirty minutes, but the road continues in full flood for another hour or two. We make the best of our time by botanizing in the rain, and we find several cattle and cacti. Botanists, beasts, and plants—all soaked, all forlorn.

Once the water drains off the road, we start out again. We are lightly loaded and have four-wheel drive, so we are not worried about getting stuck. Unfortunately, several big trucks and buses have become mired up to their axles in mud and cannot move. Long lines of cars are stranded because of them. As we talk to other drivers waiting for the road to clear, we hear that truck drivers are often suspected of turning across the road when they realize they are getting stuck—that way no one can get by and it is in everyone's interest to help the truck. It sounds to us like grumbling, but we do notice that stalled trucks tend to be in the middle of the road instead of on the right-hand side where they should be. The vehicle immediately ahead of us is a pickup filled to capacity with ears of corn, their weight giving the rear wheels good traction. We and the pickup driver conclude that we can just squeeze around the truck. Waiting is not an attractive option because we know it will be a long time before anyone can move a giant truck as muck-bound as this one. We edge around the truck and go on our way. Ahead of us, the pickup with the corn is struggling. Its wheels, although finding traction on the flat ground, are spinning uselessly on even slight inclines, so we jump out of our pickup, climb onto the truck's back bumper, and begin bouncing up and down to give it enough weight and traction to make it move. Jumping up and down on a back bumper amidst a bunch of corn on the cob and with mud flying everywhere—this is proof that we are enjoying the sophisticated life that was guaranteed us by all those years of college education. At least the truck is not carrying pigs and chickens.

One of our traveling companions was a truck loaded with corn that needed
an extra push up the hills. R. Kiesling demonstrates the glamour of fieldwork.

Riding in the open on the back of a corn truck is a great way to look for
plants. What a view. Although we had been noticing some kind of *Cereus* all
day, we ignored it as yet another tall columnar cactus. But as we continue, we
notice that they are unusually narrow and tall, and definitely slender for
Cereus. When the corn truck stops for a moment, we jump off and collect
some stems and ripe fruits. This is undoubtedly *Cereus hankeanus*, and
although it seems to be a very generic *Cereus*, its narrow stems are elegant, a
little more than 2 inches (5 cm) wide and 12 to 15 feet (4 to 4.5 m) tall.

The drizzle never really stops, and by the time we reach Camiri, clouds
hang low over the town, the lower clouds raking buildings on the hilltops.
We find a nice hotel, the J and R, a classic 1940s-style building with large and
spacious rooms. The gray sky is quite beautiful when viewed from the warm,
dry lobby. Our routine is standard: shower, eat dinner, work on plants.

From Camiri we head to Boyuibe, a small town not too far from the bor-
ders of Paraguay and Argentina. Much to our surprise we encounter brand-
new pavement and are able to drive at a full 55 miles per hour (about 90

kph), perhaps ten times our ordinary speed. From Boyuibe we turn east onto a dirt road that we believe heads toward the frontier with Paraguay, although there is no road sign indicating this is the correct route. On our first stop we find an abundance of *Gymnocalycium pflanzii* growing not in a sunny, rocky area, but rather in deep, rich soil in the shade of bushes. There is a small gully about 6 to 10 feet (2 to 3 m) deep, its sides consisting only of soil from top to bottom; there is no rock at all. Many gymnocalyciums that are growing too close to the edge of the gully have been loosened by erosion and now dangle upside down, held precariously by their roots. This strikes us as a strange place to find gymnocalyciums, and in 1996 in Argentina, we will see the more typical habitat

This is a large colony of *Gymnocalycium megatae* growing in even shadier, more moist conditions than those of G. *pflanzii*. The soil of this cliff face must rapidly crumble away, but these cacti are able to germinate and grow to flowering size before their home falls out from under them. Abundant mosses, normally good indicators of a habitat unsuitable to cacti, least of all healthy cacti, are growing alongside these specimens of G. *megatae*.

for members of this genus: rocky, flat, and drenched in sunlight. All species of *Gymnocalycium* resemble each other so strongly—their bodies are similarly shaped, their flowers are a delicate cream color, the scales of the flower buds overlap like those of a fish—that there is no question they are related. Species adapted to deep shade, such as G. *pflanzii* and G. *megatae*, are very similar to those adapted to full sun, such as G. *spegazzinii*.

In this area we also find our first *Quiabentia*, Q. *pflanzii*. It is another key species because it is part of a transitional group that is not well known. It is

In contrast to the shade-loving *Gymnocalycium megatae* and G. *pflanzii*, other gymnocalyciums such as this G. *spegazzinii* love full sun. They can tolerate both exposure to intense sunlight and water-stress all day long. In cultivation, it is safe to treat all your gymnocalyciums to more intermediate conditions.

closely related to *Pereskiopsis*, and some taxonomists even put it into that genus. But *Pereskiopsis* is found in southern Mexico, Guatemala, and Honduras, whereas *Quiabentia* grows in South America. The two genera appear to be relicts of the subfamily Opuntioideae because they have undergone little evolutionary change since the conversion of some early cacti into opuntias. Their seeds are big, hard, and white like those of all opuntias, and the plants have glochids, those numerous, tiny, bristlelike spines that make handling opuntias so annoying. *Quiabentia* leaves are quite large and fleshy; they are real leaves that are more substantial than those of other opuntias. In the same way that studying *Pereskia* is helpful to our understanding of the early steps in cactus evolution, studying *Quiabentia* is helpful in understanding the early stages of *Opuntia* evolution.

Unlike plants of *Pereskiopsis*, which tend to be shrubby, plants of *Quiabentia* are full-sized trees. Their trunks are thick and firm, not as hard as those of woody pereskias, but not as soft as those of columnar cacti. Old are-

Gymnocalyciums have beautiful flowers, and even their flower buds are wonderful.
The overlapping scales of this plant of *Gymnocalycium chiquitanum* here are diagnostic
for the genus—few other genera have flower buds like these.

oles have many spines, so they must be producing new spines year after year.
Like most opuntias, these plants are jointed, and although they seem to have
leaves everywhere, only the terminal joints actually do. Leaves seem to fall
off when they are a year old, but triggered by what? Cold? Drought? Age? We
notice that there are two types of terminal joints: those that are narrow,
short, apparently young, and without many spines; and those that are wider,
longer, much older, and with more spines. However, both types of terminal
joints bear leaves. We do not see any flowers—we are too late for that—but
there are many ripe fruits that are full of seeds. Although we collect these
seeds and later sow them, few germinate, and the seedlings that result are tender, elongated, and tend to fall over.

There are only a few plants here but soon we come to an area that is
really amazing, a forest that consists almost exclusively of trees of *Quiabentia
pflanzii* and *Pereskia sacharosa*. What a sight. *Quiabentia pflanzii* is shaped like
a giant jade plant with spines. Its leaves are fat (about 1½ inches [4 cm] long

This individual of *Quiabentia pflanzii* is a large tree. Quiabentias grow so profusely in southeastern Bolivia that they create their own forests. Because of their shiny leaves, a summer rainstorm makes the entire forest a dazzling sight.

by about 1 inch [2.5 cm] wide) and shiny enough that the plant appears to glisten. Like opuntias, each branch of *Quiabentia* grows only for a limited period, then one or several new branches emerge from its tip. Because one new branch grows more or less parallel to the original branch while the others grow outward, it appears as if there is continuous growth of one trunk with sets of new branches every foot or so. As if *Q. pflanzii* and *P. sacharosa* were not impressive enough, there are thousands of *Gymnocalycium megatae* growing in this forest too.

From Boyuibe, we explore in various directions. Near Palos Blancos in the west we see *Harrisia guelichii, Monvillea cavendishii, Pereskia sacharosa*, and several species of *Echinopsis*. To the northeast we search for *Gymnocalycium mihanovichii*, but the area has been explored for oil drilling and dirt roads lead in every direction. It is impossible to know where to go without getting lost, and many roads are almost overgrown now that they have been abandoned. Although we do not find *G. mihanovichii*, we come across many wonderful plants of *Monvillea spegazzinii*. This particular species is famous for stems that are mottled with small patches of blue and gray. Some of the plants here are more dramatic than any we have seen in collections, and they would be a great addition to those already in cultivation. But we do not have permits to export living cacti—those are almost impossible to obtain—and not one plant has fruits.

Leaves of *Quiabentia pflanzii* are fat and
shiny, much thicker and broader than
those of other opuntias.

Although quiabentias look like giant jade plants, their spines and glochids clearly
differentiate them. In our experience, quiabentias have the most painful spines of all cacti.
Our cultivated plants have survived mild frosts in Texas and are beautiful plants,
but their spines are so painful it is difficult to recommend them for home gardens.

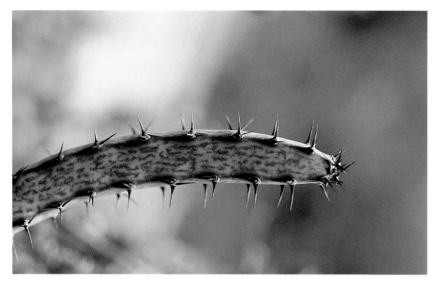

Stems of *Monvillea spegazzinii* feature small patches of blue and gray.
Various clones differ in the number of patches on the stems and the intensity of the color.

While examining these plants of *Monvillea spegazzinii*, we notice that as they scramble through the branches of surrounding bushes, their stems occasionally touch the soil and form adventitious roots. This is not surprising; many cacti root easily when they contact the ground. What is unusual here is that these roots of *M. spegazzinii* are large swollen taproots that resemble short fat carrots, a form that is more typical of the first root of a seedling (for example, roots in *Peniocereus greggii* or *Pterocactus tuberosus*). We take a sample to study its anatomy and later discover that almost every aspect of this root is exotic. For example, swollen roots of carrots, beets, and radishes consist mostly of a very soft, starch-filled wood, as do these roots of *M. spegazzinii*. In addition, the centermost wood cells of the cactus root undergo extra cell divisions, creating even more tissue in which water and starch can be stored, and the outermost wood cells develop as fibers instead of dividing.

Adventitious roots of *Monvillea spegazzinii* become greatly enlarged and carrotlike. Water and starch that are stored underground in roots are less likely to be found and eaten by animals. Soil never becomes as hot or cold as air, and its humidity changes more slowly, so nutrients that are stored in roots are in a safer, more uniform environment than those stored in cactus shoots.

It is now the end of March. We have finished all the exploring we are able to do on this trip and are ready to begin our return to Santa Cruz, our final stop in Bolivia. We will return by a direct route that runs almost due north along the foot of the mountains that eventually become a part of the Andes, so avoiding both the mountains we crossed earlier this week and the swamps and bridgeless rivers of the week before.

Everyone told us this is a good road if dry. It has, of course, been raining all night, and apparently this year's dry season has not yet arrived. We load the pickup and head out, but at the edge of Camiri we encounter guards and a barricade. The road has been closed because of an overturned truck, and the guards do not expect to have it cleared until some time after noon. We go back to town to buy food and water so that once on the road we will not have to stop. Returning to the barricade, we get out and examine every plant in sight, trying to look as scholarly and botanical as possible. One of us (the one

We receive another surprise on our way back to Santa Cruz—a dual-purpose bridge.
Where there are not too many cars or trains, there is no need for two separate bridges,
provided a car is fast enough to get on and off in time.
We are extremely glad we came to this bridge before dark.

who speaks fluent Spanish) makes small talk with the guards. He tells them we are botanists studying Bolivian plants and asks if the guards know what the plants are like a mile down the road. One of us (the one from the United States) tries to look like an Important Foreign Scientist. Before we know it, the barricade goes up and we have permission to go down the road a mile or two to botanize. (The guards probably want to get rid of us so they can get some peace and quiet.) Once out of sight of the guards, we are on our way, "accidentally" not noticing that we have gone more than the permitted distance. Although areas of the roadbed that are flat or depressed are still mud, even the slight elevations are completely dry and turning hard. Before long we are beyond the overturned truck and the many vehicles stranded on either side of it. We proceed with no great trouble, driving slowly enough so we can peer out the windows in case any new cacti appear.

As night falls we come across a pleasant surprise—pavement. We imagine we can race to Santa Cruz and arrive before it is too late. However, the

Bolivian cows are learning that it is much warmer to sleep on pavement than in wet mud. The cows are, of course, not the white, easy-to-see breed; they are the black, blend-in-with-the-blacktop cows. We zigzag our way around each of the bucolic bovines as we head to Santa Cruz, where we conclude our exploration of cacti in Bolivia.

4

NORTHERN PERU:
Fog on the Coast and in the Mountains

The coastal area north of Lima does not look like cactus country at all. In fact, it does not look suitable for any living thing. Whereas the region around Santa Cruz, Bolivia, had seemed too wet for cacti, this stretch of Peruvian coast seems too dry. Deserts are dry, of course, but if rainfall is too sparse, not even cacti survive. Here there is nothing but blowing sand.

Two roads lead north from Lima, and the one from the airport in Callao (now engulfed by Lima's growth) is amazing. It seems to have been bulldozed out of the sides of giant sand dunes that plunge from several hundred feet high down to the breakers of the Pacific Ocean. Everywhere along the road, sections of sand up to 100 feet (30 m) wide have lost the battle against gravity and cascaded down onto the road. How does the road stay on the steep sides of these dunes? Does it? We think it best not to drive too slowly, and anyway, there are no cacti here. In fact, we see no plants of any kind.

The second road heading north from Lima lies a few miles inland and runs through the small town of Puente Piedra. The surrounding landscape is surreal, like an undulating sea of sand dunes, but there is at least no ocean for the road to slide into. We have been told that it never rains here, but the fog is heavy enough to support patches of lichens that grow as a thin black film over the sand's surface. Undoubtedly, bacterial relatives called cyanobacteria, an extremely primitive life form, are a part of this film. This must be what the world looked like for hundreds of millions of years before the first land plants evolved—an endless, barren expanse of rock, sand, bacteria, and lichens.

Traveling on this road out of Lima, we seem to have gone back in time half a billion years.

It is March and the weather is cool and overcast. The barren, sandy terrain still surrounds us as we drive toward the coastal town of Chancay. Like all towns on the coast of Peru, Chancay is located at the mouth of a river, the Río Chancay, which supplies the town's drinking water. There is no hope of finding fresh water in areas between the rivers, and the blue waters of the Pacific, stretching westward far into the distance, cannot sustain human life despite their refreshing beauty. The mountains in the east are close by, and the short, small rivers typically give up their water to irrigation projects rather than to the Pacific. After crossing miles of dry hills of sand, we see below us a narrow strip of green fields along a riverbed. The coastline divides our world neatly in two: on the left is an azure ocean of brine, and on the right is a brown ocean of sand. Transecting our northward route is the green line of the river valley. Crossing the cultivated area takes us only a minute or two, and then we climb back into the desert. Fields flowing with water are separated from natural desert by no more than 2 feet (60 cm). The plants that constituted the natural vegetation of this valley before it was cleared for agriculture will probably never be known. These small rivers have been used in the cultivation of farmland for thousands of years; a culture appropriately known as the Chancay lived here one thousand years ago. We stop in the hills to search the dunes for cacti, and although that was fruitless, we did find a large Chancay clay jar almost perfectly intact lying in the sand. Perhaps it held water for people traveling from one river valley to the next and was abandoned once empty.

Slightly north of Chancay, we stop and walk inland from the road. We seem to wade through the loose sand rather than walk. This is a known site of *Haageocereus tenuis*, and we find the plant only a few yards from the road. Over the years, one particular photograph of haageocerei has been popular— that of struggling plants lying on their sides, half dead, more covered by blowing sand than not. The plants of *H. tenuis* that we find here certainly match that picture. Procumbent, they grow on their sides in small colonies, their few

This is about as beautiful as *Haageocereus tenuis* gets in nature.
The white dots on the cactus stems are feathers that blow across the sands from the nearby
chicken farms. Although these plants appear dead, we find the occasional green piece.
If the brown-black surface is cut away, the interior of most of these branches
is very moist, green, and healthy.

branches spreading in various directions, the base dying because it is often unable to extend above the drifting sand. As if their struggle against the sand is not bad enough, these poor plants suffer the further indignity of being covered in chicken feathers. Yes, chicken feathers. Somewhere upwind of us is a chicken farm, and on these windswept dunes there is nothing to catch the blowing feathers except the spines of *H. tenuis*.

Although we could not say they are thriving, the plants of *Haageocereus tenuis* persist. The lower sides of their stems produce roots that swell to almost carrot size and store water whenever any is available. How do they get water? This is a low-lying area close to the ocean, so fog probably sweeps through here frequently. Perhaps fog is their only reliable source of water. Perhaps there is an occasional rain (meaning once every year or two), and although there is no sign of water erosion, any trace of rain or runoff would be lost as soon as all the loose sand dried out and began blowing again.

This plant of *Haageocereus chrysacanthus* is growing on barren rock and sand slightly inland from Pativilca, Peru. The bright golden spines at the tips indicate the plants are not simply growing but are thriving, even in extraordinarily severe conditions. Spines several years older and lower down on the stems retain their nice color for years despite the intense sunlight. In cultivation, the entire plant is covered in beautiful yellow spines.

Plants must be adapted to the conditions in which they live, and often we mistakenly think that means they are well adapted to that area, or even that the area is the best site for that species. But the truth behind a plant's adaptability is often different, especially for haageocerei. These plants that look so terrible in nature would be beautiful in cultivation, their bodies robust and covered with clean, brightly pigmented spines. We are almost certain this species was part of the river valley vegetation before agriculture wiped them out, and what we see here is probably not the true, original habitat but instead a site where they barely survive. If most of the trees on a Colorado mountain were cut down except for a few struggling, stunted specimens at the treeline, botanists might form an erroneous picture of the species and its habitat because they would not realize that they were not seeing the trees' natural condition. Imagine the cultivation tips those botanists might write: grow only in rocky soil in areas of year-round low, sometimes freezing temperatures; do not fertilize because these plants are miniatures. If someone were then to cultivate sample trees in good soil with adequate water and warmer temperatures, he or she would declare the resulting giant firs or pine trees abnormal because of improper cultivation.

During the next few days we see several more species of *Haageocereus*. We find plants of *H. chrysacanthus* near Pativilca and of *H. pseudoversicolor* east of Pacasmayo. Later, when we explore southern Peru, it will seem as if haageocerei are everywhere there as well. Every one of them will be in dry, desolate places, but many are full of water, are healthy, vigorous, and have either flowers or fruits. *Haageocereus chrysacanthus* grows in the bottom of a dry river where it is surrounded by sand and black lava boulders, but we find few other plants nearby. It is as barren and desolate an area as that near the chicken farm, yet the plants of *H. chrysacanthus* are tall and upright. The old spines at their base are weathered and sun-beaten, but the new spines near their shoot tips are an exquisite golden yellow. They could not be more beautiful if they had been pampered in a greenhouse.

Plants of *Haageocereus chrysacanthus* are not completely on their own here. We find *Mila caespitosa* growing nearby, although only on the banks of the dry river. What environmental conditions could possibly control this distribution of *Mila* on sloping ground and *Haageocereus* on flat ground? It seems inconceivable that the flat ground is too wet for *Mila* or that the bone-dry banks of the river are any drier than the valley bottom where *Haageocereus* flourishes. Perhaps only a long-term perspective explains what we have seen. An occasional flow of water in this river, even one that occurs every several years, is enough to keep the soil moisture sufficiently high for *H. chrysacanthus*. Perhaps the small plants of *Mila* cannot tolerate the shifting of sand that would occur as a flash flood, even a small one, swept through the riverbed.

After leaving the *Haageocereus tenuis* we drive north along the coast road, which is the only north-south road, as it runs through Pativilca and Chimbote to Trujillo. We see virtually no other cacti. The next day we travel to Pacasmayo, then turn inland into the coastal range and follow a river with a wonderful name, the Río Jequetepeque (pronounced heck eh te peck eh).

Even the slight gain in elevation as we travel inland produces an incredible increase in the amount of vegetation we see, from virtually zero to abundant populations of *Espostoa lanata*, *H. pseudoversicolor*, *Melocactus peruvianus*, and *Neoraimondia gigantea*.

Let's start with *Neoraimondia gigantea*. No matter how experienced you might be, these are cacti that will bring back the excitement you felt when you first fell in love with plants. They are really magnificent. The name "gigantea" is appropriate because they are true giants with up to thirty stems, each as much as 18 feet (5 m) tall. Like all Peruvian neoraimondias, these plants have no trunk. Each stem is surprisingly broad and massive. The older ones show all the scars and decrepitude of their age, but the younger stems appear bright green and pristine without a mark or blemish, their freshness a striking contrast with the harsh desert surroundings. When we look at the stems more closely, we discover an unusual feature: an unexpectedly large amount of new growth on some stems. It is easy to recognize the growth that occurred this year because of its clean, gleaming skin, whereas the older stems look dull, their waxy cuticles oxidized and weathered. Plants adapted to severe climates such as these in coastal Peru typically grow very little each year and produce only a small amount—1 to 2 inches (2.5 to 5 cm), sometimes less—of new shoot material at the tip of each branch. By contrast, some of the stems of *N. gigantea* have 1 to 2 feet (30 to 60 cm) of stem tip that looks so fresh and nice that it must have been produced this year. Other stems are old, scarred, and covered with bark all the way to their tops, and they appear not to have grown for many years, even decades.

Neoraimondias have a remarkable capacity to concentrate their resources into one stem. They use most of the water, sugars, and other available nutrients to give that one stem a tremendous boost, sending it growing upward like a weed. The rest of the plant must do without, receiving just enough supplies to keep it alive and functional while not actually growing. Once the favored stem achieves a particular length, its supply is restricted. In the following year, the bulk of the resources are used to accelerate the growth of another branch, usually a small basal branch. We wonder if large, old, moribund branches are ever reactivated and force-fed into renewed vigorous

This is a big but not exceptional plant of *Neoraimondia gigantea* near Saña.
There is only enough moisture here to support a few leafy shrubs, and most of the soil is bare.
The top 2 feet (60 cm) of the leftmost stem appears to be this year's growth because
the epidermis is fresh and unblemished. The three tallest stems, however,
appear quite old because of the bark covering them and the typical elongate areoles.

growth. If so, the branch should have an old, bark-covered, weathered base, and an upper part that is either still fresh or at least looks newer and younger. We did not notice any such branches on the plants we examined, but it would be worthwhile for someone to undertake a more careful study.

Associated with the localized, focused growth of neoraimondias is the repeated flowering of its areoles. Neoraimondias are related to the neocardenasias of Bolivia (*Neoraimondia herzogiana*, discussed in chapter 3) and also have the characteristic elongate areoles (short shoots). In many cacti, an areole produces spines and then a flower, sometimes immediately, sometimes after waiting several months or years. In both situations, the areole usually becomes completely dormant after it has bloomed, and then never flowers again. Only occasionally might it grow out as a branch or small offset. But in plants of *Neoraimondia*, an areole is capable of blooming again after it has already bloomed, sometimes even producing two flowers at once. We find areoles that are as long as $3\frac{1}{2}$ inches (9 cm), which is pretty long for something that usually has no length, and we find several that branch. The repeated flowering of each areole is an excellent adaptation; every time the plant needs another flower, the only cost involved is that of the flower itself and a tiny bit of narrow short shoot. Plants always face the dilemma of expending scarce resources on flowering or on growing, and the elongate areoles of *Neoraimondia* reduce the cost of flowering to a minimum. Areoles of the neoraimondias are certainly some of the most extraordinary in the entire cactus family.

The two things we do not find much of on neoraimondias are flowers and fruits. We do not give this much thought at first, but during the rest of the trip, and during several others, flowers of *Neoraimondia* continue to be rare. Near the south-central Peruvian city of Arequipa we find a couple of plants each with a flower or two, but considering that each plant has dozens of stems each with hundreds of elongate areoles, the flowering potential is great. Why are there so few flowers? Have we simply been unlucky enough to miss the flowering season? Although many types of plants do flower briefly, they also require a month or more for fruits to develop, so we should

Flowers of *Neoraimondia roseiflora* are beautiful, if a little small
(only about 1½ inches [4 cm] long and 1 inch [2.5 cm] across when fully open).
We are surprised at how few we have found, and we also wonder if there is a season
when a plant like the one we found near Saña on the coast of northern Peru
would bear hundreds of flowers all at once.

be encountering flower buds, flowers, or fruits. All are rare here. There are
virtually no studies of *Neoraimondia* and very few published photographs; we
know of not one that shows a giant plant in full bloom. Does that ever happen? Certainly the plants cannot always flower as feebly as this because pollinating insects must find several flowers open at the same time if they are to
carry pollen from plant to plant. Perhaps neoraimondias have episodic flowering, blooming massively only in years when there has been an exceptional
rain, and blooming poorly or not at all in other years. This type of episodic
blooming is called masting, and it occurs also in trees such as ash, elm, oak,
and willow. Episodic blooming is beneficial because in good years the tree
produces too many seeds and fruits for animals to eat, and so some seeds survive. During the non-flowering years, animals go without food and die, and
their reduced populations mean that there are fewer animals the next time
the tree blooms. If the plant bloomed an average amount every year, there

would also be food for animals every year, which in turn would make seed predation severe. There is so little other vegetation here that *Neoraimondia* seed must be a main food source, and masting may be necessary to protect the seeds. So little is known about *Neoraimondia* biology that it would be great for some Peruvian students to study a few dozen plants and record when they grow, flower, fruit, and so forth.

Another mystery, although a smaller one, is that neoraimondias are almost never seen in collections. Even for those who do not want to dedicate their entire garden to a single plant of *Neoraimondia gigantea* or wait several decades to see the first flower, the seedlings of *Neoraimondia* are short, vigorous, unbranched, and beautiful columnar plants. In addition, they typically bear some of the longest known spines. If you like plants with character, *Neoraimondia* seedlings are for you.

Plants of *Melocactus* grow alongside the neoraimondias, and although they have also confronted the need to balance growth with flowering, their solution is different from that used by *Neoraimondia*. *Melocactus* plants grow as juveniles (meaning they are incapable of flowering) for many years. This juvenile state is common among plants. For example, if you plant an apple seed today, do not expect to be making apple pies until several years from now. While the appearance of many juvenile plants does not change much once they become old enough to start blooming, *Melocactus* plants change considerably. The juvenile body looks like that of an ordinary ball-shaped cactus in that it is fat, round, and green with low ribs that bear a few areoles with long spines. When it finally becomes mature enough to flower (probably when it is at least five to ten years old in nature), all further growth looks very different. The new stem growth is much narrower, is not green, and has no ribs; its areoles are so close together that the spines of one interlock with those of surrounding areoles. This new growth is the adult phase—called a cephalium—and it is the part of the body that can flower. The vatricanias of highland Bolivia have lateral cephalia in which the plant produces a cephalium on one side and juvenile tissue on the other three sides simultaneously. By contrast, once a plant of *Melocactus* is old enough, all further growth on all sides is cephalium. Since plants grow at the tips of their shoots, the cephalium is located on top of the juvenile body. Because cephalium areoles are located very close together, the plant can produce many areoles (and thus many flowers) without expending much energy making any more stem.

As with the neoraimondias, we know little about melocacti. Some with fairly small juvenile bodies are only a few inches tall and the size of an orange, so they must become old enough to convert into adults after only a few years. Others have larger bodies, almost as large as a football, and they must spend many years as juveniles before making the transition. A similar transition from juvenile to adult occurs in animals: mice become reproductive adults in only a few months, elephants require years, and humans reach reproductive capacity after about twelve to fourteen years. Because a *Melocactus* stops making green tissue once it becomes an adult, its photosynthetic machinery becomes older every year and is not replaced or supplemented with new green cells. This aging process must be detrimental, and perhaps very old plants— those with exceptionally long cephalia—become moribund and produce fewer flowers each year. Studies of adult plants in natural populations in habitat would be of enormous benefit to botanists because so little is known about the aging of plants in general.

Some species of *Melocactus* have large juvenile bodies while others' bodies are much smaller, and this discrepancy indicates there is an internal metabolism controlling the transition from juvenile to adult plant. The plant must measure how big it is, but what does it measure? Is it shoot volume, the number of areoles, the number of years it has lived, the amount of starch it is storing? Many non-cactus plants can be induced to bloom earlier if given fertilizer high in phosphate. Would similar treatment stimulate a young *Melocactus* plant to produce a cephalium while still small, or would it merely cause the plant to flower more abundantly when it got around to making a cephalium?

A second mystery surrounding the genus *Melocactus* is its uniformity; anyone can recognize an adult plant after seeing just one. All adult melocacti have good, well-formed cephalia. Since cephalia are ubiquitous in the genus *Melocactus*, the evolution of cephalia must have been one of the very first steps in the origin of this genus. But they must have come about gradually, not in a single evolutionary step, so we might expect to find a species or two that are left over from the transitional stages, species that make a stem with some characteristics of a cephalium. However, although dozens of *Melocactus* species have been discovered, not one is transitional, and all bear full-fledged cephalia.

Producing flowers, fruits, and seeds inexpensively and safely is as important to other cacti as it is to neoraimondias and melocacti. It is worthwhile at this point in our story to discuss the flowering processes in more detail.

CEPHALIA

G rowth and flowering are closely linked in ordinary cacti. Each year a plant grows a bit, making perhaps twenty or thirty areoles, sometimes more. Each areole is able to make one flower. What if a plant needs to grow but not flower? For example, a young specimen of *Brasiliopuntia*, *Cereus*, or *Samaipaticereus* that grows in the shade should use all its resources to become as tall as possible and elevate its photosynthetic tissues into brighter light in the forest canopy. Shade plants like these repress their flowering and focus all their energy on growth. Once the shoot has reached brighter light, the plant may not need to grow any taller because it has the height it needs and so focuses its resources on flowering. For most cacti, shifting from growth to flowering creates a problem. To make another flower, cacti must make another areole, and that means making more stem, whether or not they need it. If the stem is succulent and wide, the plant must make a lot of unwanted stem simply to get a fresh areole. Some cacti solve this problem with an alternative solution: they make a cephalium. In a cephalium, ordinary growth is reduced such that areoles are produced so close to each other they are almost packed together. Although the plant still must make some stem to get a fresh areole for a flower, it is able to make the minimum possible.

Parodia ayopayana, like most cacti, produces one flower per areole.
As it grows and makes more areoles, it makes more photosynthetic
green stem and has increased flowering capacity.

This specimen of *Melocactus bellavistensis* has grown as a green ball for several years and areoles made at that time cannot produce flowers. The tall, red, narrow structure at the top is the cephalium. Its stem is slender and its spines and hairs are packed so tightly together the stem is not even visible. The plant will continue to grow only as a cephalium now; it cannot add to the green tissue at the bottom.

Cacti normally protect flower buds with spines and hairs, but if they were to make too many, those spines and hairs would shade the stem and reduce photosynthesis. But in a cephalium, the small amount of stem that exists is not needed for photosynthesis, so the plant is free to provide as much protection as necessary. Cephalia become fortresses of spines and hairs that are so abundant they form a solid pack that is impenetrable not only to insects, but also to larger animals and fungi. Flower buds are now able to develop with little risk, and when they are ready, they absorb water, swell to project beyond the spines and hairs, open, and wait for pollinators. After cross-pollination, the petals wither and leave behind only the ovary where seeds will develop, and because the ovary is deep in the cephalium near the base of the spines, it is still well protected. Once seeds and fruit are mature, the fruit quickly absorbs water and swells beyond the spines where birds can get to the fruit's seeds. There will be several months between the initiation of the flower bud and the maturation of the seeds, and during that entire time, the flower ovary is completely protected except for the few hours when the flower is open and projecting beyond the cephalium.

Cephalia come in various models. For example, the elongate areoles of *Neoraimondia* could be considered mini-cephalia. In other genera like *Discocactus* and *Melocactus*, the cephalium is terminal, meaning that it is located at the top of the stem. The plants of these genera grow as a round, green, immature ball for several years until, when it is old enough, the ball changes so that all further growth is as a cephalium. In some ways it is like the metamorphosis of a caterpillar into a butterfly. The caterpillar represents the growth phase of a cactus, and the butterfly is the reproductive phase. The problem with a terminal cephalium is that once the plant switches to making a cephalium, it can never again make any ordinary stem. As the plant ages, so do all its photosynthetic cells; it will never have any nice new photo-

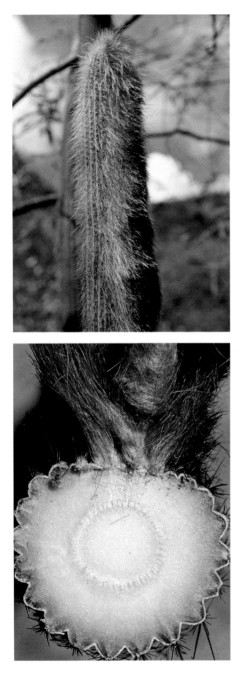

This plant of *Espostoa* (*Vatricania*) *guentheri* has a lateral cephalium. Several ribs develop as adults (they constitute the cephalium) and are capable of flowering, while at the same time other ribs are developing as juvenile ribs with areoles that cannot flower. The plant is therefore able to produce flowers in a well-protected area at the same time it produces photosynthetic tissue.

This stem of *Espostoa guentheri* has been cut in cross-section to show the abundant hairs and spines of the cephalium. A large flower bud is almost ready to emerge.

synthetic tissue, and so must gradually become moribund. Plants in the genus *Backebergia* also have terminal cephalia, but they spend so many years as juveniles that they become tall, branched columnar cacti before becoming adults.

Plants with lateral cephalia, such as *Espostoa* (*Vatricania*) *guentheri* in Bolivia, have solved the problem of not being able to make ordinary stem once cephalium growth begins. These plants produce only a few ribs every year as cephalium, and the remainder develop as ordinary photosynthetic green ribs. These plants have the best of both worlds because every year they are able to make large numbers of flowers in a really safe location while also creating new photosynthetic tissue. There is an odd aspect to lateral cephalia if one analogizes their development to human development. When a plant of *Melocactus* undergoes its transition into making a cephalium, it is like a young person going through puberty and developing adult characters like a beard or breasts. When a plant makes a lateral cephalium, however, it is as if only one narrow strip of a maturing adult undergoes puberty while the rest of him or her continues to be a kid, albeit a giant version of that kid. Maybe it is best not to think about it this way after all.

In addition to *Espostoa* (*Vatricania*) *guentheri*, lateral cephalia also occur in numerous South American genera. For example, *Espostoa, Pseudoespostoa,* and *Thrixanthocereus* (in Peru), *Coleocephalocereus, Espostoopsis, Facheiroa, Micranthocereus* (all of which grow primarily in Brazil), and *Pilosocereus* (which is found in humid coastal areas from northern South America through Central America and into Mexico). *Cephalocereus* (the old man cactus that is usually seen in cultivation as small seedlings) from Mexico also has a lateral cephalium for many years, but as the shoot grows upward, more green ribs gradually act as cephalium ribs until finally all the ribs are involved, at which point the cephalium has become terminal.

After spending several hours examining neoraimondias and melocacti, we continue to follow the Jequetepeque and gain elevation until we finally stop at a large hydroelectric dam. It is an impressive sight, but not as interesting as the several plants of *Espostoa lanata* on the other side of the road. These too have lateral cephalia, their brown cephalium spines contrasting with the snow-white spines on the rest of the body. As we continue inland to higher altitudes, the sparse *E. lanata* becomes forests covering entire hillsides. It is otherworldly to view our first *E. lanata* as a full-sized, cephalium-bearing plant after we have known it only as a 6-inch (15-cm) seedling in a collection. Seeing the second adult is just as exciting; seeing thousands of them as a forest extending as far as you can see up the valley is transfixing. To be surrounded by so much beauty is both elevating and humbling. We feel thrilled to walk among them, and sometimes we touch them to make sure they are real. We are also inspired to be better caretakers of the plants in our collections; if we put *E. lanata* into bigger pots and give them more fertilizer, they will form a cephalium for us. Only hours ago when we had been surrounded by neoraimondias, we thought we could experience nothing better. We were wrong. In the next few weeks, we will see more exquisite cacti that will give us this same awed feeling. And we will realize there is no point trying to understand how *Neoraimondia* can be the most wonderful cactus when *Espostoa* is too, as are *Haageocereus*, *Armatocereus*, and countless others.

Although *Espostoa* is related to the vatricanias we had seen in Bolivia, espostoas branch profusely, whereas vatricanias are more sparsely branched, each branch forming a very tall column. Some of the espostoas are bowl-shaped because of their many upward-curving arms rising from the short trunk. While vatricanias have such short spines that their bodies appear a brilliant emerald green, many espostoas are clothed in such a thick layer of spines and long hairs that they look completely white. A similarity does exist, however. Like vatricanias, all espostoas have a prominent lateral cephalium running up one side of each mature stem. Protected by the long spines and hairs, flowers and fruits can take their time developing without being detected by animals. We know the thick, impenetrable mass of hairs

These are young plants of *Espostoa lanata* growing near the Río Jequetepeque in northern Peru. The size of the shoot in the foreground indicates that it is has become old enough to start making its cephalium only in the last few years. The uppermost tan colored hairs at the top might produce flowers later in the year, but more likely in the next growing season.

is perfect protection for the critical processes of reproduction because during our dissections we must first pick off all the hairs, otherwise our preservative solutions do not penetrate to the underlying tissues we want to study. Pulling off all the hairs is really very tedious because there are thousands in every square inch of cephalium, but it is also very necessary.

In many species of cacti, flowering occurs from either young or old areoles, not both. Because espostoas are so abundant here, we are able to examine many to see if the same holds true for this species. What we notice is that on some plants, flowers and fruits do indeed emerge from young areoles near the top of the cephalium. What is unusual is that we occasionally find a fresh fruit in the very oldest parts of a cephalium near its base, even though this part of the cephalium must have formed twenty to thirty years ago; apparently they can also flower from very old areoles.

By the time we climb to about 5000 feet (1500 m), the air is cooler, and many areas on the hillsides are green with grass. Not dry, sunburned desert grass, but green pasture grass. Although the area does not look like cactus country, we learned our lesson in Bolivia and keep watch. We are rewarded with a single plant of *Borzicactus cajamarcensis*, another species that is too rare in cultivation, or at least in landscaping. A medium-sized, scrambling plant,

Seedlings of *Espostoa*, although beautiful, do not prepare you for the stunning sight of large, mature plants such as this *E. mirabilis*. Plants branch freely at the base and each shoot arches gracefully upward. Stems have straight, parallel ribs until cephalium production begins when the plants are about 3 feet (1 m) long. Notice that cephalia are on the side of the stem that faces away from the center of the plant.

Because ribs in the cephalium do not grow as much as the surrounding ribs, symmetry is affected and ribs cannot run straight up the stem. At many sites on the stems, new ribs are initiated and run to the cephalium. Each foot of cephalium has many more ribs and areoles than an equal length of juvenile stem.

its slender stems form an arch, root, sprout upward, and then arch over again before rooting and spreading further. This growth pattern is not suitable for flowerpots in a greenhouse, but these plants may be cultivated outdoors in warmer climates. We do not know if they are frost tolerant, but there is a good chance they could take some freezing. From the looks of their habitat here, they would appreciate plenty of water in the growth period. This species is worth such care in a garden, and your reward would include stems that are bright emerald green with strong creases around the areoles that make them attractive even while not in flower. Their flowers are particularly nice, 2- to 2½-inch (5- to 6-cm) long pink tubes that do not open wide. The tips are darker pink, even purple, and vivid in their brightness. When pollinated, they produce round, bright yellow fruits covered with small scales.

Borzicactus is a genus often combined with Cleistocactus because the flowers of both do not open wide. Instead of flaring or spreading outward, tip petals project forward, giving the entire flower a tubular form. When we look at B. cajamarcensis flowers, it is easy to see why some taxonomists classify them as members of Cleistocactus. But when we look at the stems of both plants, it is just as easy to understand why other taxonomists keep the two genera separate. The areoles are so far apart and the spines so sparse in B. cajamarcensis that the stems are almost naked. In direct contrast, the stems of cleistocacti are famous for being heavily covered with spines. We are not sure what the benefit is of classifying plants that are bright green together with those that have so many spines they are snow-white, and yet not many people have accepted Backeberg's opposing approach, which was to create a new genus Clistanthocereus for several of these species.

We continue traveling eastward for another hour until we are at 9000 feet (2770 m) above sea level. The vegetation continues to become more abundant and green. Although the natural vegetation forms a thick layer on the mountainsides, much of the region has, unfortunately, been completely clear-cut and replanted with eucalyptus trees (various species of the genus Eucalyptus). Botanists are virtually unanimous in detesting eucalyptus, at

Most plants of *Borzicactus cajamarcensis* we encountered had a profusion of flowers. We are sure they would be excellent garden plants in warm areas, and they may even survive light frost.

Stems of *Borzicactus cajamarcensis* are attractive because of the strong angularity of their ribs that are furrowed almost to the point of having tubercles, and because of the rib edges that are all sharply defined rather than rounded. Every stem we examined had this nice sculpturing. Spines are initially brown but then immediately turn pure white.

Perhaps one reason we like borzicacti so much is that they tend to grow in scenic areas. This is the Cordillera Blanca near Huaraz, Peru, and slightly behind us is the Cordillera Negra. One range really is white and the other black.

least whenever it is encountered outside its native Australia. Here, as in so many places around the world, it has been planted for many reasons that seem reasonable: it grows quickly, stabilizes deforested hillsides, prevents erosion, and is a better source of firewood than slowly-growing native trees. Unfortunately, eucalyptus has a big downside because almost nothing grows beneath it, no ferns, no wildflowers, no shrubs. Dead eucalyptus leaves and bark are the only vegetation underfoot, and as they lie on the forest floor they release chemicals that are toxic to other plants. Because there is no undergrowth at all, the birds, mammals, insects, and fungi that would be supported by such understory plants are not here. If natural forests remained, they would shelter matucanas, lobivias, peperomias, and other wonderful shade-loving succulents. A eucalyptus reforestation area is close to being the most severe type of ecological destruction possible. We do not spend much time here because it takes only a few minutes to confirm that this eucalyptus plantation is as barren as we had suspected.

Before arriving at Cajamarca, we cross a pass that has occasional treeless, grass-covered slopes beside the road. *Matucana aurantiaca* reportedly grows on these hillsides, and we are eager to explore for what would be our first small, globular cactus on this trip. Our bus driver is hesitant to stop though, preferring to go directly on to Cajamarca before the fog becomes too bad. Fog? There are some clouds, and rain looks vaguely possible, but we see no fog anywhere. We coax the driver into stopping for at least a few minutes and, sure enough, we find small matucanas in abundance. The driver continues to fret, and from our vantage point on the hillside we can indeed see a white mass moving inexorably toward us as it climbs eastward up the valley we had just passed through. Giant swirls of fog move toward us, the great bulk of it flowing quietly up the valley while huge wisps slosh high against the enclosing mountainsides looking for a way out. Perhaps the driver is right to worry. Besides, it is 4:30 in the afternoon, windy and cold (we are almost 2 miles [3200 m] above sea level). Since we hope to see the matucanas the next day, we might as well head to Cajamarca now. It would be a welcome novelty to find a hotel and have a shower and dinner at a decent hour of the evening.

As we turn toward the bus, the fog hits us. It has somehow traveled miles up the valley in only seconds. The air is now a sea of mist (some droplets are so large we can see them) as it blows horizontally and completely enshrouds us. We cannot see even a few feet ahead, and the entire field of matucanas has disappeared into the wet grayness. Our skin and clothing are suddenly damp and the cold penetrates more deeply. How can matucanas live in a place like this? Obviously this is not a rare fog or the driver would not have expected it and been so anxious. Like the rebutias we had seen high above Puente in Bolivia, these mountain matucanas must have adapted to cold, wet climates by staying small and huddling near rocky soil. We decide to continue our exploration of this area the next day, and plan to arrive well before the fog.

We return the next morning and find that the weather has changed completely. It is 10:00 A.M., the sky is crystalline blue and perfectly clear, and although the air is cool, the sun feels warm. We leave the bus wearing T-shirts

This is the habitat of *Matucana aurantiaca* near Cajamarca, Peru,
on a typical March evening. The fog is so thick it is difficult to see anything or to walk,
and the wind, although not strong, is cold. All the plants become thoroughly wet,
and while we might have expected to see *Rhipsalis*,
we did not expect terrestrial cacti.

instead of the jackets and sweaters we had worn the afternoon before. The matucanas grow here in abundance, but now that the visibility has improved, we see that we had earlier been fooled. Rather than squat little globes, the matucanas are short columnar plants almost buried by mosses that grow more than halfway up their bodies. Many are 1 foot (30 cm) tall, some 1½ feet (45 cm) tall, a really amazing sight if you are accustomed to seeing matucanas in 4-inch pots in a greenhouse. And they are as healthy as possible, with no sign of rot or fungal damage. At the base of most of the matucanas, numerous small pups barely protrude through the mosses. It is difficult to tell if these are offsets or plants that have grown from seeds dropped from the central, tallest plant. Once again, we resolve to give our plants richer soil and much more water when we return home.

Cajamarca is arguably the most historic town in Peru. This is where Francisco Pizarro met the Inca king Atahualpa, then held him for ransom.

After the fog lifted, the sun shone brilliantly, and we were able to see what had been
obscured only the day before. The area was covered with hundreds of plants of
Matucana aurantiaca, most of which were struggling to stay ahead of the mosses
growing up their sides. Fortunately, the cushions of mosses are good sites
for germination of *Matucana* seeds.

Even though a room was filled with gold as was demanded, Pizarro killed
Atahualpa and slaughtered thousands of Indians, including the nobles and
leading warriors, thus ending the Inca empire and bringing most of western
South America into the Spanish empire. In his book *Guns, Germs, and Steel:
The Fates of Human Societies*, Jared Diamond gives a vivid account of the
meeting between Atahualpa and Pizarro and of the ensuing battle, even
describing the layout of the land where tens of thousands of Inca troops and
people were camped on land that is now covered by the city, matucanas, and
eucalyptus forests. Many colonial artifacts are intact; even the building that
was filled with the ransom has been identified. Inca ruins are also everywhere
as Cajamarca had been an important ceremonial site before the arrival of the
Spaniards.

   After exploring habitats around Cajamarca for a day or two, we set off to
Celendín, a quiet town about 60 miles (100 km) east of Cajamarca and a lit-

Matucana flowers are very nice with their anthers clustered tightly around the stigma. Stamen stalks are white at the base and orange at the tips. This is M. *intertexta.*

tle below 8000 feet (2400 m). This town will be our base of operations for exploring further east in the valley of the Río Marañón (pronounced mah ran yon). Although little has been written about cacti of South America—and most of that has been in German—the name Marañón comes up again and again. This is a big river, a main tributary to the Amazon, and because it runs so close to Peru's coast, it looks as if it should drain into the Pacific Ocean. However, its westward route is blocked by the mountains west of Cajamarca, and it cannot flow eastward because of a low range of mountains near Chachapoyas. Thus the Marañón flows northward for miles, and as it approaches Peru's border with Ecuador, the lowest area of the Andes, the Abra de Porculla, comes into sight. But even those "small hills" (over 6000 feet [1840 m] high) are too much of a barrier, and the Marañón makes a leisurely turn to the east. Near Celendín, the river is only a little more than 3000 feet (900 m) above sea level—and thousands of miles from where it will enter the Atlantic as part of the Amazon River. By the time it makes its large turn to the east, the Marañón has dropped considerably and is flowing through the low, flat plains of the Amazon rainforest. When it joins with the Río Corrientes and the Río Ucayali slightly to the west of Iquitos, it has only a 300 feet (90 m) drop to carry it to the Atlantic. Technically, the Marañón and the area it drains are part of the Amazon drainage basin, so when we see the river, we will be in the famous Amazon.

By 3:30 in the afternoon we have found a hotel (there were only three to choose from), and we decide not to wait. We are too close to the Marañón to wait until the next morning to begin exploring. We can set out this afternoon, and although not much daylight remains, we hope to explore the first part of the way and reduce the next day's work a little. More importantly, we can catch our first glimpse of this famous place. Our driver gives us an incredulous look—which we were expecting—but he has learned that we cannot be dissuaded when it comes to cacti. A short drive east takes us to the top of a ridge where, from the summit, we look into the wide, dry valley with its ribbon of brown at the bottom, the Río Marañón. In that valley we will find *Armatocereus*, *Corryocactus*, *Gymnanthocereus*, and one of the strangest and almost completely unstudied cacti, *Calymmanthium*. We have to wait until the next day, however, because the little ridge we climbed coming out of Celendín drops away into a tremendous canyon on the other side. Even though we drive down the canyon for half an hour before darkness falls, the river and the desert it flows through remain far below us. We return to the top of the canyon, and as we recross the ridge, we enjoy a radiant sunset in a clear sky and think about the adventures that await us.

There is a light rain falling in Celendín the next morning, falling through a heavy fog. The weather will not be a problem because the warmer temperatures at lower altitudes that we will descend to should keep the air clear and desertlike. We imagine that just as in early spring at Arizona's Grand Canyon, snow might be falling at the visitor center on the rim but there is sunshine and 90°F (32°C) temperatures at the bottom. Off we go through the early morning darkness and drizzle. We are soon retracing our steps across the ridge and anticipating the hot, sunny valley that will warm us up after the chilly morning. But from the ridge we do not see the cactus-rich valley of the day before. There is, instead, a sea of white; the valley is an immense bowl of fog. We are standing at the edge of a Chinese watercolor, unable to distinguish the gray sky from the undulating gray vapor filling the canyon. The dark mass of a mountain peak occasionally teases us by becoming almost visible, but it recedes again behind a swirl of mist. We are entranced by this liquid beauty and watch it until the cold becomes too much. Then we begin our descent, placing bets on how quickly we will emerge from the bottom of this cloud world. We descend to the lowest point we reached the day before, and still the fog obscures whatever plants are beside the road. After another half hour, we are still enveloped. By the time we have descended to the town of Limón, or rather the signpost that says we are in a town, we can at least see 100 feet (30 m) into the vegetation. We see *Espostoa lanata* growing here and wonder if we have been driving by it all this time without being able to see it. At a widening in the dirt road we stop to botanize, and as we step out of the bus, we come face to face with *Corryocactus chachapoyensis*.

Corryocactus is part of a group of species that can best be described as confounding. About thirty species have been named, a dozen of which are sometimes classified as *Erdisia*, although most taxonomists leave them all in *Corryocactus*. If all species are placed together, *Corryocactus* becomes an odd-ball group. Its members mostly have lanky, slender, scrambling stems that look like a mass of rambling blackberry canes (without the leaves, of course, but definitely with the stickers). After arching upward, the stems bend over, touch the ground, establish adventitious roots, then send out several more curving branches like those of *Borzicactus cajamarcensis* but with skinnier stems. If the plant falls over, its stems lie on the ground and shoot up branches here and there that only rarely produce something other than a scraggly mass. They are not thick, succulent plants, and their wood is hard, tough, and very fibrous; we need a saw or clippers to cut through even the narrow stems of most species. They somewhat resemble *Leptocereus* of the Caribbean, plants that barely qualify as succulents. Although most corryo-cacti are only a few feet tall (they spread outward rather than grow upright),

The fog and the overlying shrubs combined to provide almost no light
for photographing this specimen of *Corryocactus chachapoyensis*.
It sprawls across the almost permanently shaded rocky bank of the road cut,
and the bromeliad growing with it indicates that fog must be common here.

the species *Corryocactus brevistylus*, which we later encounter in southern Peru, is exceptionaly large with columns that are easily 10 feet (3 m) tall and as broad as 4 inches (10 cm) across.

The plant of *Corryocactus chachapoyensis* in front of us is quite the opposite of *Corryocactus brevistylus*. It is growing in the open soil of a road cut as it lies on the soil's surface and spreads over rocks and dirt. Several stems struggle upright, others sprawl horizontally. All are thin, not even ¼ inches (2 cm) thick, but each is covered with 13 fine, narrow, low ribs. Areoles are packed together, and because each rib has seven areoles per inch (2.5 cm), the spines, which are surprisingly soft, overlap despite being short. At first glance, this plant resembles *Wilcoxia poselgeri*. What surprises us about this particular plant of *Corryocactus* is that it must be growing in the shade almost all the time; morning sun is blocked by the cliff, overhanging plants stop the noon light from reaching the plant, and the facing side of the ravine prevents any direct light from falling on it in the afternoon. Perhaps this lack of light

We find this plant of *Corryocactus huincoensis* growing east of Lima.
Many of its features are similar to those of *Erdisia*,
and its beautiful flowers and small size make it an attractive garden plant.

explains why it is more rangy than compact. Despite an extensive search, we do not find even one more plant of C. *chachapoyensis* here or elsewhere, so we have no other specimen for comparison. Finding a rare species like this is a great way to start the morning and we feel a slight thrill.

Around the corner we get a thrill that is far from slight. While we have been searching long and hard for more *Corryocactus chachapoyensis*, *Gymnanthocereus pilleifer* is awaiting us only a few feet away on the other side of the hill. Not one plant, not two, but thousands of big, multiarmed giants form a complete forest. *Gymnanthocereus* is a name many people will not recognize. The genus was created by Backeberg, although he himself changed the name at various times. Few people now use the name *Gymnanthocereus* or Backeberg's other name *Seticereus*, but instead place the species into *Browningia*.

Each plant of *Browningia pilleifera* (or *Gymnanthocereus pilleifer*, whichever you prefer, although notice the different spellings of *pilleifer*) is

Much of the canyonside between Limón and the Río Marañón is covered with
Browningia pilleifera. The dense brush is at least partly due to the heavy evening fog
that fills the canyon and lasts until noon. Other cacti that poke their heads above the brush
in this area are *Armatocereus* and *Espostoa*. A plant of *Corryocactus* is growing in the shade.

large, up to 15 feet (4.5 m) tall, with a stout, well-defined trunk, and many
branches. Most plants have about twenty or more branches, and each branch
turns upright quickly as it grows erect. What immediately draws our attention
is the white top on each branch. The last few areoles of each rib are so close
together they look almost like a cephalium, the mass of white spines and hairs
making the branch tip look frosted. However, these cannot be considered
cephalia because as the stem tip continues to grow, the areoles separate into
an ordinary arrangement. As we look out over the thousands of branches of
B. pilleifera on the hillside, the white apices give the landscape a polka dot
appearance.

The fruits of *Browningia pilleifera* reveal another strange aspect of this
species, their flat, transparent scales that resemble cellophane. These unusual
scales on the fruit also occur in Mexico's *Escontria chiotilla*, and plants of the
two species also resemble each other in size, shape, and spination. Could the
closest relative of this Peruvian cactus be a Mexican cactus? Maybe. There

are a few species that also have scales (examples include *Anisocereus lepidanthus*, *Pachycereus weberi*, and *Polaskia chende*), and *B. pilleifera* and *E. chiotilla* differ in several significant aspects, so it seems unlikely that the two species are closely related. Still, the idea that some of these species (or their near ancestors) might have been involved in the migration of cacti between South and North America is exciting. Further studies are needed to determine how many characteristics these two species have in common and how closely related they might be.

Another feature of *Browningia pilleifera* comes as a surprise—a real handful of a surprise. We climb a huge boulder next to a particular plant to get a good picture of a fruit and its papery scales. We hold on to one of its branches and lean out, farther, farther, farther. All of a sudden the supporting branch breaks off. It is a big branch, about 4 to 5 feet (1.2 to 1.5 m) long and several inches thick, yet it snapped off the main trunk as if it were a breadstick. The wood is incredibly weak. It seems impossible that such a big branch can be maintained by such flimsy wood, so we try breaking off another large branch and get the same result, a handful of broken branch. Considering how fragile the wood is, we expect to find broken branches everywhere on the ground, but there are none. Similarly, we expect the branches to be twisted and drooping like branches of saguaros (*Carnegiea gigantea*) in Arizona, but they are straight and upright. How bizarre.

We have conducted anatomical studies since collecting this specimen, but even they have not shown anything strange about this wood. One sample we always collect is a piece of wood from the base of a trunk so that we can examine the anatomy of wood where it is thickest. We are able to get a fresh, green sample from the very bottom of the trunk of an entire tree of *Browningia pilleifera* that recently blew down, and in the process are again astonished. Instead of the machete cutting easily through the base of the trunk as it did with the large branches, it merely bounces off as if it were encountering steel. This is definitely among the toughest woods we have collected. Because we are smart scientists, we quickly turn this work over to several young, strong, enthusiastic graduate students. They battle the trunk for

Plants of *Browningia pilleifera* have only about seven to ten low, broad ribs.
Stout spines are sometimes present, but not over much of the older parts of the stem.
Areoles at the top of every stem are crowded together and have long hairs that
make the stem tips appear white.

about half an hour and are sweating and breathing hard when they finally saw
all the way through. There is one final surprise: after a short while, the cut
surface of the trunk turns black, just as it does with *Escontria chiotilla*.
Browningia pilleifera has enough exotic aspects to make it one of our favorite
cacti. Our only disappointment is the lack of seeds. Although we collected
many fruits, all the seeds were immature and not one has germinated.

Mixed in with the forest of *Browningia pilleifera* is an occasional plant of
Armatocereus, and in this area near Limón, it is *A. rauhii*. Over the next several days, we encounter various species of armatocerei, but because they are
in full glory in southern Peru, we will describe them in greater detail in the
next chapter. In general, these large columnar cacti grow with a jointed
appearance like chollas (*Opuntia*), each joint representing one year's growth.
But each plant we encounter looks much older than its number of joints;
plants with only twenty joints already show signs of old age.

We have descended halfway down the canyon and the Marañón is still far below us. The sky has finally cleared completely, the clouds having lifted or simply evaporated. The landscape now appears dry and desertlike, and it rapidly becomes more so as we continue downward. Even before we reach the river, we drop below the forested elevations and there are no longer any signs of *Armatocereus*, *Browningia*, or *Corryocactus*. At the river's level, the terrain has become open and dry with few shrubs between the cacti. It could not be more different from the cold, misty hills covered with *Matucana aurantiaca* near Cajamarca, but the first plant we encounter in this hot, arid place is *Matucana formosa*. These two species should certainly not be treated the same in cultivation. However, their body shape and flower structure show they are closely related, and we are confident that it has not been a taxonomic mistake to combine a moisture-loving species with a dryness-loving one.

Another species here, *Thrixanthocereus blossfeldiorum*, clears up a long-standing mystery. This is a mystery that has probably troubled hundreds of people who have cultivated *T. blossfeldiorum* in their own collections. Hobbyists know many cacti just as seedlings because the young plants are small, manageable, and attractive, whereas the adults are too gigantic for personal greenhouses or take too long to nurture. Examples include *Cephalocereus senilis* (commonly known as old man cactus), *Pachycereus*, and *T. blossfeldiorum*. Many of us have ordered *T. blossfeldiorum* from a nursery, and the first thing we noticed on opening the package is that the seedlings are covered in an abundance of very long, thin spines. Try as we might, we cannot get the plants to continue producing those spines in our own gardens or greenhouses. What secret trick do nurseries use to get the plants to make long spines? And why is it that no matter what type of fertilizer we give the plant, no matter how much—or how little—sunlight or water we provide, the plants make only short spines? Here in the wilds of Peru, the answer is finally revealed: the plants simply grow that way. Seedlings, being small, are especially vulnerable to attack by herbivores, even little ones like mice, so a tangle of long spines that forms a brush of sharp points around the seedling is

very effective protection. Once
the plants grow to about 6 inches
(15 cm) tall, they no longer need
to continue producing such long
spines. By this time, their base is
wearing a skirt of spines that project downward and outward, a
barrier that few animals would try
to penetrate. The only way an animal could get to the juicy stem
would be to leap completely over
the basal spines and land on the
upper part of the stem, but that
too has an effective shield of short
spines. This variation in spine
growth is a great modification
because the plant is not using
resources to make long spines
throughout its life. Instead it
makes enough basal spines to

Thrixanthocereus blossfeldiorum
growing in nature, its skirt of long spines
covering the first few inches of growth,
and shorter spines growing above that.

ensheath only what is needed to protect the whole stem.

Four species of *Thrixanthocereus* have been named, and many people use
this genus name. Their close relationship to *Espostoa* is easy to recognize
because all species of *Thrixanthocereus* are columnar with a lateral cephalium.
Some taxonomists have split this group of species up by creating *Espostoa*,
Pseudoespostoa, *Thrixanthocereus*, and *Vatricania*, even though they all have
lateral cephalia and similar flowers. One reason we are in northern Peru is to
collect material for studies of the anatomy of this group, and our results indicate that all species are so similar that it is difficult to justify maintaining separate genera. *Vatricania* occurs only in Bolivia and has the greatest number of
unusual features in the group, a finding that is consistent with the great geo-
graphic separation of *Vatricania* from the Peruvian/Ecuadorian taxa. It prob-

After plants of *Thrixanthocereus*
become 4 to 5 feet (1.2 to 1.5 m) tall, they
undergo the transformation to adults
and initiate a lateral cephalium.
Vegetative areoles incapable of flowering
(those on the right) have short spines and
almost no hairs, but the floral,
cephalium areoles have such long,
curving spines that the entire side
of the plant is hidden.

ably became separated from the others long ago and has been reproductively isolated since then, unable to interbreed with the others. All thrixanthocerei, by contrast, occur only in Peru. They grow with the espostoas, and anatomically, the two are very similar to each other. Almost certainly, all pseudoespostoas and thrixanthocerei will soon be known as species of *Espostoa*. In fact, many espostoas near the Río Marañón also have a basal skirt of long spines, and while not quite as obvious as that of *T. blossfeldiorum*, it is a distinguishable enough feature to indicate a strong relationship between the two genera.

From a cultivation standpoint, thrixanthocerei have a lot to recommend them. Their stems are very slender—at most only 3 inches (7.5 cm) in diameter—and they become elegantly tall. Some plants reach as much as 10 feet (3 m) in height. They grow well in cultivation with abundant water and fertilizer in the spring and summer growing season, and they begin making their cephalium while still only a few feet tall. It does not require too much patience to see thrixanthocerei produce flowers. The true espostoas are much slower to flower, and your chances of buying a seedling and seeing it produce a cephalium are not very good. We have found that if we cultivate cacti with very little water, they will survive and grow at a leisurely pace as if such conditions were optimum. However, once they are established in a bed or large container where their roots have adjusted, many will grow surprisingly rapidly if we water them every few days and regularly fertilize them. In sunny climates, this does not cause the plants to become weak or spindly, and espostoas, pilosocerei, and vatricanias can really shoot upward, adding from several inches to more than 1 foot (30 cm) of height every year. It seems that many commercial nurseries have discovered this growing method because they have superb, healthy plants that quickly reach a large size.

This plant of *Calymmanthium fertile* is growing without the aid of a tree. The shape of this plant resembles those in *Acanthocereus* or *Leptocereus*. We wonder if they are closely related or merely a result of convergent evolution, the three resembling each other only by accident.

Now that we are on the valley floor beside the river, our main objective is to find an extremely rare species, *Calymmanthium fertile*. We cross the Marañón at the little town of Balsas, drive past the shop selling roasted *cui* (guinea pigs, which appear to consist mostly of skin and bone), and continue a few miles up the opposite side of the canyon through a sparse forest of spiny trees, shrubs, and cacti. Three plants of *C. fertile* come into view.

Calymmanthium is a combination of two Greek words, *calymm-* referring to something being clothed, and *-anthium* indicating that it is the flower. The only two species in this genus (*C. fertile* and *C. substerile*) have flowers so strange as to warrant a special genus name as well as an explanation. Every flower, even in non-cactus plants, forms at the tip of a section of shoot.

This is a flowering branch of *Calymmanthium fertile*.
The flower itself is emerging from the torn, green branch tissue
that had completely enveloped the flower.

Indeed, sepals, petals, stamens, and carpels are typically considered to be modified leaves, and the whole flower is thus a specialized branch. When a flower develops, all its parts are initiated as tiny groups of cells, called primordia. As the stem tip grows upward, it first makes sepal primordia, then petal primordia, followed by primordia for stamens and carpels. As the flower matures prior to opening, the primordia grow to their final size; sepals therefore grow at the base of the flower and carpels at the top. This process is easy to see in cherry tomatoes. Even if you do not have the chance to watch a fruit develop, you can see the mature red fruit (carpels) above the green sepals in the grocery store (petals and stamens have fallen off). Because the carpels are above all other parts, the flower is said to have a "superior ovary."

Cactus flowers, on the other hand, are a little different and are most easily explained if we consider apples. After all a flower's parts are initiated and start to develop, the growth rate of the apple stem that bears the sepals and petals accelerates. The stem enlarges more rapidly than the other parts and swells over the bases of the stamens and carpels. This accelerated growth rate and subsequent swelling happen while the flower is microscopic, and by the time the flower is developing into a fruit, the part of the stem that surrounds the carpels also develops to be fruit tissue. When we eat the outer, sweet flesh of an apple and its skin, we are actually eating stem and not the true fruit. The inner part that contains the seeds—the core that we throw away—is the true fruit, the developed carpels.

Cacti are constructed similarly: leaves, scales, areoles, and spines (stem features) occur on what appears to be a fruit. What we call a flower is more accurately a combination of stem (on the outside below the petals) and true flower (on the inside). Such a flower has an "inferior ovary," meaning that the ovary where the seeds develop is located below (inferior to) the sepals, petals, and stamens. Carpels and ovaries that grow at the top of the flower stem in superior ovaries are exposed to insects, fungi, and bacteria. Inferior ovaries, by contrast, provide more protection for the developing seeds because they are buried in and protected by stem tissue; bugs and microbes have to penetrate several layers of protective tissues, including tissues that can have spine-bearing areoles and other effective deterrents. Many non-cactus species have superior ovaries, but all cacti except a few pereskias (for example, *Pereskia aculeata* and *P. diaz-romeroana*) enjoy the protection of inferior ovaries.

Calymmanthium goes one step further in protecting its developing seeds. While still tiny, the entire flower becomes enveloped—clothed—by growing stem so that the stem closes up over even the top of the flower. The whole flower, not just the bases of sepals and petals, becomes surrounded by stem. All further flower development takes place inside this pouch of stem tissue, completely hidden from view. We cannot see any kind of a hole at the top of this pouch, even when we use a hand lens. Few animals could detect that there is a flower inside with many nutritious parts to it that would be good to eat. Once the flower is mature, it swells and grows rapidly, bursting out of the stem by tearing it open. Ripping part of its own body open is a very strange thing for a plant to do because it both damages itself and creates a possible point of infection in the torn area. Obviously, the plants survive the damage. And it may not be as dangerous as it seems because after pollination, this part of the pouch turns yellow and dies, whereas the base remains green and becomes part of the fruit. It is a real stroke of luck to find *Calymmanthium* plants while they are in bloom because we can get plenty of specimens for anatomical study. And much to our surprise, one branch we collect has a flower ready to open. It begins the process of tearing and emerging much later that evening, or more accurately, at 1:30 A.M. the next day. Although we were not too happy about working that late past midnight, we could not pass up the chance to see this flower open.

After getting over our excitement at seeing *Calymmanthium* flowers that we had previously only read about, we start to notice that numerous features of these plants are unusual. If we had been dropped here blindfolded without having any clue as to our locality, a logical guess would be that these plants are members of *Acanthocereus* and that we are close to the Caribbean. Each plant is a highly branched tangle of long, narrow stems, each with four, 1-inch (2.5-cm) tall, thin ribs. Areoles are widely spaced (there are about fourteen in each foot [30 cm] of rib, which means they are about 1 inch [2.5 cm] apart) and the spines are about 1½ inches (4 cm) long. The branches lead back to a main trunk that is solid and woody, and each branch also has a central strand of very hard wood. We find it difficult to cut through the wood to collect samples, but despite the strength of the branches, they do not support themselves. They rest on the limbs of the host tree they are growing under, and if the tree does not have a limb in the right place, *Calymmanthium* branches dangle down and rest on the ground.

These are the first plants of *Calymmanthium* we find, and we presume that they must be the ones surviving on the edge of this species' range. Plants in the more central part of the range should have better conditions and be more healthy. We hope that is the case because these specimens here are ratty-looking. Large patches of ribs have died, and the holes and gaps they leave behind reveal nothing but a strand of naked wood. While these plants would not win any blue ribbons for their looks, we cannot see any signs the plant is suffering because the stem beyond these holes and gaps is still alive and green. Cultivated specimens at the Jardin Exotique in Monaco, by contrast, are gorgeous, healthy, bright green, and without any dead spots.

Luck abounds for us here. Not only have we found three plants, and not only are some flowers already open and opening, but we also find that real treasure, a mature fruit with ripe seeds. The seeds have germinated well for us, and we now have a little forest of *Calymmanthium* seedlings growing in Austin. Despite its novel features that would endear it to many collectors, this species is virtually never offered for sale.

As much as we would love to continue on a little farther and perhaps find another ripe fruit or two, darkness is falling and we are a long way from home for the night, the town of Cajamarca. It will be 11:30 P.M. by the time we get there, and we will eat dinner at midnight. At least we can say we stood in the Amazon (even though rainforest conditions are not within hundreds of miles of here) because when we crossed the Marañón, we also crossed into the state of Amazonas. The Marañón valley is anything but the Amazon rainforest; it is hot, dusty, and dry, very much a desert. We turn around and leave the Río Marañón behind.

We have so far explored an east-west corridor from the coast to Cajamarca to Balsas, so next we travel south from Cajamarca. We are still east of the foggy, cold pass where we encountered *Matucana aurantiaca*, and we are also still in the drainage system of the Marañón and Amazon rivers. As we pass through the towns of Namora, Matará, and San Marcos, we are not traveling through one well-defined canyon, but rather through many small, intersecting valleys. This area is dry, but not at all desertlike. The hillsides, many of which are gently sloping and rolling, support a dense cover of low shrubs. The region reminds us of the coastal hills between San Diego and Los Angeles in California. We see a few columnar cacti poking up through the shrubs, but they are quite rare. After having so recently traveled through real forests of large cacti, we find it strange to see so few in this seemingly suitable region. Although we notice some interesting species here, including species that need study, we can find only a few plants of each and none with flowers. *Armatocereus mataranus* is present as very large trees with huge woody trunks. Its ripe fruits are growing on the topmost parts of the branches, and although we try to knock them off by throwing rocks, we soon discover that we all have very bad aim. (Goliath would have been in no danger from us.) We are at greater risk from misguided rocks than are the fruits, but we do finally collect several whose seeds are mature. The seeds have germinated very well for us, and the seedlings are growing well, if slowly. It will be fascinating to watch these seedlings grow because armatocerei appear to be plants that can grow rapidly or remain dormant for many years. We will discuss these plants in greater detail in the next chapter.

We also come across a single plant of *Weberbauerocereus albus* and one of *Lasiocereus rupicola*. These are both vanilla cacti because they do not have any distinctive features that would make it obvious whom they are related to. Both species consist of tall, branched, columnar plants, neither distinctively thick nor distinctively narrow. The spines are abundant, but not remarkably so, and of course their length could be described as average. *Lasiocereus* is thought to be related to *Haageocereus*, which is not too much help because almost a dozen genera are closely related to *Haageocereus*. Plants of *Lasiocereus* are virtually never offered for sale by the nurseries, but the one plant that we see can only be described as beautiful. The yellow spines glow in the afternoon sun, and the branches have an elegant curvature that we admire as if it were a graceful piece of statuary. The plant of *W. albus* is tall and gangly, sparsely branched, and with a nice ripe fruit. The presence of the plant here fits a pattern that we are not yet aware of, that the four species of *Weberbauerocereus* we will encounter are adapted to a very broad range of dryness. The species *W. albus* and *W. cuzcoensis*, for example, grow in moderately dry areas, *W. johnsonii* occurs in a very moist, green farmland, and the third species, *W. rauhii*, grows in a super-dry area where there are no other plants at all.

The only direction left to explore from Cajamarca is northward, and so that is our next destination. We must initially head west and cross back over "fog hill" where this morning there is no fog, only heavy clouds threatening rain. We continue west, retracing our earlier route along the Río Jequetepeque, passing back through the forests of *Espostoa lanata*. The "forests of *Espostoa*"—even writing it now seems otherworldly. Both sides of the canyon are covered in trees of this species that we had previously known

Plants of *Lasiocereus rupicola* are highly branched and grow to about 10 feet (3 m) tall, but their strong, fibrous wood is able to hold up the heavy branches. We found only a few plants.

Lasiocerei have many low, narrow ribs with areoles closely spaced along each rib. The resemblance to plants of *Haageocereus* is easy to see, but the flowers are quite different. This is *Lasiocereus rupicola*.

only as little 6-inch (15-cm) tall seedlings or as a photograph in a cactus journal. We are stunned by the sight of thousands and thousands of espostoas.

At Chilete we turn north toward San Pablo and immediately begin
climbing rapidly. As we gain altitude, the terrain becomes greener and
moister. Before long we encounter fields—not a good sign for cacti. Fields
usually mean that large areas have been cleared of all natural vegetation.
Urban development also destroys natural vegetation, of course, but even
small farms are larger than stores and parking lots. Our fears are well
founded. When we finally reach Zangal (the habitat of *Weberbauerocereus
johnsonii*), there are fields everywhere. The forests that must have been here
have been cut down. There is no way we can know if *Weberbauerocereus* had
ever been abundant or was always a sparse population. The only plants that
grow here now are those in areas too steep or rocky to be worth farming,
and they must share the little space with *Borzicactus samnensis* and
Haageocereus zangalensis.

Several dozen plants of *Weberbauerocereus johnsonii* are scattered about,
but we are quickly drawn to one patriarch that is at least 20 feet (6 m) tall
with a trunk 4 inches (10 cm) in diameter that supports about thirty
branches. Because the remaining plants are growing in the steepest slopes,
we can examine their tips by climbing up on rocks at the edge of a cliff so
that we are near the tops of plants rooted far below us. An unusual feature
of the weberbauerocerei here is that most are covered with lichens, and several are suffering the ignominy of having big bromeliads growing on them.
This region is definitely not a desert. Once again we determine to give our
plants more water when we get home, and perhaps install a mist system.
Our resolution will get stronger as we continue exploring in Peru and
Argentina because we learn that while many cacti can survive in dry conditions, they grow naturally and best in really humid areas. So far, many
areas we have been exploring have been remarkably cool, at least at night.
Cactus greenhouses should almost certainly be air-conditioned down to the
60°sF, maybe even the 50°sF (10 to 15°C) at night.

Like *Weberbauerocereus albus* near San Marcos, *W. johnsonii* here is a little nondescript. It is big and highly branched, with tall, narrowish (about 3 to 3$\frac{1}{2}$ inches [7.5 to 9 cm] across) branches that have many (thirty-one) low ribs. The length of the branches is striking; they seem remarkably narrow for their length. A tuft of hairs grows along one side of each branch, but only near the tip. It looks like a branch of *Espostoa* just starting to make its lateral cephalium, but that cannot be the case because no other branch has a real lateral cephalium running down its side. Then we notice that all the tips look this way. We have certainly not arrived a month after all

Flowers—and later the fruit—of this individual of *Weberbauerocereus albus* are covered in long hairs. Old reports indicate that these flowers are up to 4 inches (10 cm) long, light pink, and able to remain open for several days. It is a pity we arrive too late to see them.

branches simultaneously matured. What is going on? Maybe these plants do flower only on one side and only near the tip, and maybe they produce extra hairs while flowering. If so, and if the hairs fall or break off after the fruit is mature, then the cephalium-like condition would be visible only near the tip. We would like to periodically examine these plants through several growing seasons and to keep track of individual shoot tips and areoles. Our seedlings in the greenhouse are now about 4 inches (10 cm) tall. How many decades will it be before they are old enough for us to understand the unusual tuft of hairs growing on one side of each branch? We had better plan another trip to Peru.

Weberbauerocereus johnsonii shows two unusual features, its ability to grow in a moist area
(despite being covered with lichens and bromeliads), and the tuft of hair on the tops
of two stems. Perhaps the tufts of hair are simply flower buds.

Our study of this genus will be completed when we encounter *Weberbauerocereus rauhii* inland from the famous Nazca Lines in Southern Peru. Plants of *W. rauhii* are large (often they are very large), and they branch at ground level. Their branches can spread across several square yards. Each branch then turns upward, and although the plants never get as tall as those of *W. johnsonii* here, they still tower over us and reach at least 12 feet (4 m) tall. There is no hint of an apical tuft of hairs or any type of a pseudocephalium. Instead, they produce dozens of flowers in many places on their stems, from areas near the tip to the very old, lower parts of the stem. They too have lichens on them, despite being in a barren, seemingly arid habitat.

The road stops at San Pablo, and we are only a few miles from San Miguel de Pallaques, an inviting town that would have provided a different road for our return to the coast. However, those few miles between San Pablo and San Miguel de Pallaques contain a mountain and a canyon, but no road. We must backtrack along the Río Jequetepeque to Pacasmayo on the coast, then drive north to Chiclayo, another coastal town. We arrive at 10:30 that night, our usual arrival time. Our carefully planned itinerary calls for us to arrive at all these cities at about 6:00 P.M. in time for a leisurely, civilized dinner. At least we are fortunate enough to have a driver for the bus and we can get some rest. We begin dissecting a little after midnight and finish in time to get about two hours of sleep before getting up at 6:00 A.M. to start another day. Thank goodness South American coffee is rich and strong.

It is early in March 1997 when we head inland a little to the north of our earlier route to Cajamarca. It is a short trip, only a few miles to the town of Oyotún, which will be our northernmost point on this trip. The coastal area here is as sandy and dune-covered as the rest of the coast from here to Lima, but there is no vegetation to speak of. The road is paved and our progress quick, and in only about a half hour, we see rocky hills protruding above the sand. Rocks are always a good sign; rocky soil is stable soil that allows roots to anchor a plant firmly and hold it in place so that it does not blow over. Sandy soils offer plants no similar chance at permanence. The only plants that can hope to survive in sand are low, spreading, prostrate plants that cannot topple, such as haageocerei. But even they still face the danger that wind will either bury them in a dune or blow the sand away, thus exposing their roots to the burning sun. Even with the rocky hills still in the distance, we can see plants of *Neoraimondia gigantea* covering them. This area is so barren, and yet the neoraimondias are abundant. If we had time to check, we would probably also find many little haageocerei, which must be some of the most drought-hardy plants in the world.

Less than half an hour later we have climbed a little farther inland to the dizzying altitude of 600 feet (185 m). Without an altimeter, we would have guessed we were driving over perfectly flat territory. Even this tiny rise must somehow affect the climate and produce more rain or heavier fog because we now see an abundance of *Haageocereus pseudoversicolor*, *Melocactus peruvianus*, and *Neoraimondia gigantea*. The sight of such abundance does not, however, prepare us for what we next encounter at Oyotún, a dense forest of neoraimondias. There must be millions of them covering every square yard of soil. Between their gigantic branches is a lawn of melocacti. "Lawn" is the appropriate word because the plants grow so thickly that we cannot walk among them without stepping on some. There is not even a patch of bare soil large enough for a boot. *Neoraimondia* and *Melocactus* must regard Oyotún as paradise. Why, then, do other cacti not grow here? Could it be that the roots of *Neoraimondia* and *Melocactus* occupy all the soil, that their roots are so adept at grabbing any available water that roots of other cacti would die of thirst? We do not know the answer, only that we have discovered another phenomenon in need of study.

Near Oyotún we enter the wide flood plain and river bottom of the Río Saña. Like so many of Peru's rivers on the west side of the mountains, as the Saña nears the coast its valley spreads out to almost a half mile (800 m) wide, providing a large, flat, fertile area farmed with irrigation water taken from the river farther upstream. To say that driving through some of the world's most severe deserts before entering a valley of rice fields is an incongruous experience is to only hint at the enormous contrast. Rice, of all things, an aquatic crop that here is surrounded by desert.

We come across a narrow strip of natural vegetation that lies in that otherworldly region just above the cultivated fields and slightly below the barren sand. Among the shrubs are several cacti, one or two plants of *Armatocereus oligogonus*, a few *Espostoa lanata*, some scattered *Monvillea pugionifera* (often considered *M. diffusa*), and a new species for us, *Rauhocereus riosaniensis*. Rauhocerei are easy to recognize once you get to know them, but at first they can be a real puzzle. Here they are almost indistinguishable from the monvilleas growing alongside them. Both are scramblers; some narrow branches grow straight up for 5 to 6 feet (1.5 to 2 m), and others arch over and root before sending out more arching branches that root and continue spreading and so on. Plants of both genera have only a few ribs (five in *Rauhocereus*) with areoles about 1 inch (2.5 cm) apart, each with a few short, nondescript spines. Trying to tell *Rauhocereus* from *Monvillea* is about as difficult as distinguishing between *Monvillea* and *Harrisia* in Bolivia, and we scrutinize many individual plants trying to be certain which is which. When one of the plants has a flower or fruit, the plants are easy to distinguish. Both the flowers and fruits of *Monvillea* are smooth with a few large scales, almost like giant versions of *Gymnocalycium* flowers, but those of *Rauhocereus* have many small scales. Unfortunately, most plants here have neither flowers nor fruit, but as we become more accustomed to the plants, we find it easier to identify the subtle differences. The areoles on each rib of *Rauhocereus* are set off from the others by strong, angular creases that give the stems a notable pattern. We find this a little difficult to recognize at first (and we want to be certain that we are not fooling ourselves), but soon it is so obvious that we feel foolish at having had any trouble.

Rauhocereus riosaniensis is another of the many species of cacti rarely encountered in collections and gardens, which is a real shame. The areole creases create such a striking appearance that the plants are attractive even when not in flower. Unfortunately, we do not have much more to say about *Rauhocereus* because not much is known about it and almost nothing has been written. There is only this one species, with two subspecies, *R. riosaniensis* subsp. *riosaniensis* and *R. riosaniensis* subsp. *jaenensis*.

Flowers of *Rauhocereus* are similar
to those of *Browningia* but not to those
of the monvilleas that grow with them.
Petals are short and spread wide enough
to display the stamens and stigma.
This flower was opening in early evening
while twilight was still bright.
Les Cèdres Botanical Garden.

Ribs of *Rauhocereus riosaniensis* are
divided almost into tubercles by deep
fissures, and strong angularity is obvious.
Each tubercle has six sides with ridges
running horizontally from the areole,
and even though these are low ridges,
they are crisp and not the least rounded.

After collecting samples of *Rauhocereus riosaniensis*, we have completed our work in the north. We return south along the coast and travel easily on the excellent road. A quick side trip just before we reach Lima takes us along the Río Chillón, a small valley that has a high diversity of cacti. We quickly encounter several types of cacti in this area including *Armatocereus procerus*, *Haageocereus acranthus*, *Loxanthocereus faustianus*, *Mila nealeana*, *Neoraimondia roseiflora*, and an exotic, strange little opuntia, *Opuntia pachypus*. This is the only area in which we will come across *Mila* and *O. pachypus*, so they merit discussion here.

Mila is a small genus of small plants. Although thirteen species have been named, it has been suggested that all should be combined into only four species. The plants themselves are mostly small, spiny balls that, to be perfectly honest, are not especially attractive. We had seen *Mila caespitosa* and *M. nealeana* a few years before on another field trip, and we were not impressed by either one. Milas are obstinate in a greenhouse, and most prefer to die gradually, probably because they do not recover very well from transplant shock. Although they are small, spiny balls, milas do not resemble mammillarias, those favorites from Mexico and the southwestern United States. Whereas every *Mammillaria* plant is a beauty, the poor little milas we had seen here before were simply not. So we are pleasantly surprised to see the transformation that a little rain can bring about. Instead of looking like dry, shriveled lumps of spines, the milas here are big, fat, and so full of water that their bodies have expanded and pushed the spines apart to reveal a shiny, dark green epidermis. What makes the plants even more attractive is that they are in full bloom with large yellow flowers so wide they completely cover the little bodies. Flashy splashes of yellow are visible everywhere, each one advertising itself to pollinators. We realize that this area has thousands of plants, all of them thriving. The plants in this condition are so different from what we had seen before, but there is no reason to ask which condition is more typical because the plants no doubt go through these phases regularly during their lifetime. Just as a maple tree in winter bears little resemblance to one in summer, both represent normal

Mila nealeana during an August drought will not win any beauty contests,
although it is a pleasant little plant.
These are slightly sunburned and shrunken because of lost water.

After March rains, plants of *Mila nealeana* are swollen and green.
Although they are flowering now, the presence of fruits indicates they have been flowering
for several weeks. Flower buds are present but are too small to see here;
this plant will continue flowering for many more days.

phases of the tree's life. Still, when we remember the desiccated milas we had seen here several years ago—almost certainly these same plants—we are reassured to see how nice they can be. If only we could get milas to be happy in the greenhouse.

A number of cacti seem as recalcitrant as milas. They arrive nice and healthy from a nursery, we plant them in what should be a suitable potting mix, and then they do nothing but slowly and steadily shrink and become moribund until they finally die. The Río Chillón valley is home to a number of these difficult species, such as *Haageocereus*, *Loxanthocereus*, and *Mila*, and some of the Chilean globular cacti like *Copiapoa*, *Horridocactus*, and *Neoporteria* are equally difficult to transplant. Every once in a while a plant that has been withering for months in the greenhouse will return to life and begin growing, apparently happy and healthy, with few problems after that. What has caused the transformation? We do not know the answer, but many species that display this syndrome originate in areas with very long dry spells where extended periods of dormancy are common. Perhaps when the nursery uproots the plants for shipping they are triggered into dormancy because they are expecting severe conditions for months or years. Perhaps a certain amount of time must pass before watering will stimulate them. Or maybe other aspects of a rainy day, such as a sudden drop in temperature or a change in atmospheric pressure, bring about renewed growth. One treatment we have occasionally found helpful is to put the plants in the dark, either before we pot them or after we place them in a pot but have not yet watered them (after all, they are cacti and will survive weeks without water). If an ordinary plant were treated this way, it would become tall, spindly, and yellowish. This is called etiolation, and an etiolated plant might be stimulated to produce hormones that induce growth. We have given some of our plants heavy shade (we placed them in a paper grocery bag) for three or four weeks, and that has been effective in getting them to grow after being transplanted. If you try this, keep the plants dry and watch them carefully because you should put them back in soft light before they start to elongate and turn yellow.

The body of *Opuntia pachypus* is a short
cylindrical stem that grows slowly and is only
about 1 foot (30 cm) or less tall. Flowers appear
near the apex and grow like a young side shoot
covered with areoles, spines, and small leaves,
but then red petals appear revealing that
it is a flower and not a branch.

Our final find on this trip in Peru is *Opuntia pachypus*. If you look at these plants and immediately think *Opuntia*, you deserve a prize. The plants look like nothing but thick, straight sticks that stand upright in the dirt. The stem is very solid and tough, and it has no ribs. The areoles are joined by low furrows that form a diamond-shaped pattern. Because the stems are cylindrical and prominent, some taxonomists considered these to be a member of the genus *Austrocylindropuntia* (southern cylindrical opuntias). Most do not branch, do not have the long nasty spines of most opuntias, and lack the flat pads of prickly pears. But when we look closely, we see the key feature, the small, round, cylindrical leaves that any *Opuntia* species produces at some point in its life. Leaves on *O. pachypus* are tiny but unmistakable. If you are lucky enough to see them in bloom, you'll get another treat: these are among the few opuntioids that have red flowers. The species epithet *pachypus* means "wide foot;" after blooming, the ripe fruits fall to the ground and, instead of rotting, take root. One bud then sprouts and grows into a new plant. Consequently, the new, young plants consist of a slender stem emerging from a big fruit, and the plants look as if they have a wide foot. Plants of *Opuntia pachypus* may be difficult to grow in cultivation, but they are undoubtedly worth the effort.

Once we come across *Mila* and *Opuntia pachypus*, we have completed our objectives for this trip. Now all that is left is a short drive back to Lima, followed by years of study.

5

SOUTH CENTRAL PERU:
Cacti and Snow

Our objective on this trip through south central Peru is to make a transect south from Lima along the coast to Nazca (home of the famous Nazca lines), then turn inland and climb to Puquio. After reaching Puquio, we will head north into the real Andes, a land of snow and cacti. Our drive from Lima looks a lot like our drive in northern Peru a few weeks ago—a lot of sand, that is. We are surrounded by sand dunes. Although our objective is to find cacti that grow among ice-cold snowdrifts, we begin our exploration in swelteringly hot sand dunes. Although seasons in the southern hemisphere are reversed from those in the north, this July 1997 does not feel like winter at all.

The first cactus locality is a few miles down the road. We see cacti everywhere, even though the bus roars past without stopping. These *Haageocereus olowinskianus* plants suffer—or benefit—from the same fate as many cacti in the United States since they grow on a gigantic military base that is off-limits to civilians. Their habitat is well protected from collectors, but not from tanks, jeeps, or target practice. Their only vegetable neighbors are drifts of a bromeliad, *Tillandsia latifolia*. The bromeliads are in drifts because they are unrooted; they simply lie on the soil where strong winds have blown the plants into windrows. Without a real root system, they get water from occasional fog and mist, much like their epiphytic relatives Spanish moss (*Tillandsia usneoides*) and ball moss (*T. recurvata*) do. As we look at these tillandsias and remember the poor chicken-feathered *Haageocereus tenuis*, we conclude that the search for life on Mars does not seem so futile. Could conditions there really be much worse than here on the Peruvian coast?

At Pisco, the road turns slightly away from the coast and heads toward Ica. As an aside, it is worth mentioning that Pisco is the area where a strong liquor (called Pisco, of course) is made, and when drunk as Pisco sour or Pisco with cola, it is quite good. From Ica we travel directly inland following the trickle called the Río Ica through Los Molinos toward Huamaní. The river valley is dry to begin with and becomes even more so the farther inland we drive. There are some sprawling colonies of *Loxanthocereus brevispinus* and surprisingly large numbers of *Armatocereus procerus*. We have seen *Armatocereus* near Cajamarca and know that not only does it extend far north into Ecuador, but also almost as far south as Chile. At this point we can discuss this exceptional genus.

Armatocereus—a perfectly good genus that even the most ardent lumper does not combine with anything—is another of the South American cactus genera that many people have never heard of, seen in a botanical garden, or read about in a nursery catalog. Perhaps, except for its big size, it is just too ordinary. Most people do not have room for a full-sized, highly branched *Armatocereus procerus*, and although its flowers are nice, *Cereus* will produce a greater abundance of similar flowers much more quickly. Many other cacti (for example, old man cactus *Cephalocereus senilis*) look as unexceptional as those of *Armatocereus*, but because they have such attractive seedlings, young plants are in almost every collection. Unfortunately, *Armatocereus* produces homely seedlings with scraggly spines and gangly bodies of an unremarkable color (a mix of green, gray, and blue). They are also the ultimate in slow-growing cacti, and although they do not die, they often do not grow at all for years. Two plants of *Armatocereus* in the greenhouse at the University of Texas remained absolutely unchanged for twenty-two years; we had seen no signs of growth, and none of death, distress, shrinking, or shriveling. Then, after seeing how beautiful armatocerei can be in habitat, we gave one plant a new pot and moved it outdoors into full light and fresh air, and every stem began growing within a week. Each stem put on about 1 foot (30 cm) of new

In the most recent growth period
(the uppermost segment of the stem),
each rib of this *Armatocereus mataranus*
produced twelve areoles, and because
there are five ribs, this segment produced
sixty areoles. Did this segment have good
growing conditions? Did neighboring
plants grow the same amount in the same
year? Such questions are difficult to study
on cacti that lack constrictions.

The visible part of this *Armatocereus
procerus* has eight segments.
The one at the top is the newest,
and the one surrounded by the bush
was formed eight growing periods ago.
It seems unlikely that a shoot could have
grown so tall in only eight years
in this habitat, especially when a nearby
hillside is completely barren.

growth, and the following year (1998), the stems grew equally well. The other plant that remained in the greenhouse might as well be made of plaster. Clearly, *Armatocereus* is not going to be everyone's favorite cactus.

The ability of *Armatocereus* plants to sit for years is critical to their survival. Such tenacity, combined with their jointed shoots, makes it possible to carry out important scientific studies of their biology. Each shoot of a columnar cactus grows in length only at its tip or apex. During times of dormancy, such as a winter rest period or prolonged drought, the apex stops growing until good conditions return, at which point it continues making the stem longer. When growth resumes in *Armatocereus*, a constriction is left in the stem where growth was halted, and that constriction never grows to a full width. In virtually all other columnar cacti, no constriction is left, and all parts of the stem are as wide as any other. Because of the constrictions present in armatocerei, we can count the number of growth and dormancy periods the plants have had. It is similar to counting the annual rings in the wood of a tree, except that the constrictions in armatocerei cannot possibly be annual. Plants that look very old and appear to have suffered for many years have only ten to twenty constrictions, but they must be older than that. Even the epidermis and spines of the topmost segment, the one formed most recently, do not look like this year's growth. The plants look as if they have been out in the sun and wind and blowing sand for a very long time. We conclude that this year's springtime was too dry for these cacti and that the lack of rain prevented shoot tips from growing. From the haggard appearance of these plants, the prior year was no wetter. When we notice the complete lack of other plants in the area, we realize that this is not merely a dry area, but a barren one. Maybe a typical year is one without any rain at all. A year with rain could be the real exception.

Perhaps the key to understanding the biology of armatocerei lies in something that we experience a few days later, when we return to Lima: the first rains of the 1997–1998 El Niño. This is the yearlong period in which the waters of the Pacific become unusually warm, causing vast quantities of surface water to evaporate into the air. That air then blows onto the west coast of the Americas where it falls as rain, spawning flash floods from Chile to California. El Niño years come irregularly but at intervals of three to fifteen years. Is it possible that *Armatocereus* is adapted to droughts that last up to a decade and a half, being able to use their stored water so sparingly that they can survive for years when there is no hope of rain? We believe this must be the case because when we visit this area again in January 2000, every branch on every plant of *Armatocereus* has a fresh, bright, shiny tip segment that appears to be about two years old. If each segment and constriction represent an El Niño rainfall, then a plant with ten segments might be anywhere from 30 to 150 years old. They certainly look as if they could be that old. If true, then the annual cycle of ordinary plants has been stretched to a decade-long cycle. Does this mean that flowering, fruiting, and seed production also occur only in El Niño years? If so, what do pollinators live on for the many years between flowerings? Certain insects can go into long-term dormancy, so is it possible that just as El Niño rains trigger growth and flowering in the cacti, they also trigger an emergence from dormancy in the plants' insect companions? What a host of questions to be studied regarding these plants. From a scientific standpoint, these armatocerei could be some of the most thought-provoking plants in the world.

Our road east from Nazca follows a river valley for only a few miles before climbing up the dry mountainsides and through valleys that appear never to flow with water. The terrain near the coast is barren rock devoid of all life. If you have not actually seen this place, you would struggle to imagine just how completely lifeless parts of this earth can be. Once we ascend to about 2000 feet (615 m) in altitude, our old standby *Armatocereus procerus* appears, right on schedule. It has been an almost constant companion at this altitude everywhere along the Peruvian coast. We can count on it staying with us until we climb to approximately 4000 feet (1230 m). At 3600 feet (1100 m), *Weberbauerocereus rauhii* makes its appearance. The landscape becomes more unusual; the tops of hills and ridges consist of fine soil hundreds of feet thick. Small creases that cover the soil indicate that water has run down the hillsides at some time, but when we touch the soil, it is soft

Flowers and fruits of *Armatocereus* form very high
up on the tall stems and
are difficult to collect. But where there is a
will—and students—there is a way.
These incipient cactologists are from the
Universidad Nacional Agraria "La Molina."

and powdery. One real gully washer would melt the entire region, yet the hills still stand. Certainly rain is a rare phenomenon here, and probably only enough falls at one time to moisten the surface. There are no plants, not for miles, and the air is so clear that our view is unobstructed. It is not entirely accurate to say there are no plants; every once in a while there is a plant of *Haageocereus turbidus* and *Loxanthocereus clavispinus* (this even has a fruit), and a colony of *Opuntia sphaerica*. We are puzzled by the plants we find. On the one hand they are good-sized and not suffering at all despite being a little dry; on the other, if they are so well adapted to this exotic habitat, why do we not see more plants of each species? Why is each plant or colony of plants separated from the others by miles?

At 6000 feet (1840 m) elevation we come across one of the most wonderful cacti of all, *Browningia candelaris*. This species extends from Arica in northern Chile almost as far north as Lima, and probably the easiest way to see these plants is to fly into Arica, rent a car, and drive up the road toward Bolivia (there is only the one road, so you do not need more detailed directions). The road climbs steadily, and when you are at about one mile (1600 m) altitude, you will suddenly come to a population of *B. candelaris*. After another mile on the highway, you will have gained enough altitude to be out of *B. candelaris*'s zone. While there is never a dense population of *B. candelaris*, it is not terribly sparse either. Looking across the mountains, we notice

Plants of *Haageocereus acranthus* are dormant in August, as are the trees in the background, but the cacti are healthy and have only a few dead stems. This plant grows at about 5000 feet (1540 m) elevation, as does *Weberbauerocereus rauhii*.

A flower of *Haageocereus turbidus* shows its long tubelike structure, spreading petals, and mass of stamens. The tube is not spiny like it is in the related *Lasiocereus*, nor is it bent as in the similar *Loxanthocereus*.

Fruits of haageocerei open spontaneously when ripe, revealing a thin fruit wall, white pulp, and small dark seeds. This yellow-green *Haageocereus pseudomelanostele* fruit is unusual because most *Haageocereus* fruits are red. This species is endangered because its habitat is near the ever-expanding outskirts of Lima.

Loxanthocereus (*L. piscoensis* in this photograph) is difficult to distinguish from *Haageocereus* while they have no flowers. Plants of these two species have similar growth forms and sizes, and they occur together in many areas.

there are browningias as far as we
can see in this one narrow strip of
altitude, but we see none above or
below this height.

The bodies of *Browningia candelaris* plants are as exotic as their
restriction to a narrow altitudinal
band. Each plant, without exception, has a single stout trunk that
grows unbranched until it is about
6 to 7 feet (1.8 to 2 m) tall. This
trunk is one of the most formidable of the cactus world. It is protected by vicious spines 6 to 10
inches (15 to 25.5 cm) long that
are so abundant no animal would
ever try to get through them to
the trunk, no matter how great its
thirst. When it reaches 6 feet (2
m) tall, the trunk stops growing,
and several of the uppermost areoles release from dormancy and

Flowers of *Loxanthocereus* are completely
different from those of *Haageocereus*
because they are narrower—even tubular—and
curved. This specimen of *L. pachycladus*,
from Cañete and Pisco valleys, is unusually large
and thick-stemmed for a *Loxanthocereus*,
and it somewhat resembles one from *Oreocereus*.

begin growing out as branches. The trunk grows upward as straight as a ram-
rod, but the branches extend out more or less horizontally until they gradually turn upward. They often cannot support their weight, so ultimately twist
and hang down. There are many peculiar shapes.

Another way the branches of *Browningia candelaris* differ from the trunk
is that they do not have long spines. We still have to be careful of the few,
tiny, bristly spines, but we can handle the branches with our bare hands. The
branch epidermis, which is not hidden by long spines, is bright green with
some hints of sunburn, and it is covered with many narrow, low ribs. The
change in growth and spination of *B. candelaris* reminds us of the modifications made by *Thrixanthocereus blossfeldiorum* (discussed in chapter 4), the

This plant of *Browningia candelaris*
shows the typical branching pattern and
spine cover. All branches grow from just
above the spiny section, do not produce
long spines, and have a surface
that stays green for years.
Notice how barren this area is.

All parts visible here
of this *Browningia candelaris* are brown
because bark has formed, but they were
green when young. Early formation
of bark is unusual in columnar cacti,
and we wonder why the trunk did not
stay green to retain its green pigments
and boost photosynthesis.
We notice animal droppings in this area,
so despite the barren habitat,
they must live and eat here.

plant that produces an impenetrable skirt of downward projecting spines thick enough to keep animals off its base while also producing short spines above that base. If no animals can reach beyond 5 feet (1.5 m) to bite *B. candelaris*, then the plant does not need to protect anything other than that first 5 feet.

Of the many strange things about this species, the strangest may be that *Browningia candelaris* fruits have large leaves. We have seen *Browningia candelaris* in Chile several times, but here on the road to Puquio, the plants provide the very rare treat of fruits. Many large fruits still grow on the plants, and even more lie on the ground. All cactus flowers have stem tissue around them, which is why they can have areoles and spines (see the discussion on *Calymmanthium* in chapter 4) and often scales (sometimes called bracts). The scales are the leaves of the stem that encloses the true flower. The scales on these *B. candelaris* fruits are amazing: they are up to ½ inch (1.25 cm) wide, at least ½ inch long, and sometimes as long as 1 inch (2.5 cm). Leaves this size would be nothing on *Pereskia*, but these scales are larger than anything else in ordinary cacti (that is, the subfamily Cactoideae) and larger than any of the leaves in *Opuntia* and its relatives (excluding *Pereskiopsis* and *Quiabentia*). How do they survive in this dry region?

We observe one more noteworthy feature of *Browningia candelaris*. Most of its fruits are lying on the ground, yet they look perfectly healthy. They have not fallen off because they are diseased or aborted. It seems the plants have let them fall so they can continue ripening while on the ground. We wonder if this is possible, but because the nice, black, mature-looking seeds we collected have not germinated, we do not know the answer.

All the plants of *Browningia candelaris* at 6000 feet (1840) elevation are big, mature plants with many branches, but a few miles farther up the road, and at a significantly higher altitude—about 9000 feet (2770 m)—we come to another population of *B. candelaris* in which every single plant is a juvenile with only the one, unbranched trunk. None is old enough to have started branching. How could all plants in this area be the same age? In other areas, an evenly aged stand like this occurs after a forest fire, but that is obviously not the explanation since there is no forest or brush here that could

Browningia candelaris occurs only in the driest habitats, and such giant scales on its flowers and fruits must allow water to be lost from the plant. Although many fruits had fallen before ripening, the scales were somehow still fresh and alive, not wilted or withered.
We encountered immature fruits and fallen flowers in abundance at Hualhua and Arequipa, Peru, in August 1997, but have not seen flowers.

burn. Perhaps some rare freeze or fungus killed all the plants in the area without harming the seeds, and although the population succeeded in reestablishing itself by seed germination, it will be years before there are any mature individuals here.

We continue climbing to 7500 feet (2300 m) where we stop for a remarkable plant, a gigantic *Weberbauerocereus rauhii*. We have seen *W. rauhii* here and there for many miles now, most of them with all five or ten branches (sometimes fifteen) reaching upward. But this one has at least fifty branches and is by far the largest we see on our entire trip. The plants of *W. johnsonii* we had seen in the north near Zangal had hairy flowers and fruits only near the stem tip, but these plants of *W. rauhii* have flower buds all along the stems except at the very base. The fruits, which are at various stages of maturity, are mixed together along the stem with the flowers. An additional notable feature of *W. rauhii* is that all the flowers and fruits grow on only one side of the

This is the largest plant of *Weberbauerocereus rauhii* we encountered.
Some branches are 12 feet (4 m) tall, easily towering over the students.
Lichens on the stems indicate that fog or mist must occur here,
yet the area is very barren.

stems (the side facing our camera), while the opposite sides of all those stems have no buds at all.

At the place where we find *Weberbauerocereus rauhii* there is another real treasure, *Corryocactus megarhizus*. Mega- means "large," of course, and -rhizus means "root." It seems a poorly named species because while a tiny stem such as this one might have a largish root by comparison, we doubt it has a large root, and certainly not a megarhizus. We begin to dig light-heartedly, then in earnest when our digging does not reveal the bottom of the root. We discover that the shoot is a tiny fraction of the plant's total size, and that the root is indeed very large. If only we had a set of scales to weigh the root, or some other method of accurately measuring its volume. *Corryocactus megarhizus* is almost certainly a suffrutescent plant, one in which the stem lives for years as long as conditions are good, but which in bad years dies back almost to the root. Deep underground, a little nub of stem remains alive on top of the root

Hairs on flowers of *Weberbauerocereus rauhii* are not nearly as long as those on
W. albus or *W. johnsonii*, but they are plentiful. They do not seem long enough to offer
much protection from intense sunlight or to inhibit water loss.

until good conditions return. When they do return, the stem sprouts, and one of its areoles quickly grows out as a branch that emerges above the soil to photosynthesize and perhaps even produce a flower or two. Garden bulbs such as tulips or lilies are common examples of suffrutescent plants. The stem of this *C. megarhizus* will endure until retreat becomes the better part of valor. Because it dies back every few years, the stem never becomes large, and so the plant always appears just a few years old. In actuality, however, the bulk of the plant lives underground for years, where it is safely protected from extreme temperatures and drying winds. Every time the shoot ventures upward, it sends any extra carbohydrates it makes down to the root for safekeeping. The stem does not become especially voluminous over many years, but the root does.

The same type of suffrutescent life occurs in *Cereus aethiops*, *Peniocereus greggii*, and *Pterocactus*. *Peniocereus* is available through most nurseries, and many readers may have one or two in their collections. Cultivated peniocerei

This plant of *Corryocactus megarhizus* may look like either a seedling or a very young plant, but its roots are each nearly 1 foot (30 cm) long. Although it was cool in August when we found this plant, it must be hot and dry much of the year.

The roots of *Corryocactus megarhizus* are very soft and they snap easily in two.
Since they store water and starch, the shoot can be smaller and less easily detected
by hungry and thirsty animals. As with *Cereus aethiops* and all species of *Pterocactus*,
each shoot is temporary and dies back during times of stress,
then one or more new shoots emerge from deep underground.

provide an inadequate picture of the possible root size. In the olden days of field-collected plants, peniocerei with roots bigger than a football and stems slightly larger than a pencil were commonly dug up and sold. Most such plants have been wiped out by now, and people really get excited to see one with a root the size of an orange. We wonder if we would have found even larger roots if we had been able to search for more than the two plants of *Corryocactus megarhizus* that we see here.

Beyond this point (we are still at 7500 feet), the road climbs a little distance then runs along the edge of a rocky cliff. We notice a scattering of leafy shrubs, the first significant non-cactus vegetation we have seen since leaving the coast, so there must be more than just occasional rain at this high altitude. We come across another giant, *Corryocactus brevistylus*. Having seen *C. megarhizus* only a few minutes ago and now this monster *C. brevistylus*, it is difficult to understand how anyone could combine these into the same genus. The plants of *C. brevistylus* tower above us, their stems consisting of seven low, wide ribs, each larger than an entire stem of *C. megarhizus*. There are no flowers, but fruits the size of large oranges are plentiful. Each shoot has many fruits arranged up the ribs; it has been a good year for flowering and pollination. These plants use every strategy to protect themselves. Shoots have only sparse spines, but each is at least 3 inches (7.5 cm) long, and even the fruits have hundreds of tiny spines, each one as sharp as it is short. The students with us have much better aim with rocks than we do, and soon a harvest of fruits is raining down. No one volunteers to catch them, so we let the fruits hit the ground and roll wherever they want. These plants mean business.

While photographing *Corryocactus*, we notice that our camera exposures are becoming much longer. The sky is now heavily overcast with a high sheet of clouds. They are flat clouds, not the puffy cumulus clouds that drop rain. There is no reason to expect rain up here in this dry, cactus area, and we would be tremendously lucky to experience a rare rainfall here. We drive on.

We emerge onto the top of an altiplano, a high plane. The topography is still slightly rough with big gullies and hills all around us, but nothing that could be called a mountain rises above us. There are no canyons either.

The funnel-shaped flower
on this *Corryocactus brevistylus* is one
reason why some people combine
Corryocactus and *Erdisia*, which also has
small funnel-shaped yellow or red flowers,
in the same genus. The shape of the flower
bud is characteristic of *Corryocactus*
because it is like two small flattened balls,
the lower one smaller for the ovary and
the upper one larger for the petals.

These plants of *Corryocactus brevistylus*
had a very good year for pollination.
When the fruits are fully ripe,
their spine clusters fall off and the fruits
are harvested and sold in markets.
The rocks in the background and the stem
to the right of the photographs have
bromeliads growing on them,
so the fog, mist, and overcast skies
that we are experiencing
must be frequent here.

Small clumps of bunch grass blow in the wind, and woody shrubs are also swaying. The clouds overhead have gotten heavier and lower; it almost looks like a winter's day. On the hillside to our north, white tufts become visible: *Oreocereus hendriksenianus*. At first we see only one or two widely scattered individuals, but soon they are so abundant that most plants are within a few yards of one another. We stop to examine them. The cold shocks us. It had been warm enough to wear only a jacket a few minutes ago at the *Corryocactus brevistylus* locality, but here the cold makes coats and sweaters necessary.

Oreocereus is a wonderful genus. It is restricted to high altitudes, and these plants of *O. hendriksenianus* grow at 10,000 feet (3075 m), which is on the low end of their preferred altitude range. Their lofty habitats are cool to cold all year, of course, but is it safe to say they are never hot? We compare climate data for Cuzco, Peru, which is at the same altitude but inland a few hundred miles. The average temperature for Cuzco for the whole year is 54.1°F (12.3°C), and the lowest average monthly temperature is 50°F (10°C) in July (midwinter). The highest average for a month is in November at only 57°F (14°C). Thus, the coldest time of year is almost indistinguishable from the hottest. But because these are average temperatures, an average temperature of 57°F (14°C) does not mean that every day is cool; there could be hot days interspersed with cold ones. Oreocerei thrive in gardens of hot climates like Arizona and southern California, and they even survive well almost everywhere in overly hot greenhouses. However, they would almost certainly prefer to have their greenhouses air-conditioned rather than heated. By comparison, Phoenix, Arizona, that well-known cactus locality, has one average monthly temperature similar to Cuzco's hottest month (56°F [13°C]), but that occurs in February at the end of Phoenix's winter, not in midsummer. Regardless of all the climate theory and data, we are very cold while we examine these oreocerei, and our fingers become stiff as we take photographs.

Oreocerei are some of the most beloved cacti because even as seedlings or juvenile plants too young to flower, they have beautiful bodies. All have long spines, usually yellow, that project straight out from the body. There is

Many plants of the white form of
Oreocereus hendriksenianus grow at 10,000
feet (3075 m) near Pampa Galeras.
We caught the end of the flowering
season—only two or three flowers were
still present in this area—and
unfortunately no fruit had ripened
completely. We suspect that
fruit maturation is very slow.

The dark, overcast sky prevented us from
getting a bright photograph to really
show the beauty of this yellow-orange
form of *Oreocereus hendriksenianus*.
All three color forms grow together in
this one location. Despite the cold,
this one flower was open,
waiting for a pollinator.

also a cloud of very long, wispy hairs ensheathing the stem, sometimes completely hiding the green epidermis. The effect of the brilliant yellow spines protruding out from the mass of white hair is stunning, and these plants always look great.

Here in this one spot near Puquio we find oreocerei in three distinct color forms. This variability is probably the same kind of variability we find in people, most obviously in the different hair colors of children from a single set of parents. One color form we discover is of hair that is as white as snow (yes, it is a cliché, but it is true: the hairs are pure white). The *Oreocereus* hairs look as if they have been cultivated by the most meticulous gardener who has never let a drop of water touch them. We also notice others whose hairs are a distinctly grayish, smoky color. These plants appear somber in the fading, late afternoon light of the overcast sky. Without doubt, the most beautiful of all three color forms is the third form we see on plants with hairs that are colored somewhere between orange and gold. In some plants, only the youngest hairs near the shoot tips have the strong, full color, whereas the older hairs have faded slightly to gold. Other plants, by contrast, have the full, rich color along their entire length. This last group of oreocerei would be superb in gardens, and perhaps someone somewhere does have them, but we do not know of this color form in cultivation. Some of the plants have fruits, but all are immature with a solid flesh. Fruits of *Oreocereus* are hollow when mature, like a bell pepper. Although the seeds appear ripe, not one has germinated for us. Because it is almost impossible to get permits to bring living cuttings from Peru to the United States, our hopes of being able to introduce this nice form of *Oreocereus* into cultivation are unfulfilled.

From 10,000 feet (3075 m) elevation, the road continues to climb almost imperceptibly to slightly below 12,000 feet (3700 m). The area around us is flat, and the low hills in the distance are similar to the high plains of southern New Mexico or even Wyoming. Herds of vicuñas (wild, ruminant animals that are related to the llama and alpaca) become a common site as we pass through Pampa Galeras, a national reserve for their preservation. The site of the peacefully grazing vicuñas is wonderful by itself, but the scene is soon enhanced by a few flakes of snow. Snow? Yes, snow. Having spent the last several days in areas so dry they have not seen any rain for months, years, or perhaps even a decade, we are stunned to see flakes of falling snow. Pandemonium breaks out because most of these Lima college students have never seen snow. Within fifteen minutes there is an actual frosting of snow on the bushes and grass, enough to warrant a stop to let the kids experience it firsthand. We nevertheless insist that the bus continue without stopping, not out of meanness, but because of a secret plan. The snowfall becomes heavy—a real snowfall instead of just a few flakes—and when there is almost an inch of accumulation on the ground, we stop the bus. The students pile out to touch the snow, and they are utterly amazed by it. And as we suspected, they have no clue about snowballs. The professors do, however, and we exploit our advantage mercilessly by pelting the astonished students with an all-out barrage. This is great fun—until the students show themselves to be quick learners and the professors become outnumbered and outgunned by about ten to one. It is time to move on.

Snow continues to fall faster and faster, and some begins to stick to the highway. The driver, who is also from Lima, is not familiar with driving in snow, so we worry a little but not much. The most amazing thing is that there is any precipitation at all. The vegetation here indicates that moisture does fall, and although this area is not nearly as dry as the coastal lowlands, the amount of moisture we see still seems like a lot for this area. A few miles west of Puquio, the road begins to drop, and soon we are low enough that the falling snow melts to rain. We drive through a drizzle that is a heavy rain by the time we enter Puquio itself at 9600 feet (2954 m). Clumps of cacti are barely visible through the darkness and rain, but we are sure we can make out *Oreocereus hendriksenianus* as well as the taller and more massive *Trichocereus puquiensis*.

Puquio is a typical small mountain town, and one of its many attractions is that it has not yet been invaded by much of modern culture. There are no hamburger chains and no strip malls with the ubiquitous famous-name stores that you simply cannot escape in the United States. There are some modern conveniences such as electricity, but there is only enough generating capacity for half the city at a time. Every other night, part of Puquio has electricity until 10:00 P.M. while the other part does not. There are three small hotels, none large enough for all of us. The students choose to stay in the hotel with electricity the first night, and the professors go to the one with candles. Our single small candle is a real marvel, providing not only all our light, but also all our heat. The tin roof does not leak, but if you have ever been under a tin roof in a heavy rainstorm, you need no description of the noise. The roof, like the candle, had a dual purpose: it guaranteed that we heard every single raindrop, and it also conducted away all heat in the room. It was one of those nights—rare, but not rare enough—that we put on extra clothes to go to bed. The bathroom is down the hall, or more accurately, across the open courtyard and down an uncovered passageway. Most of the courtyard has a roof, but key portions between us and the bathroom are solid columns of rain. The bathroom is perhaps nicely illuminated on those nights when this part of the city gets electricity, but it is not possible to carry the candle with us on our potty runs, so everything must be done using the Braille method. A night like this makes morning seem wonderful.

And morning is wonderful. We are early risers anyway, and at the first sign of morning's light we jump out of bed, fully clothed and ready to go. Stepping outside, we see that Puquio is ringed by mountains, all of which are completely covered by snow. There is no snow in the town itself, but there are patches on the town's outskirts. We are sure that the oreocerei we saw earlier must be covered in snow. We go to the students' hotel where some of them are coming back to life, although others need some intensive efforts to get them going. We all eventually find breakfast of one sort or another and then pile into the bus for the journey northward.

Driving out of Puquio, we see that the columnar cacti we had passed coming into the town are indeed plants of *Trichocereus puquiensis*. Strangely, many plants are deformed; the knobby growth on their tips looks as if they have been infected by a virus or bacterium. Fortunately, other plants are healthy, and we have caught them at the height of their blooming season.

Still covered with water drops from last night's rain, a flower of *Trichocereus puquiensis*
awaits pollinators. These might make very nice garden plants
even in areas that have cool winters.

Large open flowers are everywhere (many plants have ten or more open at once), and there are plenty of buds that will flower over the next few weeks. We have not gone far from Puquio, so we know it was really cold here last night, though perhaps not freezing. Obviously these plants withstand very cool temperatures, perhaps even a hard frost. Later, just before we cross the pass near La Oroya east of Lima, we will come into stands of *Trichocereus peruvianus* high in the mountains at 9500 feet (2920 m) elevation, and they too will be blooming vigorously in cold, wet conditions.

When we arrived in Puquio, it was dark, and we had not noticed the smaller cacti, *Corryocactus quadrangularis*. Plants of this species are perhaps more typical of the genus than the gigantic plants of *C. brevistylus* or the tiny ones of *C. megarhizus*. Like the corryocacti we had seen in Bolivia, these shrubs of *C. quadrangularis* are rather sorry-looking plants. They scramble through bushes and are barely able to support themselves, instead falling over and rooting, never becoming very lush. They have also been grazed on, despite their plentiful spines—some animal must have been very hungry. At one site along the road, we come across a set of plants that has many fruits, most of which appear ripe. We collect them and clean the seeds. Although many have since germinated for us, we do not have a huge collection of corryocacti because these cacti have been among the most difficult to grow. The seedlings are weak and fragile; they suffer from damping-off long after they have germinated. The young plants lack vigor, and many, after failing to elongate beyond the first few inches, gradually become moribund. This is especially surprising because the plants in habitat look weedy and tough, as if they could survive almost any conditions.

We later dissect some of these *Corryocactus quadrangularis* samples for examination of their anatomy, which is what we do with all the species we collect. We cut them into pieces a little smaller than a sugar cube and place them in a preservative solution of formaldehyde, acetic acid, alcohol, and water. After a day, this mixture is washed out with 50 percent alcohol (which is the same as 100 proof alcohol) that is then poured off and replaced with fresh alcohol in which we store the samples. There is usually nothing special about the first alcohol that is poured off most cacti. If a plant (for example, most opuntias) is really mucilaginous, then the alcohol mixes with the mucilage and also becomes slimy; when a plant is especially mucilaginous, the alcohol mixture can become disgusting. Samples of C. *quadrangularis* may be the all-time champions. They cause the alcohol to become so thick that we have to pick the pieces of cactus out with tweezers because the liquid cannot be poured. Imagine how we feel picking cacti out of slime after spending a night in a freezing, unlit hotel.

We come across what has become an old favorite of ours, *Matucana*. There must be some connection between matucanas and exotic weather. We first saw M. *aurantiaca* in the fog near Cajamarca, then M. *formosa* in a roasting desert near Balsas on the Río Marañón; now we encounter M. *hystrix* covered in snow. There are many plants of M. *hystrix*, some that are solitary balls, others that are large clusters. All have many fruits that have split open and let their seeds fall out. Are they as surprised by the snow as we are? There is no way to know if the snow has damaged the plants or not because any freeze damage would show up only after a few days of warm weather. Our guess is that they are not at all bothered. At this high altitude so far south of the equator, these plants are guaranteed frosty nights, perhaps on a regular basis. We visit this population of matucanas two years later in January 2000, and again find them very healthy and obviously able to survive the snow with no trouble. During that second trip, we had to fight our way to Puquio through a blinding snowstorm, so we are now certain that not only can *Matucana hystrix* and *Oreocereus hendriksenianus* survive occasional frosts, but also that cold winters are a common occurrence for both of them.

From Puquio we climb northward toward Chalhuanca, an area that is high altiplano. The road is excellent and we make rapid progress. About 30 miles (50 km) before Chalhuanca, the road suddenly begins descending into the valley of the Río Pachachaca. The valley is wide with steep sides, and rain clouds sweep in low enough to obscure the mountaintops around us. Waterfalls cascade on either side of us as a steady drizzle falls. When we reach the lower altitudes of the valley floor, cacti begin to appear, but we see mostly opuntias and an abundance of *Trichocereus peruvianus*. Just before entering the city, we see something that makes our hearts fall. We have come to the end of pavement and the beginning of dirt roads. Our travels in Peru have almost all been on modern highways that are well paved and have good signs and guardrails. Because of the good infrastructure, plant exploration in Peru is feasible, even relatively easy. Even the dirt roads we travel on between here and Huancayo are good and solid, definitely not in danger of being washed away by rains. Even so, it is simply not possible to drive fast on such roads. We do not know it yet, but over the next several days, we will often travel only 50 miles (80 km) per day.

After following the Río Pachachaca, we reach the land of *Weberbauerocereus cuzcoensis* at Abancay. Like the plants of *W. rauhii* to the south, these are large and highly branched with narrow stems. They occur sporadically about halfway between Chalhuanca and Abancay. Although the river valley near Abancay is broad and flat with a thick layer of sediment brought down from possible ancient floods, here the river has eroded a narrow channel into the plain. On all level surfaces is a forest of *Weberbauerocereus* and, in places, *Azureocereus*. We have found weberbauerocerei in the north beyond Cajamarca and in the south beyond Puquio, and although in some places within this vast range it grows abundantly, for the most part it is completely absent. If nothing else, Peru is a country of widespread genera.

Our transect from Abancay to Andahuaylas puts us into new territory, which means new types of cacti for us to study. A trip like this through the Rocky Mountains of the United States or the Alps of Europe would entail endless climbing and descending from one set of mountains to another. While the passes might be at high altitudes, all the roads themselves would either climb or immediately drop away again. Peru's mountain roads do not do that. Here the road climbs to a very high altitude and then runs more or less flat for 50 to 100 miles (80 to 160 km). Abancay itself is at 6800 feet (2000 m) elevation, and we are above 12,600 feet (3870 m) as we traverse the "pass" of Abra Huayllaccasa. This area consisted of such gently rolling hills, if we had not had an altimeter with us, we would not have known when we reached the summit before beginning our descent.

The road from Abancay climbs quickly through the weberbauerocerei and continues upward until it abruptly levels off on a flat, grassy plain. It is easier to believe we are in eastern Montana or Wyoming than in central Peru. We call it a road, but it is nothing more than the narrowest strip of dirt in an expanse of grass, barely visible as it meanders aimlessly around low knolls and modest depressions. The land around us has only a little undulating topography, but far in the distance we see serious mountains in every direction. Even though we are already more than 2 miles (3250 m) high, the mountains tower above us. Shallow pools of meltwater are scattered across the flattest regions, and there are sedges and rushes growing at their margins. True to the lore of mountains, weather at this altitude lasts for only minutes. Heavy clouds gather and a light drizzle sweeps across us, but after half an hour the rain is interrupted by a clearing in the clouds that races past and allows full sunshine to pour down on us. The sunlight is cold up here, and we can do no botanizing without a coat or sweater. But the botanizing is wonderful.

The orange balls are *Oroya depressa*, and the white patches are
Austrocylindropuntia tephrocactoides. The site was this sunny for only a moment before the
clouds and fog swept through. Although this area is at 12,350 feet (3800 m),
there are potato fields wherever it is not too rocky to plow the soil.
Even at this altitude, habitat destruction is extensive.

These altiplanos are the home of high Andean cacti such as
Austrocylindropuntia tephrocactoides, *Oroya depressa*, and *Tephrocactus floccosus*. These are not cacti that merely tolerate cold, wet habitats; they prefer
them. Altiplanos at this altitude are the only places where these cacti are
found, and transplanting them to lower, more moderate climates will not
make them happier. We drive for many hours through lower altitudes that
have the same aspect as the altiplanos—similar grasses and topography—but
we see no cacti. Only after we climb high enough do these cacti make an
appearance again.

The oroyas grow as globose cacti that are nestled close to the ground,
half-buried by mosses and little mountain herbs. On cloudy days, or if the sun
is high, they can be difficult to spot, but when the sun is low enough to backlight their spines, they glow brilliantly so that whole hillsides are dotted with
their orange luminescence. Their abundance (in some places hundreds of

Reproduction was successful this year for *Oroya depressa*,
and many plants had multiple fruits. Harvesting the small fruit was difficult and slow because
when we plucked them they tore at the bottom and the seeds fell out.
The population here included individuals of all sizes,
from tiny seedlings to large specimens like this.

plants grow in a space the size of suburban backyard) shows they are by no
means merely surviving. We are amazed at the size of some of the plants we
see here. Diameters up to 9 inches (22.5 cm) and heights of 6 inches (15 cm)
tall are fairly common, whereas in cultivation they are always much smaller.
This is a small genus, though, and only seven species have been named. A
reclassification in 1999 suggested that six of those should be just one species,
Oroya peruviana.

One species we find here, *Austrocylindropuntia tephrocactoides*, looks like
drifts of snow. Its low stems sprawl on the ground like those of *Haageocereus*,
barely protruding upward more than 6 to 8 inches (15 to 20 cm), but because
each stem bears so many long white hairs, a colony really can look like a
patch of snow. The illusion is so effective that even when we examine a hillside covered in these plants that we know are cacti, we still occasionally mistake a clump of them for snow. Of course, this mistake is made easier by the

The sprigs of grass clearly indicate the miniature size of these plants of
Austrocylindropuntia tephrocactoides. Hidden by the hair are the small,
green leaves one would expect to find on a relative of *Opuntia*.

presence of the many real patches of snow here. Another species in this
region, *Tephrocactus floccosus*, is even more famous for this mimicry because
it is much more widespread. In certain areas, colonies are so dense that entire
hillsides are covered with a layer of pure white. *Austrocylindropuntia* catches
our attention because it is less well known and so small. The term *cylindropuntia* refers to opuntias that have a cylindrical stem like the chollas of North
America, rather than those that have a flattened stem (known as *platyopuntia*), such as prickly pears. Originally, *cylindropuntia* referred to all opuntias
with a cylindrical stem, but later it was decided to separate the South
American opuntias into a new genus *Austrocylindropuntia* (*Austro-* means
"south" or "southern"). Most members of the genus are large plants; indeed
A. subulata can be a small tree, and in Argentina we will come across many
that are 2 to 4 feet (60 cm to 1.2 m) tall. These plants of *A. tephrocactoides*,
by contrast, do not poke up much and instead remain low to the ground and

out of the cold wind. Their thick stems (about 2½ inches [6 cm] in diameter) branch frequently, and old plants can end up covering a square yard or two (about a square meter). They have such copious white hair that they appear to be imitating either snowdrifts or plants of *Tephrocactus floccosus* imitating snowdrifts. In fact, these plants were named *tephrocactoides* because of their strong resemblance to *Tephrocactus floccosus*. We are about to finish our examination when a student spots a single plant in bloom. Its three yellow flowers, although starting to wilt at the end of the day, still show their perfect *Opuntia* form.

It is wonderful to be able to drive up to a population of high Andean cacti, study and photograph them, take measurements and samples, climb back into a warm vehicle that keeps out the wet, bitter cold, drive to a restaurant for a good meal, and then check into a hotel with a hot shower and warm bed. The early plant collectors traveled this area on horseback or by foot. Even if they could take a railroad to a mine in the area, any further exploration would have been arduous. Imagine having to take enough food, water, and other provisions for trekking across these endless miles of altiplano, all of which are high, windswept, and unable to provide shelter or even wood for a fire. Our reflections become all the more real when a leaf spring on the rear axle breaks and threatens to puncture the gas tank. We cannot drive another foot. We are traveling between Andahuaylas and Ayacucho, and having climbed to altiplano at 13,780 feet (4240 m), we realize that during our five-hour drive, the only sign of life has been three trucks coming the other way. Walking back to Andahuaylas is obviously impossible. We estimate how far ahead the next town might be and decide that it is also too far away (it turns out to be four hours away by car, not foot). In total, we are nine hours between towns with no intervening houses, no fields, no pastures of grazing vicuñas, not even a fork in the road. In fact, we will later discover that there is nothing in this entire area except a single camp for workers who are building an electrical power transmission line. This camp is about ¼ mile (400 m) from where we break down, and most fortunately of all, the only welding machine within 200 miles (320 km) that can fix our leaf spring is right here within sight. It is also the only place with a dormitory big enough for us all, and the only place with a kitchen. The supervisor puts the camp and its facilities at our disposal. Clearly, if we were going to break down, doing so next to a repair shop was a great stroke of luck.

Night has fallen, and cold rain whips across the open plains. We decide to wait till morning to do the welding. The cook boils water for hot coffee and instant hot chocolate. Space heaters are brought out to warm the small mess area—dining hall would not be the proper term—because we lowland, coastal types are obviously not as inured to the cold as these highlanders. Before long, we are warm enough to do some work (our fingers are no longer stiff), so we bring out our bags and boxes of plants, dissecting tools, and notebooks, and we work into the night by the light of kerosene lanterns. The dormitory is a long, low room with two rows of bunk beds and a pile of mattresses and blankets. Because this is a construction camp high in the Andes, there are no sheets, pillows, or heat. Toilets are outside, at the end of the building, and not lighted. The rain does not let up all night. Once again, instead of undressing to go to bed, we put on all the dry clothes we have and wish we had not drunk quite so much coffee. In the morning the leaf springs are welded back into shape in short order. Breakfast consists of more hot chocolate, and then we head off for another day of science.

We soon find two wonderful cacti. We encounter the first, *Morawetzia doelziana*, as soon as we drop into lower altitudes where the climate is hot and dry. It is now often combined taxonomically with *Oreocereus*, and the plants at first sight do look like smaller, more slender versions of *O. hendriksenianus*. Their fruits too are the large, yellow, hollow fruits typical of *Oreocereus*, so large that the black seeds rattle around inside. The first sign that morawetzias are unusual is that they are growing in a low, hot habitat. The second sign is their lack of hair. *Morawetzia doelziana* forma *calva* is particularly naked (*calva* means "bald"), although *M. sericata* does have enough hair to resemble a specimen of *Oreocereus* that is thinning. The most significant difference is that *M. doelziana* has a peculiar growth pattern. While young, the stem grows upward as a slender column, incapable of flowering. When it is about 2 feet (60 cm) tall, all elongation stops, and the shoot tip—but not the rest of the

The branch on the right of this *Morawetzia doelziana* is old and its spines have been weathered white, whereas the stem on the left has fresh, young, yellow spines and is obviously still juvenile. The top of the right stem is slightly wider than the rest of the stem, and although it is not yet old enough to have become distinctly club-shaped, it is now capable of flowering.

shoot—gradually widens and starts producing flowers. This has been called an apical cephalium, although it could never be confused with the cephalium of *Melocactus*. Even in an old M. *doelziana* plant, the apical cephalium does not grow up as a typical cephalium; instead, only the very end of the stem becomes somewhat club-shaped. As the plant ages, new branches will emerge from basal areoles. Old plants are highly branched clumps covering a square yard or more (one square meter). Although there are hundreds of *Morawetzia* plants here, we did not see any with branches that had become really thickened and obviously woody.

The second cactus here, *Azureocereus hertlingianus*, is one of those species rarely seen except as a small seedling in a nursery. As seedlings, though, they are among the most beautiful of all plants. The *azureo-* in their name relates to their blue color—and it really is blue—that is due to the type of wax that protects their stems. Golden yellow spines against the blue skin are what make this plant so attractive. Because mature flow-

Plants of *Morawetzia sericata* are good landscaping plants.
They never become tall but instead form compact clumps that do not spread
too vigorously, and they produce red flowers reliably.

ering plants are very rare in cultivation, most people never have the
opportunity to see another striking feature of A. *hertlingianus*, its almost
completely black flowers. Some taxonomists classify this species as
Browningia hertlingiana, and its flowers definitely bring to mind those of B.
candelaris because they are completely covered by prominent leaflike
scales. The scales of A. *hertlingianus* are smaller, black, and have an elab-
orate, fringed margin. When we visit this area on another trip in January
2000, we arrive slightly late in the flowering season, but we do encounter
several flowers. Mostly, however, we find many developing fruits. After
pollination, the outer end of the flower withers and dries out, but it still
clings to the developing ovary for some time. The basal ovary enlarges
into the fruit, retaining the flower's scales. The presence of blue stems,
golden spines, and black flowers makes this an exceptional plant that
could become among the most attractive landscaping plants in gardens of
southern California and Arizona.

We came across thousands of plants of
Azureocereus hertlingianus near Huanta, Peru,
ranging from seedlings to juveniles to mature
adults. Like so many columnar cacti,
they flower at a height where it is not possible
for us to get a good photograph.
Of all the many plants available here,
none had flowers nearer than 8 feet (2.5 m)
or so to the ground.

We begin our return to Lima and pass through Huancayo, encountering *Tephrocactus atroviridis* on the way. It seems to be a hairless form of *Tephrocactus floccosus*, and without the abundant white hairs, it would never fool anyone into thinking it was a patch of snow. In most areas, *Trichocereus peruvianus* appears as a tall, columnar plant, but sometimes it is nothing more than a low shrub only a few feet tall. In both forms, however, its large, white flowers are abundant. We must cross one more pass to begin our descent to Lima, and this is a real pass, straight up and then down again, no altiplano at the summit. This pass, called Ticlio and located near La Oroya, is at 15,873 feet (4884 m), high enough that we do not want to spend too much time here. Doing anything strenuous, such as having a snowball fight, would guarantee an attack of altitude sickness.

The rest of the trip back to Lima is uneventful. We are still thrilled to see each species, even those we have encountered before. The sky is gray and heavy, but we expect to be back in the invigorating sun and heat as we drop down to the coast. That does not happen, however; our descent continues under overcast skies until we reach Lima itself. Before long a mist, not quite a drizzle, is moistening everything. The next morning, while we are working on plants at the university, the mist turns into a light rain and then a real

Although plants of *Azureocereus* are too tall to photograph in the wild,
they are more accommodating in the Jardin Exotique in Monaco.
Note how black the buds are, and the fringe on the flower scales is just visible
at this magnification. This plant also proves it is possible to raise a plant of
Azureocereus to adulthood in cultivation, a project well worth the effort.

rain. Rain on the coast of Peru—not an impossible event by any means, and
it does not surprise us as much as all the snow we have just passed through.
But this rain does not let up. The El Niño of 1997—98 has begun. In a few
weeks, many roads we have driven across will be wiped out by floods, and the
completely dry rivers we have "forded" will be raging as they carry boulders
down from the mountains. Without a doubt, those poor, long-suffering armatocerei will get some relief, and their roots will be absorbing water as fast as
they can, which puts a smile on our faces. This may be their only chance for
water until the next El Niño, and when will that be? Probably in the next
millennium.

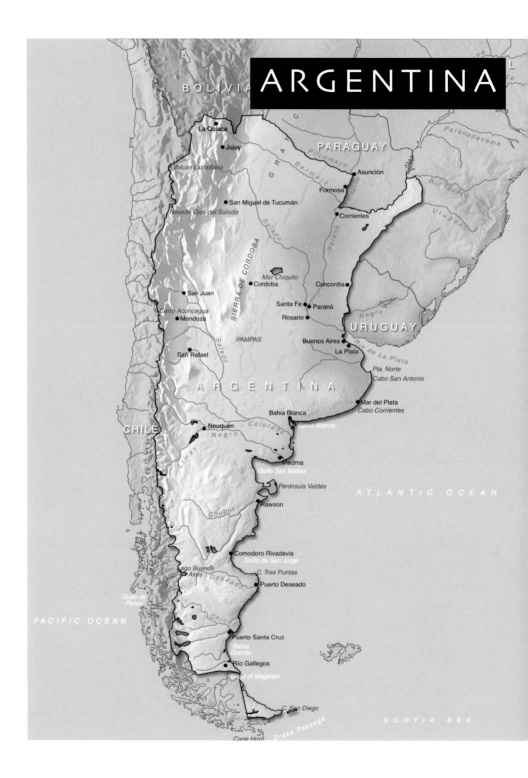

ARGENTINA

BOLIVIA

PARAGUAY

La Quiaca

Jujuy

Volcán Llullaillaco

Asunción

Formosa

San Miguel de Tucumán

Corrientes

Nevado Ojos del Salado

SIERRA DE CORDOBA

Mar Chiquito

Cordoba

Concordia

San Juan

Santa Fe

Paraná

URUGUAY

Cerro Aconcagua

Mendoza

Rosario

PAMPAS

Buenos Aires

La Plata

Río de La Plata

San Rafael

Pta. Norte

Cabo San Antonio

A R G E N T I N A

Mar del Plata

Cabo Corrientes

Bahia Blanca

CHILE

Neuquén

Colorado

Bahia Blanca

Negro

Limay

Viedma

Golfo San Matias

Peninsula Valdés

Chubut

Rawson

ATLANTIC OCEAN

Comodoro Rivadavia

Golfo de San Jorge

Lago Buenos Aires

Deseado

C. Tres Puntas

Puerto Deseado

Golfo de Peñas

PACIFIC OCEAN

Chico

Puerto Santa Cruz

Bahia Grande

Río Gallegos

Strait of Magellan

C. San Diego

Cape Horn

Drake Passage

SCOTIA SEA

6

SOUTHWESTERN ARGENTINA: The Search for *Maihuenia*

A rgentina is the land of the pampas—grasslands that extend to all horizons, enormous cattle ranches, and cowboys that would be at home in any Wild West movie. It is also more than that. To the south is Patagonia, flat plains swept by a constant wind that is known to have driven people mad. To the west are the Andes, their peaks separating Argentina from Chile. In the northwest are the provinces of Salta, Tucumán, and Jujuy, a mixture of lowlands, hot deserts, rainforests, salt deserts, and high, cold deserts known as altiplano. In the northeast are extensive plains, part grassland, part marsh, that rise barely above sea level and through which the Río Paraná and Río Uruguay run. Only the central, eastern region of Argentina is truly pampas. This is a country with a multitude of habitats, climates, ecologies, geographies, and just about every region is home to numerous species of cacti. Diversity and abundance are not as great here as in Mexico and Peru, but there are still plenty of cacti, and many are exotic.

Our first objective on this trip is to find *Maihuenia*, a poorly known genus of small cacti that grow in the southernmost region of Argentina, the area known as Patagonia. This is the narrow strip of land that tapers south forming the needlelike point of South America. On the west side of Patagonia are the Andes, whose Pacific slopes drop almost directly downward into the ocean. On the east side, desolate grassland forms a flat shelf between the mountains and the Atlantic. Patagonia is a cold country, a windy country that lies as far to the south of the equator as Seattle and Vancouver are to the north. The little vegetation that survives here, a grass called *Stipa*, grows as clumps with all its leaves held upright together so that they all move synchronously in the wind like a flame. When the late afternoon sun reflects off the yellow flickering leaves, it appears that all of the plains are burning. That wind comes out of the Arctic and seems never to cease or bring warmth. This is Patagonia, the home of *Maihuenia*.

As if it did not find the lowlands severe enough, *Maihuenia* also extends its range up into the Andes, across the mountains, and into part of Chile. It is early March, a bit late to start a trip to Patagonia since summer is over and fall well under way this far south. An early snowfall could keep us from the cacti we seek. We were lucky in Peru, finishing our exploration of the southern valleys not even one full week before El Niño rains washed out roads and bridges. We were not as lucky in Bolivia where rains stopped us from reaching the western habitats of *Oreocereus celsianus*. We do not want to miss seeing *Maihuenia*.

We drive west from the Buenos Aires airport and cross the immense pampas. These plains are clearly marked by an abundance of pampas grass (*Cortaderia selloana*), which is popular in gardens in warmer parts of the United States. Here in their native habitat, the leaves arch at least 6 feet (2 m) into the air, and because it is autumn, each of the millions of plants has a multitude of long, graceful tassels. Exquisite in bright sunlight, pampas grass becomes even more elegant when the setting sun shines through the tassels, turning them brilliant white.

The road is an excellent highway, and our progress westward is rapid with only a few stops. The countryside is remarkably featureless: no mountains, valleys, or even hills. Featureless cannot be equated with boring, however. A small lake beside the road is filled with hundreds of flamingoes, and in the occasional groves of *Prosopis caldenia* (a cousin of the North American mesquite), we find an exceptionally unusual plant, a root parasite called *Prosopanche americana*. As far as we know, there is no club or hobbyist society dedicated to the cultivation of parasitic plants, but there should be.

Prosopanche americana in the family Hydnoraceae is not a cactus by any means.
Visible here is only the very exotic flower; the rest of the plant is an irregular mass
called a tuber, which draws nutrients from the roots of an unwilling plant of *Prosopis*.
In Africa, an even more exotic root parasite, *Hydnora*, parasitizes a cactuslike *Euphorbia*,
and in Chile, *Trichocereus chilensis* is attacked by the mistletoe *Tristerix aphyllus*.

The mistletoes (*Viscum* and *Loranthus*) so familiar at Christmas are perhaps the most mundane of parasitic plants with their ordinary leaves, stems,
and flowers. Whereas all cacti are so closely related they constitute a single
family, parasitic plants have arisen in evolution so many times that there are
about a dozen families of parasitic plants. Many parasitic plants are like
mistletoes in that they attack shoots of their host plants; such parasites often
have recognizable stems and leaves, although these can be highly modified in
some parasites. Certain other parasitic plants attack the roots of their host
plants. Some, like Indian paintbrush (*Castilleja*), look more or less like ordinary plants, while others spend almost all their time deep underground after
they have attached themselves to their host. Being subterranean, they have
little need for stems and absolutely no need for leaves. Root parasites often
grow in such a way that they end up with lumpy, knobby, or scaly bodies that
always remain underground. These parasitic plants always grow in the dark,

drawing water, sugars, minerals—everything—from their host plants. When they have extracted enough nourishment from the host, they produce a flowering stalk that extends upward, breaks through the soil surface, and elevates the flowers where they can be seen by pollinating insects. The flowers of some root parasites are truly beautiful, while others are best described as interesting since their parts are so extensively modified that it is difficult to know which part is which. *Prosopanche* fits into both categories. The flowers are beautiful, even to non-botanists, but trying to figure out what the parts are is not easy. There are few studies of the anatomy of parasitic plants, so we are more than willing to make our first specimen on this cactus-collecting trip the plant of *Prosopanche* rather than *Maihuenia*.

TRICHOCEREUS CHILENSIS AND TRISTERIX APHYLLUS

Collecting specimens of *Prosopanche* reminds us of one of the strangest parasitic plants we know, *Tristerix aphyllus*, which attacks cacti growing in Chile. Cacti and parasitic plants are abundant in many parts of the Americas, and although they often occur close to each other in a particular area, cacti are for the most part immune to the parasites. Perhaps the thick fleshy stems of cacti are the key to their immunity. The seed of a parasite must germinate on a host stem, break open the host epidermis, and then insert its root (the root is so highly modified it is called a haustorium) into the host's vascular bundles. Although the thick, tough skin of cacti resists being torn open by the parasite's haustorium, if the haustorium does break through, all it finds is watery, non-nutritious cortex. Cell after cell inside the cactus is cortex; there is no vascular tissue with sugars to steal. Seeds of many parasitic plants have germinated on cacti, have beaten the odds and broken through the tough skin, only to die of starvation as the haustorium elongates to its maximum length still inches away from the cactus' deeply placed vascular bundles.

Natural selection has produced one species of parasitic plant, the mistletoe *Tristerix aphyllus* (in the family Loranthaceae), that is able to successfully overcome every defense available to a cactus. How it lives on the cactus *Trichocereus chilensis*, which occurs slightly north of Santiago, Chile, has been studied in detail by Gloria Montenegro and Jim Mauseth. A mistletoe seed is typically deposited by a bird on the host plant either as the bird cleans its beak or as it defecates. *Tristerix* seeds stick to the cactus epidermis, spines, or trichomes, and then germinate. The haustorium emerges from the seed and grows away from light, which in this case guides it toward the dark green surface of the cactus. The haustorium tip is covered with glandular cells, and once contact is made with the cactus epidermis, the cells secrete a glue that welds parasite and cactus together. The haustorium then expands radially, growing wider but not longer. Because it is glued to the cactus, the haustorium's sideways growth stretches the epidermis of the cactus sideways as well. Before long, the cactus' waxy cuticle is ripped apart, opening a hole in the first line of defense. There is no hole in the epidermis, so the haustorium still cannot penetrate it the way a root penetrates soil. Instead, some haustorium cells elongate, stretching themselves into long threadlike shapes so slender that each cell can get inside an epidermis cell of the cactus. The mistletoe's cells grow right through the epidermis cells and into the first layer of hypodermis cells, then into the next layer, and the next. The extreme slenderness of the haustorium cells allows them to pass right through cactus cells until they finally reach the cactus cortex. Cortex cells are mostly just water with too little nutrient value to keep a haustorium and a seedling alive. The *Tristerix aphyllus* seed now does a strange thing: it dies. It never had a chance of surviving as a plant; it only had the ability to get some of its cells into the cactus cortex.

The few haustorium cells that make it through the surface of *Trichocereus chilensis* are so tiny that the paltry nutrients in the cortex are enough to keep them alive. They grow, probably slowly, and divide, elongate, and explore, in the process forming a narrow strand of cells inside the cactus body. We do not know if they grow at random or if somehow they sense the direction in which the vascular tissues lie, but after a time (we do not know how long), they finally reach the sugar-filled vascular bundles. Until this point, *Tristerix aphyllus* exists as a plant embedded completely inside a host plant, and its body consists of nothing but a sparse network of fine strands. Knowing that *T. aphyllus* is a plant that produces flowers and fruits, we would expect it to have stems, roots, leaves, an epidermis, a cortex, vascular tissue, and pith like all ordinary plants, and yet it has none of those things. It is living at the barest, most minimal level possible, and its very existence requires us to stretch our concepts of "plant," "plant body," and "plant anatomy" to the limits.

Once the strands reach the cactus vascular tissue and all its nutrients, the parasite's growth changes. The strands become thicker until they are many cells wide, although they still never develop any tissues we could call normal. The strands grow upward and downward in the cactus, spreading extensively. They somehow trick the cactus into putting up no fight whatsoever. We see no sign of damage, no necrosis, no corky protective layers. The outside of the cactus does not look diseased, and even when we use a microscope, it appears completely healthy.

At some point, strands of mistletoe grow outward through the cortex toward the cactus' surface. During this passage, the parasite uses the nutrients of the cactus vascular tissues to keep it going through the watery, non-nutritious cortex. When the mistletoe strand arrives at the surface, it again faces the barrier of the tough hypodermis and epidermis. Something stimulates

Tristerix cells to divide and grow into a nondescript lump about the size of a pea. Inside this lump, flower buds form. The lump somehow kills a small patch of cactus skin, pushes against it, and breaks it open. Through this hole in the skin, the parasite's flowers emerge and then open, attracting pollinators. Once fruits form, a bird arrives and carries the seed to another cactus, so starting another round of infection. After flowering or fruiting, the emergent part of the parasite (called the exophyte) may die while the internal part (the endophyte) remains alive inside the cactus, growing and preparing for next year's flowering season.

As we examine infected plants of *Trichocereus chilensis*, we notice that some exophytes are large while others are small, and that some are alive while others are dead. We also notice that a cactus with dead exophytes has endophytes that are still alive. What is going on? It is suicide for a parasite to kill its host, and if a plant of *Tristerix aphyllus* were to kill its host plant of *Trichocereus chilensis*, then it too would die. If, on the other hand, the parasite can grow and reproduce slowly and gently, then the host can tolerate it; both host and parasite will survive for years. The long life of both allows the parasite to maximize its reproduction. The death of the exophyte may also be an adaptation that helps the host. All this parasitic behavior of *Tristerix aphyllus* is occurring in a desert, and there is little chance that any mistletoe will ever evolve to be as well adapted to xeric conditions as a cactus. If *Tristerix aphyllus* were to try and keep its exophytic portion alive during hot dry summers, it would lose so much water that it would put the host at risk. After all, the water must come from the cactus, and all of the cactus' water-conservation mechanisms do no good if the mistletoe exophyte is losing water to the dry air. By letting its exophyte portion die while keeping its endophyte portion alive, the *Tristerix aphyllus* retreats inside the cactus body, and both parasite and host are now protected by the

This specimen of *Trichocereus chilensis* has a mass of *Tristerix aphyllus* flowers emerging from it. The dark flowers at the top of the mass have died, but the endophyte that produced them will remain alive. The lower red flowers are all still healthy, and many individual flowers are preparing to open. Some flowers have already pollinated and begun to form small, grape-sized fruits. Notice that the cactus looks perfectly healthy—except for the parasite that is emerging from it.

full complement of desert adaptations available to *Trichocereus*. If the summer is very mild and humid, the exophyte is not shed and instead continues to grow and flower, becoming a small "shrub" emerging out of the side of the cactus. We can think of *Tristerix aphyllus* as a kind of water plant. Its roots (the haustorium) are in a lake (the cactus), and as long as the lake is full of water, *Tristerix* remains active and healthy. Should the lake start to go dry, *Tristerix* lets its exposed parts die and it survives the drought as an endophyte.

The biology of *Tristerix aphyllus* is definitely unusual, but it is also clearly adapted to an unusual host that grows in an unusual habitat.

Amazingly, while *T. aphyllus* is atypical, it is not unique. Another parasitic plant, *Viscum minimum*, in a different family, Viscaceae, attacks a similar desert-adapted, succulent host, *Euphorbia*. Except for their different names, evolutionary histories, and ancestors, the present-day biology of *V. minimum* is almost identical to that of *T. aphyllus*.

This example of *Wigginsia tephracantha* is surrounded by grass that protects it from full sunlight.
Although they have adapted well to such harsh conditions,
these plants are also very easy to cultivate and are not at all temperamental.
Even without flowers they are really beautiful.

After collecting our samples of *Prosopanche* and reminiscing about *Tristerix*, we climb into the pickup and head toward the town of General Acha where we will spend the first night of this trip. In the morning we continue southwest to Lihue Calel, a national park that encompasses a set of low granite hills that have been weathered into gentle mounds. The pink rock is tinged green with tiny lichens clinging to its surface. Between the rocks there are open, sandy areas supporting some grasses and a few bushes. Cacti are everywhere.

The easiest cactus to find is *Wigginsia tephracantha*. These small globose or disk-shaped cacti grow primarily in the long, narrow, dirt-filled fissures of the granite, in some places by themselves, in other places alongside grasses that try to crowd them out. There is no reason for us to search for the cacti in the loose, gravelly soil around the base of the granite outcrops because they do not survive without solid rock to keep them stable. We are surprised by this preference in microhabitats because wigginsias are shaped like beets

Flowers of *Wigginsia* are strikingly attractive, and these plants are highly recommended for
hobbyists. Their red stigmas and the unusual metallic sheen of the petals make these flowers
look much like those of *Notocactus*. This is *W. sellowii* photographed
at the Jardin Exotique in Monaco.

with large, deep taproots that could undoubtedly grow more easily in soil
rather than in narrow rock crevices. What is the result of a 4-inch (10-cm)
wide plant trying to grow in a 1-inch (2.5-cm) wide fissure? A plant that
looks like a pancake. Grown in cultivation (they are very easy to grow and
thrive in almost any conditions), they are round like any ordinary plant.
Here, however, most are deformed in that they take on the shape of the fissure in which they are trapped. With their big taproots and small, slightly
rounded tops, wigginsias fill with water in the wet season and the top protrudes well beyond the rock. During periods of drought the plants shrink and
pull themselves down until they are level with the rock, sometimes even
sinking into the fissure.

A striking feature of wigginsias is the dense tuft of hair at the top of the
plant large enough to look like a cephalium. Only the young areoles at the
top of the plant produce flowers in *Wigginsia*, so flowers emerge through this
mass of hairs, further enhancing its resemblance to a cephalium. The hairs,

however, are temporary; the young areoles produce them in large quantities together with the flowers, but the hairs are fragile and break away after a few months or a year. With the hairs thinned out or completely gone, we can ascertain that the areoles at the top of the plant are exactly like those at the sides and bottom. When we see that the plant has not undergone any change of growth pattern as it matures from a juvenile to an adult, we confirm that there is no real cephalium at all. It is fairly common for a cactus to have a dense mat of hairs at the apex of its stem, especially those like *Wigginsia* plants that grow in full sunlight unprotected by surrounding shrubs. At noon, sunlight beats down on the shoot tip, which is the most delicate part of the shoot. Because shoots become longer only through growth at the tip, this is a critically important tissue. Without hairs to block at least part of the light, the shoot tip would overheat and suffer damage from ultraviolet radiation.

Wigginsia is a name that you might not come across too often when reading about cacti. The plants were in the genus *Malacocarpus* for over one hundred years, and then in 1964 the genus *Wigginsia* was created. A long-standing error arose when the name *Malacocarpus* was given to this group of cacti without realizing that the same name had already been used seven years earlier for a group of plants in a different family, the Zygophyllaceae (the family that contains creosote bush). The rules of nomenclature do not allow two plant groups to share the same name, so *Malacocarpus* could not be used for cacti. A new name was needed, so the genus *Wigginsia* came into being. Once in a while—very rarely, actually—an error like this can be corrected in favor of the second group, with the first group getting a new name. An example of this is *Mammillaria*. It was originally named *Mammillaria* in 1812, but that name had been used for other organisms, algae in this case. So the cacti were renamed *Neomammillaria* in 1923 (these things take time to sort out), but that name was universally disliked and never accepted. Finally, at a meeting of taxonomists, it was decided to use *Mammillaria* for the cacti. We are not certain what happened to the algae.

Growing in Lihue Calel's granite fissures alongside *Wigginsia tephracantha* is *Notocactus submammulosus*. We easily distinguish the two because notocacti have longer spines, are more globose, and are too big to shrink down

and hide in the fissures. Wigginsias are believed to be closely related to notocacti; like plants of *Wigginsia*, those of *Notocactus* are apically hairy. However,
notocacti are generally larger than wigginsias and their fruits have scales and
hairs, whereas *Wigginsia* fruits are naked. A 1999 publication puts both
Wigginsia and *Notocactus* into *Parodia*, and considering that the plants are
embedded in rock, they certainly do a lot of traveling, at least taxonomically.

We drive a little further south and cross the Río Colorado, which puts
us into the province of Río Negro. We drive just twenty minutes further and
come to the Río Negro itself. The river bottom is now heavily cultivated,
and orchards extend all the way to the hills. As we found with the western
rivers of Peru, the line where the river bottom meets the hills is one of
absolute demarcation; the fields stop abruptly and the desert remains intact.
The dry hills contain a surprising variety of cacti, such as *Austrocactus
bertinii*, *Echinopsis leucantha*, *Pyrrhocactus strausianus*, and a species of *Maihuenia*. We were not expecting such variety because we are very far south,
about latitude 40°S. That is the equivalent of 40°N, the latitude of New
York and Pittsburgh, which are not prime cactus regions. Perhaps a fairer
comparison is with the western United States where 40°N passes through
the Great Basin Desert of eastern Washington and Oregon. Although not
known as a cactus wonderland, this area is home to the genuine cacti
Coryphantha missouriensis, *Opuntia fragilis*, *O. polyacantha*, and *Pediocactus
simpsonii*. And whereas the Great Basin is a cold desert (temperatures drop
into the 20°sF [-5°C] almost every night in January and February), here in
the home of *Austrocactus* the midwinter month of July averages 42°F (6°C).

We find a small plant of *Austrocactus bertinii* here, a little column of
hooked spines 4 to 6 inches (10 to 15 cm) tall. The plants are so dehydrated
that they have shrunk; all the spines are pulled tightly together to the point
that we cannot see the body at all. The first plant we find is growing completely encased in the prickly branches of a small bush whose dead, gray
branches match the color of the spines and provide effective camouflage.
Spurred on by the success of finding this rare species, we search every bush
and shrub, but we encounter only a few more plants of *A. bertinii*. All the

The plants of Notocactus submammulosus were not particularly photogenic,
so we are substituting this N. roseoluteus to show a characteristic feature of notocacti,
their many beautiful flowers that open at the same time. With so many flowers open at once,
the plant increases the chances that a pollinator flying by will visit its flowers,
but this is risky biology for desert cacti because no pollinator may happen by that day.

plants we do find tend to be curved at the base as if they had fallen over as seedlings and are now growing upright. There are no flowers or fruits, but we find a few seedlings around the larger plants, an indication that despite their rarity and desiccated state, they have been reproducing. As we collect a few plants, their hooked spines tangle together and grab our fingers, reminding us very quickly of *Mammillaria*. They do not grow as easily as mammillarias, however, and our cultivated plants have been slow to add new height and so far have not flowered.

Pyrrhocactus strausianus is a popular plant in collections. Their emerald green bodies have curved, red-yellow spines, making them a standout among other plants in a group. The plants here are large for the species, up to 10 inches (25.5 cm) tall and almost 5 inches (12.5 cm) across, excluding the spines. Like the austrocacti, they grow under the protection of shrubs of *Prosopis*. We collect a plant for dissection and find that there is more wood

This plant of *Austrocactus bertinii* did not grow exposed like this; we pulled the covering shrubs away for the photograph. Although it looks ferocious here, the plants are easy to handle and their spines are not too sharp. This plant is only about 3 inches (7.5 cm) tall.

than we expected at its base. The pith is about ½ inch (1.25 cm) in diameter and is surrounded by a ring of wood about ⅓ inch (0.75 cm) thick. That may not sound like much, but take a look at a ruler—this is a lot of wood for such a small plant. The pyrrhocacti are strange beasts in cultivation. They are part of that group that often dies after transplanting: they are unable to recover from the shock and unable to produce new roots that supply the shoot with critically needed hormones. Every once in a while, especially if you just leave the plants alone without watering them, they will finally begin to grow on their own. Then they can be watered and fertilized, and they will usually grow reasonably well. We say *reasonably* because pyrrhocacti will often die overnight, even though they appeared to be fine the day before.

A clue to cultivating pyrrhocacti may lie in this habitat. Patagonia is a zone of rainy winters and hot, dry summers. Records for Maquinchao, only a few miles south of Lihue Calel and still within the range of *Austrocactus* and *Pyrrhocactus*, indicate average June and July (winter) temperatures of only about 35°F (2°C). Freezing must occur almost every night. Although the region receives very little rain under any circumstances (7¼ inches [20 cm] per year), the amount in May and June (less than 1 inch [2.25 cm] per month) is almost double that of the summer months of November, December, and January (about ½ inch [1.25 cm] each month). It goes against all our experience to water our plants in the winter when they are cold, but that is when Patagonia gets most of its rain. In the summer we try to encourage our plants to grow by giving them water and fertilizer, but Patagonian plants are not expecting water then and are not prepared for it. For many species, dormancy is controlled by internal metabolism, so giving them water does not break dormancy, it only encourages mold and bacteria. Whatever the situation is with pyrrhocacti, the harsh conditions here indicate that it may be best to give them less rather than more water.

Pyrrhocactus strausianus has the short body and stout spines typical of pyrrhocacti. All species of *Pyrrhocactus* grow in hot, dry conditions, but surrounding leafy shrubs and trees often provide some shade. This plant has sand halfway up its body that both deflects excess sun and helps the plant retain moisture. Of course, too much sand would suffocate the plant.

After passing through Neuquén, we travel southwest through Plaza Huincul to Zapala. The border with Chile is only a few miles to the west and we have already climbed to 3000 feet (900 m) altitude. The terrain here is still plains and rolling hills, the soil is almost pure sand, and plants of the bunch grass *Stipa* (which are characteristic of Patagonia) are everywhere. This is the land of *Pterocactus* (*Ptero-* is pronounced tero), a genus of subterranean cacti. These are cacti that, under the best of circumstances, have most of their body deep underground with only a small amount of stem protruding into the sunlight. When *Pterocactus* needs to get away from the heat, cold, wind, and bugs, it lets its exposed parts die and hides deep below the soil surface. These underground plants enter a state of dormancy much like that of tulip bulbs, and

This is a medium-sized plant of *Pterocactus araucanus*.
All these stems are the ends of many branches coming from one neck.
Although their green chlorophyll is hidden by orange, sun-blocking pigments,
the stems are healthy. At first glance, all these little globose stems look alike,
but some have a small crater in their tops where flower parts fell away,
indicating that they are fruits not stems.
These were growing in pure sand that we could dig with our bare hands.

they can pass months, even years, in a state of suspended animation. Yet they somehow detect the return of good conditions in the world above ground (perhaps from rain soaking deep into the soil or a change in soil temperature) and activate a dormant bud or two that then grow upward as thin, delicate "necks." Once the necks reach sunlight, they develop as short but otherwise normal photosynthetic, spiny cactus stems. These aerial parts will carry out photosynthesis in their green tissues, and under proper conditions will flower and set seed. The length of time the aerial parts survive may depend partly on conditions and partly on genetics. In mild conditions, the plants' aerial parts are more easily kept alive, and as long as they are able to photosynthesize, the plants are profiting on their investment. Allowing a healthy aerial stem to die would be a waste of resources if a plant could keep it alive through a winter that is only mildly stressful or through a summer that is not too severe.

In some cases, however, it may be that just as natural cycles cause some trees to lose their leaves in the autumn, so too do natural cycles cause some cactus plants to sacrifice their aerial stems, regardless of how mild or severe the conditions are. Leaf abscission is set by the plant's genetics, and when the plant detects the short days and long nights of autumn, the plant's genes are triggered to begin the abscission process. The same type of mechanism probably occurs in *Pterocactus*. It is better for the plant to sacrifice the aerial part in a controlled way using a layer of bark to seal the subterranean, living tissues off from those that will be sacrificed. The alternative is to keep the aerial portion alive until harsh conditions kill it, but then the plant would be faced with having dead, decomposing, fungus-filled tissue still connected to the underground part that needs to stay alive.

Simply by looking at the plants around us—and pterocacti are very abundant here—we cannot be certain exactly what abscission process these plants go through. On some individuals, all aerial stems are short; it looks as if they are all only a year old, that the plants had all absdised their aerial stems simultaneously. But some stems on other plants are long and branching, as if the topmost branches are the current year's growth, the underlying ones the preceding year's growth, and so on. These plants appear to have gambled on a mild winter and won, but it may be a risky gamble. It would be great if a student could study a large number of plants over a period of several years and see how accurately pterocacti predict the future weather.

This dying back of pterocacti has undoubtedly led many people to throw away perfectly good plants in their collection. Despite the hobbyist's best efforts, some of these species, for example, *Pterocactus fischeri*, simply go moribund and die, and then the grower throws the plant out, not realizing that the root is still healthy. The best thing to do when pterocacti begin to die back is to stop watering them and let them stay dry and dormant. A few months later, they should send up a shoot on their own. When that shoot appears, resume watering. When in doubt, unpot the plant and check to see if the root is solid and fleshy (it is alive, so keep it) or dry and withered (donate it to the compost pile).

Although they may not look like it at first glance, pterocacti are part of the subfamily Opuntioideae. They have a number of close relatives, *Puna* for instance, and also *Maihueniopsis* and *Tephrocactus*. *Pterocactus* and *Puna* share the same body plan by having a large subterranean root, a neck, and an aerial part. In *Pterocactus*, however, the flowers are borne at the very end of the neck and aerial part; it looks as if the entire neck and aerial part are equivalent to a very elongated *Opuntia* flower. *Tephrocactus* and *Maihueniopsis* species look like big branching tops of large, old pterocacti, but when they are dug out of the sand, their subterranean parts have no special modification. The underground branches are really branches that have been covered by drifting sand; they are not long and thin like the necks of pterocacti.

We come across extensive fields of *Pterocactus araucanus* and *P. valentinii* as we travel a little south of Zapala. The former looks like a large mound of *Copiapoa hypogaea* from Chile, and the latter resembles a mass of cholla joints that have fallen apart and then been swept into a pile. Plants of both species are thriving despite growing in loose sand, and when we dig around a 2-foot (60-cm) wide group of aerial stems, we find that they all come down to the same giant root. Studying plants in habitat is more difficult than working on ones in a greenhouse, but there are some measurements you can only get out here in the sun and wind and dirt. The neck of one *P. araucanus* plant here is 12 inches (30 cm) long, a full foot between the soil and the top of the root. The root itself is 4 inches (10 cm) in diameter—much larger than a carrot or most beets. Looking carefully, we notice that many aerial stems have a shallow, cuplike depression in the top, the characteristic mark that these are the remnants of flowers. The cuplike depression is the scar left when petals wither and die. Being flower remnants, they are technically fruits, but when we cut open a number of them, we do not find any seeds. We have previously found their reproduction successful and their fruits filled with seeds. Lack of pollination and seed formation during a particular year is not a serious problem for these plants, however, because they undergo vegetative reproduction, an option available to most opuntioids.

Also here in Zapala we find a specimen of our main objective, a species of *Maihuenia*, *M. patagonica*. We have beaten the weather to at least one

This is one of the smallest plants of *Pterocactus araucanus* we found;
it had only three little round stems above ground. These few aerial stems have certainly not
produced this massive root; instead, those from previous years produced it but they died
and decayed long ago, leaving only the root and neck to survive each time.

Pterocacti have dual personalities. They most often hide underground or expose only a tiny,
dull gray stem, but when they decide to flower, they go all out.
This *Pterocactus gonjianii* has large flowers with typical *Opuntia* shape.
The pink-purple color and bright red stigmas allow insects to see the flowers
from far away against the dull, ubiquitous sand.

species, and although the nights are already cold, snow is the last thing we worry about on this warm day. For such a sought-after plant, the reality is something of a let down. The plants are simply not very attractive. Only the most die-hard hobbyist or scientist could get excited about these scraggly, half-dead bushes that are not much more than a mass of spines. *Maihuenia* and *Pereskia* are the only two genera in the subfamily Pereskioideae (some cactologists also classify a few of the pereskias as *Rhodocactus*), and pereskias are of particular value because they appear to have changed little since the early stages of the evolution of the cactus family. Pereskias even now are restricted to areas that are not terribly hot and dry, areas that may be similar to their ancestral habitats. Rather than becoming increasingly adapted to ever-drier conditions, pereskias have been able to persist by not changing too much and remaining in habitats that are also not changing much.

Because *Maihuenia* is in the same subfamily as *Pereskia*, it would be reasonable to expect that it too is a type of "living fossil." But the maihuenias appear to have changed considerably during evolution. Only two species of *Maihuenia* have survived extinction, and both live in habitats that must have changed greatly in the last several million years. *Maihuenia patagonica* now occurs in the severe deserts here in Patagonia, whereas M. *poeppigii* lives at high altitudes straddling the Andean border between Argentina and Chile. One species has adapted to lowland hot deserts, the other to cold alpine deserts, but neither is now adapted to what must have been its moderately warm and dry ancestral habitat. The ancestors of *Maihuenia* probably separated from the ancestors of *Pereskia* and other cacti, and then they flourished in a variety of habitats that became progressively more severe. Throughout the millions of years that intervened, this line of evolution almost certainly produced many species of *Maihuenia*, but now, all but these two species have become extinct. We are indeed lucky to have these two species that are the last of their line; they provide us with a unique opportunity for examining the early phases of this family. We photograph the plants and take samples for anatomical study, then simply sit and have lunch next to them. It is not every day that we can dine next to a species whose story is so intriguing. When we find M. *poeppigii*, we will tell the rest of *Maihuenia*'s story.

Plants of *Maihuenia patagonica* have a dry, tough look, and when we cut them with clippers, we confirm that they are wiry and desert-hardened. Their long spines project in every direction, but they keep from skewering themselves by having a somewhat open growth form. This is a single plant with one trunk and a large root.

After spending a night in Zapala, we set off to the mountains in search of *Maihuenia poeppigii*. This species occurs only at high altitude, and in this area there is plenty of high altitude for us to search. Perhaps the most useful clue is to look for trees of *Araucaria araucana* since the two species are rarely out of sight of each other. We drive until we find the first grove of *Araucaria*, and a short search gives us our first plants of M. *poeppigii*. We are only 3 miles (4.8 km) from the pass of Pino Hachado that leads into Chile. The plants are tiny at this site, only about 3 to 4 inches (7.5 to 10 cm) across, and they nestle among the dead leaves at the bases of clumps of grass. It is easy to walk among them and not even notice them. Unlike the plants of M. *patagonica*, these plants of M. *poeppigii* each have dozens of brilliant green leaves. Digging plants out intact is difficult because their roots are completely entangled with the roots of the grass, and grass stalks have grown up through the branches of M. *poeppigii*; the two plants are completely entangled.

We have superb luck in Caviahue. The ground here is a mix of sand and gravel, and the mountains around us are thick with *Araucaria* trees, and

Maihuenia poeppigii is everywhere. The altitude is 6000 feet (1840 m), the sky
is perfectly clear but cold, and the lake beside us is pristine. Unlike the plants
we left behind at Pino Hachado, those of *M. poeppigii* here are gigantic.
Although both species of *Maihuenia* grow as low mounds, plants of *M. patagonica* can be as tall as 2 feet (60 cm) above the soil surface, whereas those of
M. poeppigii are always very low, less than 1 foot (30 cm) off the ground. Like
the high altitude oroyas and austrocylindropuntias of Peru and Bolivia, these
high altitude plants of *M. poeppigii* form cushions. Each branch is highly
branched, and those branches all have branches, all of which are packed
tightly together. Maihuenias, like pereskias, have leaves, but these are small,
sausage-shaped cylinders, barely ¼ inch (0.6 cm) long, like the leaves of an
Opuntia. Because the branches of *M. poeppigii* are so close together, the leaves
of one branch are usually pressed up against those of neighboring branches,
and the plant appears to be a solid green blob. The biggest branches at the
base of the "trunk" of both species spread out horizontally, and while those of
M. poeppigii lie flat on the ground, the branches of *M. patagonica* are slightly
elevated. Blobs of both species of *Maihuenia* are therefore much wider than
they are tall. One plant of *M. patagonica* was 9 feet (2.7 m) in diameter, and
one of *M. poeppigii* had formed a fairy ring about 10 feet (3 m) across with
branches that had grown out, rooted, and then continued to spread outward
while its center died off. The plant now exists as a ring of rooted shoot tips,
each still progressing outward.

We wonder how old such a *Maihuenia poeppigii* might be and decide to do
some measuring. It is the end of summer, so we can see the extent of growth
that has occurred this year. Each shoot tip on the *M. poeppigii* has at most ½
inch (1.25 cm) of leafy stem; many have less. A ring 10 feet (3 m) in diameter is 60 inches (150 cm) from the center to the branch tips. If the plants
grow at a rate of ½ an inch (1.25 cm) per year, this plant must be more than
a century old. On other trips, we have also encountered fairy rings of *M.
patagonica*, some being more than 15 feet (5 m) in diameter.

What is the weather like here? There is no weather station at either Pino
Hachado or Caviahue, and the closest town that might have records is a full

This is a typical landscape for *Maihuenia poeppigii*. The tree is *Araucaria araucana*,
and usually you will not find M. *poeppigii* if *Araucaria* is not around.
Although some plants of M. *poeppigii* are up to 6 inches (15 cm) tall and can be seen from
a moving car, most are so flat you cannot see them until you have almost walked over them.
Looking for *Araucaria* first will save you lots of time.

4000 feet (1230 m) lower. The terrain here looks like that of the high
Rockies; it is cold and windswept, is very severe, and has patches of bare soil
and rock that are as common as patches of vegetation. Yet the plants of
Maihuenia poeppigii are all healthy. Every one is bright green, each with hundreds if not thousands of little leaves. Many have big yellow fruits that only
add to the comical appearance of these plants—green blobs polka-dotted
with yellow bell peppers. We take samples for anatomy and find that M. *poeppigii* is soft and cuts with no resistance. *Maihuenia patagonica*, on the other
hand, was tough, dry, ropy, and almost impossible to cut. We did not think it
would be possible to slice M. *patagonica* thinly enough to study with a microscope, but back at the University of Texas, we found that it sliced with no
trouble at all, not even a hint of toughness. The anatomy of these two species
has indeed been informative, and although the details are not appropriate

An old (how old?) plant of *Maihuenia poeppigii*, growing as a cushion plant at Caviahue
in the Patagonian Andes. From a botanical standpoint, this is a tree because it has
one single trunk. All branches of this tree are so close together that their leaves
touch each other. The yellow objects are mature fruits.

here, the bibliography references a paper written about these specimens if you
are interested in those details.

   Maihuenia behaves strangely in cultivation. *Maihuenia poeppigii* is occasionally offered for sale by nurseries, but M. *patagonica* (sometimes called
M. *andicola*) never is. Plants of M. *poeppigii* are either extremely easy or
impossible to grow. A few plants will arrive from a nursery looking fresh and
healthy, but after you plant them, some will die no matter what, while others will thrive. We brought back cuttings of both species, but despite our
intensive efforts, all have died. *Maihuenia patagonica* produces adventitious
roots in nature, which is always a good sign because that usually means it
can easily make new roots if old ones are damaged during transplanting.
Sadly, our cuttings did not do that at all; they simply died. Perhaps the
three weeks that elapsed between collecting and planting was too much
time out of the ground.

Leaves at the tips of Maihuenia poeppigii branches resemble those of opuntias because
they are short, cylindrical, and sausage-shaped without a flat blade. Plants in other families
that live in similar habitats also have leaves like this as a result of convergent evolution.
This type of leaf is beneficial because it loses less water
to the dry air than does a flat, thin leaf.

The sun is now setting, and from our high perch in the mountains, we
can see the road extend all the way to the northeast horizon. Our intended
destination for tonight, Buta Ranquil, is completely out of the question.
We will instead stop in Chos Malal, and dinner, as usual, will be at about
10:00 P.M.

Before we move on, however, we feel compelled to reflect on the trees of
Araucaria that surround us and that indicate the hiding spots of *Maihuenia*.
Plants of *Pereskia* retain so many primitive features and have undergone so
little evolutionary change that when we look at a pereskia it is almost like
looking back through time and seeing an ancestral cactus. Among the
conifers, which are the plants that bear cones and not flowers (basically the
Christmas trees and their relatives), plants of *Araucaria* play the role of
Pereskia. *Araucaria* and its sister genus, *Agathis*, retain a great number of primitive features. Coniferous trees originated in evolution as long ago as about

340 million years, and their massive, strong, woody trunks permitted them to grow taller than all other plants in existence at the time. Their leaves—scales in the earliest conifers, needles in the later ones—grew above the leaves of other plants and were therefore able to get to the sunlight first and photosynthesize the best. The other plants, such as seed ferns, giant scouring rushes, and lycopods, were all shorter and more primitive. They were overshadowed and outcompeted, and many became extinct. The conifers thrived and spread quickly, diversifying as they went.

At the time when conifers originated, all continents were united in the single super-continent, Pangaea. Early, relictual genera that included *Araucaria*, *Agathis*, and *Podocarpus* were dominant in the south, while the newer genera such as pines, firs, hemlocks, and spruces dominated the north. Then the breakup that would eventually tear South America away from Africa began. The first fissure of the breakup separated a piece called Laurasia (North America and Europe) and sent it north with the modern conifers that eventually produced the vast conifer forests that blanket the northern United States, Canada, Europe, Russia, and Japan. The primitive conifers remained to the south of the rift on a continent called Gondwana (Africa, South America, Australia, Antarctica, and India).

Here at Caviahue we intrude into the forests of *Araucaria araucana*, forests so ancient that we cannot truly comprehend their age as we touch the individual trees, each of them healthy with massive cones full of seeds. We are not the first intruders here. The grasses around us are new in evolutionary terms and have been in the araucaria forests for only a few tens of millions of years. *Araucaria* was an ancient genus when the dinosaurs were starting their domination of the world of land animals, but the cataclysm that wiped out the dinosaurs left the araucarias intact. Plants evolved from the oceans about 420 million years ago, and araucarias have been around for more than half of that period, about 300 million years. Is there a way to comprehend the length of *Araucaria*'s existence? Our galaxy, the Milky Way, is a large spiral galaxy with huge arms that consist of billions of stars all rotating around the center of the galaxy. It takes the Milky Way 250 million years to complete a single rotation. Araucarias have been in existence since before our galaxy began its most recent turn. No individual tree lives longer than a few hundred years of course, but each tree we see here is heir to an awe-inspiring, long-lived, and successful legacy.

The next day we continue up Highway 40 to Malargüe, a route that runs directly north at the base of the mountains and that is never more than an hour's drive from Chile. The road is excellent, as good as any two-lane highway in the United States, and the scenery is spectacular. Although we pass through only low hills and one or two steep-walled valleys, the mountains tower over us on our left. First there is Volcán Tromen at 12,000 feet (3700 m), and later Volcán Domuyo, which is 2,000 feet (615 m) higher. At Buta Ranquil we begin traveling through an intermountain valley and there are now lower peaks on our right as well. The road follows the Río Grande (how many Río Grandes can there be in Latin America?). When we reach Malargüe we will be more or less passing out of the Patagonian zone and will enter deserts that lack the winter rains of Patagonia. We will also leave behind the habitat of *Maihuenia*, which does not occur outside the winter rain area.

The most noteworthy species we encounter on our way to Malargüe is *Maihueniopsis darwinii*. As the genus name indicates, these plants resemble maihuenias (*-opsis* means "like" or "similar to"). The name is appropriate because as we zoom along at 100 km per hour (60 miles per hour), it is difficult to tell the two apart. An easy method of distinguishing the two is to look at them with the sun in the background. Spines of *Maihueniopsis* are slightly translucent and glow when backlighted; with the setting sun behind them, these plants appear to be aflame. In general they look very much like plants of the little cylindropuntias of the southwestern United States, such as *Opuntia clavata* or *O. schottii*. They would make attractive landscaping plants, but they have all the disadvantages of opuntias—painful spines and an excess of glochids. We have tweezers with very long handles to pick them up, and when we dissect any opuntioid we put down lots of dampened newspaper to

The easiest way of identifying plants of *Maihueniopsis boliviana* is by the way they glisten when sunlight passes through their spines. This method will at least keep you away from their painful glochids. Most species of *Maihueniopsis* form small, compact mounds that bristle with spines.

catch the glochids. We always end up with some in our fingers, and no doubt many land on the hotel room floor. (We do not want to know what some of the hotel maids think of us.) *Maihueniopsis* is beautiful and worth examining, but studying it extracts a price.

After an hour's drive, we arrive at the north end of the Sierra del Nevado, a short range that forms the eastern side of our valley. At this point we turn east toward San Rafael, but at El Nihuil we turn off Highway 144 and make a loop by entering the Cañon del Atuel. The turn-off is not easy to miss because there is a big iron works right at the turn. And a hydroelectric dam. And a sign. The road traverses flat land for a mile or two, then heads into a gully that deepens and enters the canyon from one side. Even within the first mile of our descent, we stop repeatedly for the numerous cacti everywhere around us: *Denmoza rhodacantha*, *Echinopsis leucantha*, *Pterocactus kuntzei*, *Pyrrhocactus strausianus*, and *Trichocereus candicans*. We have already seen *Pyrrhocactus strausianus* and *E. leucantha* on the second day of this trip, but there is something special about the specimen of *Pyrrhocactus strausianus* here—its size. It is a full 1½ feet (45 cm) tall. This is definitely much larger than anything we have seen before, a plant of *Pyrrhocactus* almost at knee-height. Usually in this situation we resolve to give our plants more tender love and care, more water at least, but having seen *Pyrrhocactus* in Río Negro and now in these hard conditions, we decide that more water would probably not work. This plant must simply be very old.

Most of the plants we see at the top of the canyon are growing at the extreme edge of their habitat. If conditions here at the canyon rim were really proper for them, then we would have seen these plants when we were traveling through the Río Grande valley. As we enter the canyon we are at 4800 feet (1477 m) elevation, but the bottom is less than 2000 feet (615 m) in altitude and thus considerably hotter and drier. The denmozas at the top of the canyon are small ball cacti about 5 to 6 inches (12.5 to 15 cm) across, like typical small barrel cacti, but in more optimal areas of their habitat, they grow to be big, columnar plants that are about 5 to 6 feet (1.5 to 2 m) tall. We find that the size discrepancy is the same for *Trichocereus candicans*; up here it is a fraction of what we will see in the valley below.

At the base of the canyon our patience is rewarded. Plants of *Trichocereus candicans* are sprawled out in all their glory. Having seen the tall columnar *T. chilensis* in Chile and *T. puquiensis* in Peru, it is quite a shock to see a sprawling *T. candicans*. Most trichocerei are columnar plants; some are even giant plants that at first glance look like the saguaros (*Carnegiea gigantea*) of California and Arizona. Although shoots of *T. candicans* are thick— up to 6 inches (15 cm) in diameter—they are not strong enough to hold themselves erect and instead lie on the ground with their tips turned upward as if making a feeble attempt to grow upright. As the shoots elongate and become heavier, their weight forces them to sink to the ground, leaving them only enough strength to hold up the tip. The oldest branches are about 3 feet (1 m) long and 7 inches (18 cm) thick, but they have so little wood we can cut right through them with a gentle push on a machete. The wood

Trichocereus candicans is among the shortest trichocerei; several other species of *Trichocereus* also grow like this, but many species are tall, columnar cacti. Notice the few branches of shrubs above the plants of *T. candicans*. Many low trichocerei need light shade even in nurseries in Tucson where the plants are watered regularly.

is not even $\frac{1}{10}$ inch (0.25 cm) thick despite being in such a big shoot. Each shoot branches from its base, so a plant quickly becomes a mass of prostrate stems with upturned ends, some shoots lying on top of others. We are lucky enough to see one big white flower but are too late to catch the plants in full bloom. Many species of *Trichocereus* are used by plant breeders as parental material for making crosses that produce spectacularly long, wide flowers in a variety of colors, and seeing this flower here makes us realize their potential for exceptional size.

As we mentioned in chapter 1, *Trichocereus* is part of a group of genera that includes *Echinopsis*, *Lobivia*, and *Soehrensia*. A main reason for uniting these genera is their similar flowers. It can be difficult to look at just one flower by itself and be absolutely certain whether it came from a plant of *Echinopsis* or *Trichocereus*. For the most part, species that have big, tall columnar plants are placed in *Trichocereus*; those with short, wide, globose plants are in *Soehrensia*; those with small, globose, lowland specimens go into *Echinopsis*; and those with small, globose, highland plants are *Lobivia*. Additional features reinforce these classifications, but they have never been very successful. Some species seem to fit into two genera at once because certain characteristics of each genus overlap with those of other genera. One attempt to solve this overlap is to create new genera for each problematic group of species, but that has simply given us even more genera that in turn overlap others. An alternative attempt at resolution places all these species into *Echinopsis*. However, combining a 15-foot (4.5-m) tall *Trichocereus pasacana* with a 3-inch (7.5-cm) tall *Echinopsis subdenudata* does not seem reasonable.

Trichocereus lamprochlorus, like *T. candicans*, has low prostrate stems, and its huge, brightly colored flowers make it an excellent plant for landscaping and for a collection.
All trichocerei have large flowers, often in profusion, but most are white rather than pigmented. Photographed at the Jardin Exotique, Monaco.

One of our objectives on this trip is to collect wood from as many species as possible to see if there are features that may help us understand the evolutionary relationships among these genera. Most trichocerei have trunks that are so woody they have been cut down for lumber. Wood of *Echinopsis* plants, on the other hand, is soft and spongy. Looking at this plant of *Trichocereus candicans* here before us, we do not see clear-cut differences between the two genera. *Trichocereus candicans* is prostrate, so it might have soft, spongy wood like that of *Echinopsis*, or it could have hard, fibrous wood like a typical *Trichocereus*. It feels soft and spongy when we cut it with a machete, but we will have to examine it under a microscope back in the laboratory to know

This specimen of *Echinopsis leucantha* is huge and probably very old. It germinated under the protection of the *Larrea* bush (at least, we presume it did; is the bush as old as the cactus?), and even at this height it still receives some protection from full sun. Most plants of *Echinopsis* are globose, so this is an exceptionally tall specimen.

exactly what type of wood we are dealing with. We next find an exquisite plant of *E. leucantha* nearby, fully 3 feet (1 m) tall and perfectly upright, a height and stature that seem to guarantee that it has fibrous wood like that of *Trichocereus*.

Our first impressions are that wood anatomy will not offer the quick, easy answer we had hoped for, but we collect our samples anyway. Starting from *Pereskia*-like ancestors, cacti have become smaller, more succulent, and less woody in many different ways. The *Echinopsis/Trichocereus* group is certain to reveal much useful information about wood evolution, even if it does not give us the final answer about cactus classification.

The lower areas of the Cañon del Atuel are filled with plants of *Denmoza*, and with luck we might be able to find both species of this little genus. *Denmoza* contains only two species, *D. erythrocephala* and *D. rhodacantha*. The first is the red-headed denmoza, the other is the red-spined denmoza. One is supposed to have mostly white spines, the other mostly reddish spines. We have no trouble finding the two species, but then we also find some that are not quite whitish and others that are not quite reddish. As we examine more plants, we realize this difference in color is due mostly to a difference in the plant's age; while the plants remain smaller and therefore younger, there is a

Flowers of *Echinopsis* are large with a long, narrow, tubular throat that ends in petals that spread outward. Shrubbery hides a side view of the flower, which is a tubular structure almost 7 inches (18 cm) long. Flowers of *Trichocereus* look similar to this flower but they are somewhat wider; those of *Lobivia* and *Soehrensia* are both shorter and wider.

greater color difference, but when the plants become older, they look alike. Indeed, the latest taxonomic treatment (done in 1997) has eliminated *D. erythrocephala* altogether, treating all plants as *D. rhodacantha* and giving the genus only one species. The smallest plants are dominated by big, stiff, dark red spines, but as the plants grow, the newer areoles they produce begin to have a few white radial spines. Older plants have areoles in which the white radials are more abundant, and from a distance, these plants appear whiter. This gradual change in the type of areole produced is not a juvenile to adult transition (as it is in *Melocactus* or *Espostoa*) because there are numerous fruits on the small, very red plants just as there are on the larger, older plants. Both small red plants and large white ones, therefore, are able to flower. We collect the fruits and large amounts of seed, which have since germinated well. This is a species that is not in any hurry to grow. Among hobbyists, *Denmoza* has a reputation for being among the most slow-growing of all cacti. Our seedlings from Argentina conform to this completely.

This is a typical plant of *Denmoza rhodacantha*, about 5 feet (1.5 m) tall and 1 foot (30 cm) thick, with an inclined, tilted apex. Notice the numerous red flowers at the shoot apex; they are tubular with petals that do not spread out, and the flower is bent instead of straight. *Denmoza* may be related to other genera with similar flowers such as *Cleistocactus*, *Matucana*, and *Oreocereus*.

The plants of *Denmoza* in the canyon are up to 2 to 3 feet (60 cm to 1 m) tall, but later, when we are near Uspallata close to the pass on the Chilean border, we find denmozas that are routinely 6 feet (2 m) tall. Uspallata is a bit farther north, slightly west of Mendoza, and higher, at 5,253 feet (1600 m). What allows denmozas to be so large at higher altitudes and so much smaller in the canyon? We are intrigued by the factors that control the growth, distribution, and success of *Denmoza*. The genus name is an anagram of the Argentine province of Mendoza, and as you might guess, denmozas are found near Mendoza. They are not everywhere near Mendoza, and in fact there are none on the east side of the city because that area is now wall-to-wall vineyards in what is the main wine-producing region of Argentina. On the west side between Mendoza and Chile where the land is not farmed, natural vegetation still covers the rough hills, valleys, canyons, and cliffs. In some areas, denmozas are so thick it would be difficult to walk through them, but barely a quarter mile down the road in an area that appears absolutely identical, there is not a one. (When the plants are 6 feet [2 m] tall and 1 foot [30 cm] across, we do not have to do much searching to note this fact.) Five minutes later and around a bend, all we can see is a forest of *Denmoza*. The forest is as sharply edged as if trimmed by a knife, and we wonder why there are hun-

Even though their flowers remain at ground level, punas are still conspicuous because they grow in such severe, flat habitats of bare, rocky soil that there are few other plants around. The flowers can be seen from a great distance, but the plants themselves are almost impossible to see unless you are immediately above them. This is *Puna subterranea.*

dreds of these plants in one site and none in the other, particularly when there is no obvious change of soil or slope or shading from nearby mountains. Undoubtedly, this type of patchy distribution occurs with many cacti; it is just difficult to see with the tiny plants.

After spending the night at Uspallata (elevation 5700 feet [1754 m]), we return toward Mendoza (2200 feet [677 m]) by a northern route passing through Villavicencio. A few miles outside of Uspallata, the ground is bare soil and rock with almost no vegetation. The lack of obscuring shrubs or grasses makes our search much easier: we are now in the habitat of *Puna clavarioides*, another of the opuntioids that is mostly subterranean. This plant is particularly nefarious because once the neck reaches the surface, it becomes broad and flat rather than tall, and the aerial stems we are looking for are level with the soil surface rather than upright and visible. There are only two methods for finding *P. clavarioides*: walking stooped over as far as possible (ending up with a sore back), or crawling on hands and knees (ending up with sore hands and knees). By the time we find the plants, our hands and knees *and* backs are sore. In our decrepit condition, we jump for joy as best we can because these are really wonderful plants. Punas, like pterocacti, have an enlarged root deep underground that is connected to the aerial photosynthetic stem by a narrow neck. The plants we find have aerial stems that are at most 1 inch (2.5 cm) across, and their necks are less than half this wide but as much as 5 inches (12.5 cm) long and end in roots about the size of a small, short carrot.

We call them roots here, and certainly the bulk of the succulent underground structure of *Puna* or *Pterocactus* is root, but it is difficult to be certain. Roots are usually easy to distinguish anatomically from stems because stems have pith in the center and roots do not. But when roots are greatly enlarged, the innermost wood often becomes distorted and similar to a pith, and it becomes impossible to ascertain whether a pith had ever been present. That is certainly the case here; we cannot tell if a pith had developed when the structure was young. Cactus stems, of course, have areoles and spines whereas roots do not. These structures in *Puna*, however, are covered in a flaky bark, so if areoles were present, they have now been shed and have decomposed, so we still have no reliable way of being certain what this structure is. It is rare for a root to produce a brand new shoot, and the necks are definitely shoots because they have tiny areoles with miniature spines. We are almost certain that the subterranean structure is built like a carrot with the bulk of it being a root, and the very top portion a short, flat shoot whose axillary buds produce new necks and aerial shoots. We can identify the root in carrots as the orange portion and the shoot as the greenish tissue at the very top, but no such color difference helps us with *Puna clavarioides*.

With necks 5 inches (12.5 cm) long, plants of *Puna clavarioides* retreat considerably when they abandon their aerial parts and die back to the root. These are suffrutescent plants like *Cereus aethiops* and the parasite *Tristerix aphyllus*. Usually conditions even 1 inch (2.5 cm) below the soil surface are much milder than at the surface, and at a depth of 5 inches (12.5 cm), temperature fluctuations from day to night and from summer to winter are really smoothed out. When dormant, punas are in a fairly benign environment.

This plant of *Puna clavaroides* shows its aerial portion, neck, and tuberous root. The tuber is much larger than the aerial stems, which undoubtedly die back to the root periodically. How long can these plants survive in a state of dormancy—years?

Plants of *Puna subterranea* do not go to quite such an extreme as those of *P. clavarioides*. Their necks are only about 1 inch (2.5 cm) long, sometimes even less, so they are still fairly close to aerial conditions even when they are dormant. *Puna subterranea* also occurs in areas mild enough (relatively speaking) to support at least a few shrubs and grasses; it does not inhabit the barren rock and sand areas where we find *P. clavarioides*. The newly discovered *P. bonnieae* also has a short neck, but it grows in an otherwise almost lifeless zone.

The stark conditions in each area where we find a species of *Puna* intrigue us. Although punas are exposed to the full force of the sun, they have a perfect, unblemished epidermis, exhibiting no sign of stress at all. These habitats are just as inhospitable for animals, so what insects would be around to pollinate these plants, and what do the insects survive on when the punas are not in flower? We are convinced that there can only be a few punas in flower at any one time because we search for hours and find very few plants. Even if they had all bloomed simultaneously, insects would still have only a few flowers to supply them with pollen or nectar.

A full-grown plant of *Puna bonnieae* is certainly among the most beautiful of all cacti.
Puna bonnieae was discovered by two groups of taxonomists and it almost received two names,
but the discoverers decided to cooperate rather than compete.
This was almost named *P. megliolii* to honor an amateur naturalist and banker of Argentina.

Plants with long necks must have a method for digging down and bury-
ing themselves while they are seedlings. We are sure they must have what are
known as contractile roots. The root-shoot junction, the point where the
neck arises from the root, is 5 inches (12.5 cm) or more below ground in
plants like *Puna clavarioides* and *Pterocactus fischeri*. We would expect the
root-shoot junction to mark the site where the seed germinated; after all,
with germination the root grows downward, the shoot upward, and the seed
stays where it lies. But seeds of punas and pterocacti do not wait around until
they are buried with 6 inches (15 cm) of soil. Instead, they germinate near
the soil surface like ordinary seeds and allow the root to grow deeply into the
soil. At some point, probably after a rain, when the soil is especially loose and
slippery, the root contracts. Because the branch roots extend outward and
horizontally from the lower portion of the main root, the contraction pulls
the shoot downward rather than lifting the root tip upward. The amount of
contraction that occurs at any one time is ½ inch (1.25 cm) or less, but the

root is able to grow even deeper and wait for its next opportunity to contract again. After several cycles, the root-shoot junction and even the base of the shoot have been pulled far underground.

Although we do not know of any studies in which contractile roots have been definitely observed in cacti, they are well known from other families that have this same growth pattern, and so we think it very likely they also occur here. Root contraction is the reason that each type of bulb in a garden should be planted at a particular depth, the depth that their contractile roots would eventually pull them to anyway. And for a real example of this, unpot a palm seedling—its contractile roots should have pulled the seed so deep that much of the petioles of the first leaves will be underground.

Despite the slow, difficult work of looking for *Puna clavarioides*, we stop to look for these plants several times. After making a big circuit at each new site, we always find a few plants. While doing our search loop here, we have a special experience, the kind that occurs at least once on every field trip. We search for an hour or two, looping away from the car, making a circle around it, crossing the dirt road, then continuing the loop back to the car from the other side. All the time we see nothing, nothing, nothing—until we reach the car and find *Puna*. If we had stepped out on one side of the car instead of the other side, we would have found the plants in a few seconds. It is just a Law of the Universe.

We continue on, alternately descending and climbing several thousand feet every few miles. Vegetation increases to sparse grassland at lower altitudes, but as we ascend again, the shrub gives way to barren rock. At one pass above 9000 feet (2770 m), an icy wind agitates the spare, scattered grasses, and strong gusts shake *Ephedra andina*, which is the only shrub we find here. Colonies of *Maihueniopsis glomerata* are scattered about, and a tiny, thorny relative of dandelion (*Chaetanthera*) fools us several times into thinking we have found a dwarf cactus. After crossing the pass and dropping less than 1000 feet (305 m), we are rewarded with plants of *Soehrensia formosa*, 5-foot (1.5-m) tall columnar plants. *Soehrensia* is a small genus of only eight species (or less depending on one's taxonomic point of view) that is caught in the uncertainty of the *Echinopsis/Trichocereus* complex. Like many trichocerei, soehrensias are broad-stemmed—these are 18 inches (45 cm) in diameter—but usually short and globose. These plants of *S. formosa*, however, are trying to outdo their *Trichocereus* cousins by becoming columnar. There are tall plants here, but in only a small area along the road. It would be interesting to know whether this particular population is numerous enough to extend for any distance away from the road. We hope that this one group of tall plants does not represent the bulk of the population.

A few miles down the road we come to many more plants of *Soehrensia formosa*, but they are all much shorter, less than 3 feet (1 m) tall, and not at all columnar. Such a difference in plant size from population to population is not common in cacti, but it does occur occasionally as we found with *Browningia candelaris* in southern Peru (chapter 5). Although it rarely happens, an entire population can be wiped out by an insect outbreak or an unusual weather event, but later it gradually recovers from seed that was safe in the ground. That appears to be the case with our second site; all the largest plants appear to be about the same size and so are, presumably, the same age. It is as if all germinated in the same year. At the first population we encountered (the one with the tall plants), the tallest were not at all uniform in size, which makes us think they differ in age as well. Despite searching several hundred plants, we are not lucky enough to find a single flower, and even worse, no fruit. We must leave with no seeds for cultivation. In retrospect, this is especially unfortunate because seeds of the other species of *Soehrensia* that we later collect all germinate well and grow enthusiastically.

Leaving behind the high passes of *Soehrensia*, we descend quickly toward Mendoza, and before long we can see the town at the end of a long valley. The higher elevations are green with trees nestled in protected valleys, but we can see the terrain become drier and less green at each lower level. By the time we have dropped to 3600 feet (1100 m), *Soehrensia* is long behind us (it never grows at low altitudes), but *Cereus aethiops*, *Echinopsis leucantha*, *Tephrocactus aoracanthus*, and *Trichocereus strigosus* start to appear and then quickly become abundant. We have seen plants of *Cereus aethiops* sporadi-

Plants of *Soehrensia formosa* achieve the largest size of any in the genus,
although it was only at one location that we saw really large ones like this.
Other areas had plants only half this size.

cally for hundreds of miles, ever since our second day in Río Negro. The aerial part of *C. aethiops*, like that in plants of *Puna*, can die back to a subterranean root during bad conditions, but the aerial portion of *Cereus* is a big investment to throw away. We have often seen stems 3 to 4 feet (1 to 1.2 m) long and 1½ inches (4 cm) in diameter. When they are suffering, the stems certainly have a ratty appearance, something no one would add to a collection. When they are happy, however, these stems cannot be beaten. Even vegetatively the plants are stunning; a smooth, clean, blue wax covers the stem, providing a perfect backdrop to showcase the jet black spines. Their flowers are huge and white as is typical of *Cereus*, and if you are lucky you will catch one with large, red fruit adorning the stem. Plants of *C. aethiops* in our Austin greenhouse had been very lackluster growers, barely adding a few areoles and doing so very slowly. Then, after we transplanted them into a garden and allowed them to face the full Texas sun, they perked up, began growing well, turned blue, and produced the blackest spines ever. Any garden with mild winters should consider these plants. With their ability to die back to a dormant underground portion, they can probably survive pretty severe frosts.

The other cacti here each have remarkable aspects. Plants of *Trichocereus strigosus* are low and sprawling like those of *Trichocereus candicans*, but they are also different because their stems are not thick but narrow, at most about 2 inches (5 cm) in diameter. Their upturned ends do not even come to knee height, but the plants branch and clamber so vigorously that they form irregular thickets. Walking through this vegetation is like negotiating a maze. Almost every patch of *T. strigosus* grows intertwined with some shrub (probably a species of *Lycium*) whose leafless gray branches make the spare desert landscape look even more desolate. Is the intermingling of *Lycium* and *T. strigosus* coincidental or a real biological association? Both species are so abundant here that we might think the two frequently grow together by chance, and yet the co-mingling has such clear benefits for both partners. The cactus provides a spiny, formidable ground cover that must deter herbivorous animals from getting to the shrub's buds and leaves (when it has leaves, that is), and the shrub offers some much-needed shade to the cactus for part of the year. Some of the trichocerei have large fruits that are mature

Although this looks like a group of many short plants, it is actually a single spreading
individual of *Trichocereus strigosus*. Its body is basically a tree with a short trunk and
numerous branches lying on the soil. With the ground supporting their weight,
each stem can be highly branched and heavy without
putting stress on the trunk or branches.

despite still being green, and they have split open by themselves, allowing
their seeds to either fall out or be carried off by ants.

Plants of *Tephrocactus aoracanthus*, like most tephrocacti, have areoles so
deeply sunken into their bodies that the glochids do not even come to the
surface. Animals brush by these plants safely, but if they bite into one, they
will have a mouthful of agony. *Tephrocactus aoracanthus* also has a spongy covering on its seeds that makes them look like small dark puffs of popcorn. This
covering must aid seed dispersal; when we hold the seeds in our hands, even
a mild breeze blows them away, and because they are so light, they are carried
several feet before landing. These seeds also float, so the runoff from even a
brief rain might carry them quite a distance.

The cactus family is remarkable in its scarcity of specialized seed dispersal mechanisms. Many plants that are adapted to unusual sites (such as the
epiphytes) have seeds with a special sweet, sticky coating. The sweetness
induces birds to eat the seeds, and the stickiness allows any uneaten seeds to

This stem cross section of *Tephrocactus aoracanthus* shows how the stem cortex has grown around the glochids, so much so in this case that the glochids are buried and the plant can be handled safely. It cannot be eaten safely, of course; the glochids are still effective when the stem is chewed.

cling to the tree branch where the bird perches while eating or preening. Such coatings do not occur on seeds of epiphytic cacti, however. At most, the juicy fruit pulp gives them a slightly adhesive coating. The genus *Pterocactus*, closely related to *Tephrocactus*, is the one other example of a cactus that has seeds with a specialized dispersal mechanism. There is a thin flap of cells extending around each seed that forms a winglike projection that must help the wind carry the seeds. So the light, popcornlike seeds of *T. aoracanthus* and the wings of *Pterocactus* are noteworthy.

Ants carry off many cactus seeds, such as those of *Trichocereus strigosus*, because seeds sometimes have a special bit of edible tissue called a food body or aril. There is debate as to whether or not ants carrying off seeds is of real benefit to the plant: they do move the seeds to a new location, which is good, but the ants usually take all the seeds to their nest so the seeds end up crowded together in one place and too far underground to germinate successfully.

Seeds of tephrocacti (this is from a specimen of *Tephrocactus aoracanthus*) have a spongy, light seed coat consisting of highly enlarged, air-filled cells.

Seeds of pterocacti have a thin, winglike rim of cells that projects out around the edge of the seed (*ptero-* means "wing," as in the flying pterodactyl, or wing finger, dinosaurs). The wing may allow the seeds to be blown by wind or to float as rainwater runs across the desert floor.

Our trip through the southwestern parts of Argentina has been a great success. We obtained our main genus *Maihuenia* in the first few days in Patagonia, and then had great luck every day after that. From here, we turn our attention to the north of Mendoza and the northwestern parts of Argentina.

7

NORTHWESTERN ARGENTINA:
Deserts, Rainforests, Mountains, and
Oreocereus

The Andes Mountains dominate the landscape and the weather for the entire length of South America, but here near Mendoza and in the northwestern part of Argentina, they are joined by other significant ranges. In southern Chile and Argentina, the Andes are narrow and well defined, but further north they spread out. There is a high crest running through the center of Chile rather than at its border with Argentina, and an eastern spur forms the highlands of Bolivia. Northwestern Argentina, in particular the states of La Rioja, Salta, Tucumán, and Jujuy, is a wonderland of varying temperatures and rainfall that typically accompany mountainous territory. The weather here is different from what one might expect in the United States where moist air sweeps eastward from the Pacific, crosses the coastal ranges, the Cascades, and the Sierra Nevadas, then continues on across the Rockies before blasting across the Midwest. That air has picked up so much moisture from the warm, north Pacific that it can drop rain and snow on all three rows of mountains and on the plains states, making the North American Midwest a grassland and not a desert. Even the East Coast gets much of its weather from the Pacific.

The winds in South America also come from the west, but having traversed the cold Humboldt Current in the southern Pacific, they carry so little moisture that it is almost completely exhausted when it falls as precipitation on the highest peaks of the Andes. By the time the Pacific winds move eastward into Argentina, they bring no moisture. Rains must instead come from the east—from the Atlantic—and be carried across the vast pampas and plains of eastern Argentina. As it encounters the first set of mountains, the air rises, cools, and begins dropping moisture while still at a low level. Near Tucumán, the center of a rich cactus region, the mountains are covered in rainforests despite their low elevation. Trees are immense, and mosses, ferns, bromeliads, orchids, and cacti hang from every branch. Only a few miles to the east of Tucumán are the deserts of Santiago del Estero; to the west are dry, hot valleys. Atlantic winds rise over the next range of mountains and again give up some of their moisture before descending for their final run to the Andes. Having crossed various mountain ranges, the air is dry and brings little relief to the parched eastern slopes of the great mountain range. We will experience this patchwork of green, moisture-rich forests and brown, water-starved deserts in the next few days as we weave our way more or less northward from Mendoza and pass through Tucumán toward our ultimate destination, the habitat of *Oreocereus celsianus* near the border with Bolivia.

After leaving Mendoza and approaching Chilecito from the south, we come across a landscape that must be one of the most beautiful anywhere. The rock, and all the soil, is red. Not just red-tinted, but really red. Scattered about over the sand, dry creeks, and rounded boulders are patches of vivid green, most of which are low leafy shrubs or tall, magnificent columns of *Trichocereus terscheckii*. These tall plants can, like *T. pasacana*, fool most people into thinking they are saguaros (*Carnegiea gigantea*) or that this is Arizona. Here they are in perfect health, their skin glowing in the afternoon sun, and in every direction we look there is a landscape more striking than the one before. We spend several hours simply enjoying the beauty and spirit of the cacti and their home, putting off the science for a while. It takes the setting sun to remind us that we are also here to collect samples.

When there is almost no light left, we encounter plants of *Trichocereus terscheckii* with flowers. But the flowers are all clustered at the very tops of these tall columns; the lowest flowers are at least 6 feet (2 m) above our heads. Unlike saguaros, these plants' arms do not bend over and present flowers at a height we can easily photograph. Our luck seems to be both good and bad. There is a boulder next to one plant that gets us close and high enough to take a photograph, and yet the twilight offers little light. But the rule of photography is: When in doubt, take the picture. There might be better light the next day, or we might find a better plant, a more perfect flower, an improved location, but we might not. So we take the pictures with handheld, half-second exposures, thinking that they will never come out. The next day we discover that not only are plants of *T. terscheckii* night blooming, but also that their flowers wilt before sunrise. If we had not taken the photographs in the evening, we would never have gotten another chance because by the next evening, we have traveled out of their range. And the pictures did not come out so badly after all.

Trichocereus terscheckii is a South American giant. It easily achieves heights greater than 30 feet (9 m) and it has several tremendous branches. Plants of *T. pasacana* and *T. terscheckii*, along with *Neocardenasia* and *Neoraimondia*, are the most massive cacti in South America. Only pachycerei of Mexico are larger.

The specimens of *Trichocereus terscheckii* we encountered had an abundance of ripe fruits with plenty of nice, mature black seeds. We now have hundreds of seedlings, but we do not expect to see them flower any time soon, even with heavy fertilizer or tender loving care.

Also in this area we collect *Gymnocalycium asterium*, which along with *Trichocereus terscheckii*, gives us an instructive lesson in cactus biology. When we later dissect plants of these two species, we discover that their tissues are completely different. That of *T. terscheckii* is moist, almost like watermelon,

These flowers of *Trichocereus terscheckii* are similar to those of *Echinopsis*,
indicating the close relationship between the two genera. They also have a long tubular form
when viewed from the side, but they are not quite as long or narrow as those of *Echinopsis*.
Flowers of *T. terscheckii* open early in the evening right at sunset,
whereas many night-blooming cacti wait until about midnight.

and as we work with it, the whole desk becomes wet and messy with cactus juice. Cutting the plant of G. *asterium*, on the other hand, is like cutting through dried apples or apricots. It is tough and rubbery, and the knife, instead of cutting through the plant, squashes it. The plants do not appear to be suffering, dormant, or desiccated. We had seen something like this in the Galápagos when we dissected plants of *Jasminocereus* that were suffering from drought. Those plants had shriveled to the point that their tissues looked as if they were barely hanging onto their wood skeletons. Pieces of those *Jasminocereus* plants were almost impossible to cut because their insides were like dried jam, whereas their skin (the epidermis and hypodermis) was so leathery that even the sharpest, newest razor blades squashed the tissues before cutting into them. When we finally made them into microscope slides and examined them, the *Jasminocereus* tissues indeed looked awful. We have learned that a cactus can become very stressed yet still remain alive and ready to spring back to full health and vigor with just a little rain.

Speaking of *Gymnocalycium*, we see the granddaddy of them all a little north of Chilecito—if this species is truly a gymnocalycium. This is G. *saglionis* subsp. *tilcarense*, a species that also has been separated into its own genus as *Brachycalycium tilcarense*. This is a popular species in many collections and is readily available from nurseries for a couple of dollars. The plants are beautiful with a slightly (or sometimes a strongly) purple cast to their green bodies, and they always look good, being robust and healthy. People who have had these plants a long time know them to be among the larger gymnocalyciums in their collection. Even so, we are not prepared for the plants we see here in nature. These plants are up to 2½ feet (75 cm) tall and almost that large around. And we do not see just one or two exceptional plants, but many. They are growing on a steep rocky slope, and the biggest specimens are those propped up by rocks. Without the rocks, many would be in danger of growing so large that if they leaned over, they would tear their roots out of the ground and roll down the hillside. There are other gymnocalyciums that also become large, but not quite this size.

But is such an exceptional size of *Gymnocalycium saglionis* criterion enough to warrant calling this a distinct genus? The taxonomic separation of these two genera was done by Backeberg who, by his very nature, was a taxonomic splitter because he was impressed by differences rather than similarities. The differences he cited included the large size of *Brachycalycium tilcarense* and its shorter, more urn-shaped flowers with stamens that are shorter than the typical gymnocalycium. He also stated that flowers of *B. tilcarense* are borne in a woolly furrow, which does not happen with gymnocalyciums. This is a perplexing comment because wild plants in habitat do not have a furrow with woolly hairs; perhaps he saw this feature on an unusual, cultivated specimen. For most people, these characteristics merely mean that this is an unusual species of *Gymnocalycium*, not a whole new genus, and so the name *Brachycalycium* is rarely used anymore.

These specimens of *Gymnocalycium saglionis* subsp. *tilcarense* are especially valuable for us as we try to understand the evolution of gigantism in plants. Their large size is almost certainly a new feature in the evolution of gymnocalyciums, not an old, relictual one. That is to say, the ancestors of

Plants of *Gymnocalycium saglionis* subsp. *tilcarense*
grow very large; this one is over 1 foot (30 cm)
tall. Several species that are universally
considered to be *Gymnocalycium*, for example
G. *nigriareolatum*, have plants that
become almost this large.

gymnocalyciums were probably moderate-sized plants, and since the early stages of the evolution of the genus, most species have stayed about the same size and many have become smaller. This particular species, however, has become gigantic. By studying the species, we should learn how this came about, and particularly how its large size affects the anatomy of wood. Most plants hold themselves up with a wood skeleton, but the very small globular cacti like echinopsises, gymnocalyciums, and mammillarias have a soft spongy wood. If, as we believe, G. *saglionis* evolved from an ancestor with a smaller body, its ancestor probably also had the spongy wood rather than hard, fibrous wood. What kind of skeleton does G. *saglionis* have? Could such a large plant get by with only spongy wood, or is it able to make some kind of stronger, more fibrous wood? The plants we collect here may teach us quite a lot about the possibilities of wood evolution.

We travel from Tinogasta toward Aimogasta on Highway 60. The terrain is more or less flat, with species such as *Tephrocactus articulatus* var. *papyracanthus* to keep us happy. The spines of this species are broad, flat, and papery (*papyr-* means "paper," *-acanthus* means "spine") rather than round. Like all spines, the growth takes place at the base because only the cells there are capable of dividing. Cells higher up the spine have all elongated, hardened into fibers, and died, which is the reason for the spines' strength. In most

This specimen of *Gymnocalycium saglionis* subsp. *tilcarense*
displays two good *Gymnocalycium* features: nice prominent chins (the small bumps)
below the areoles, and beautiful flower buds covered by overlapping, fishlike scales.

spines, the basal cells almost always divide transversely such that the two
resulting daughter cells are stacked one on top of each other, and when they
both enlarge, the spine becomes longer. A cell will occasionally divide longi-
tudinally and produce daughter cells that are side by side, and their enlarge-
ment causes the spine to grow wider. Depending on the ratio of these two
types of divisions, some spines are very long and narrow, while others are
shorter and thicker. In cacti with flat, papery spines, the cell divisions that
result in increased width are carefully controlled because every set of two new
daughter cells is oriented such that the cells' growth causes the spine to
become wider but not thicker.

Cell divisions in flat spines have a hierarchy; those that produce
length vastly outnumber those that result in width, and those that produce
width are much more common than the very rare divisions that produce
thickness. Such a hierarchy requires a considerable amount of control and
coordination of cell division. The hierarchy has arisen perhaps only three

The height of this *Tephrocactus articulatus* var. *papyracanthus* is even more exotic than its flat papery spines. This is a real plant growing in Aimogasta (we have not altered the photo), and a number of other plants in this population are similarly tall. Such height could be due to the joints (where each segment attaches to the one below) being unusually strong, so the segments remain attached and the shoot becomes long. Most cultivated plants fall apart easily, never becoming more than two or three joints tall.

times in evolution in the flat, papery spines of *Leuchtenbergia principis*, *Sclerocactus papyracanthus*, and *Tephrocactus articulatus* var. *papyracanthus*. Both *L. principis* and *S. papyracanthus* grow in grasslands, and their papery, grasslike spines provide such excellent camouflage that finding the plants can be a real challenge. Although the plants of *T. articulatus* that we find here are out in the open (their spines are completely ineffective at disguising the plants), these tephrocacti normally grow among grasses where their spines are able to keep the plants hidden.

The surrounding territory outside of Villa Mazán consists of very low, gentle hills and flat outwashes, the type of deep, unstable soil that cacti hate. Sure enough, there is nothing here, and we can drive on without anything to entice us out of the car. A little beyond Villa Mazán we pass through a cut in the Sierra de Ambato, a range that provides rocky hills on either side of the road. In deserts, rocks usually mean cacti, and sure enough, we find numerous specimens of *Gymnocalycium ferrarii* and *Pyrrhocactus bulbocalyx*. These plants do not occur anywhere that is flat or where there is soil; they only appear on an inclined and rocky surface. When seeds fall from the fruits, some lodge in cracks in the rocky areas, others wash down from the hills and germinate in soil. The soil offers a milder habitat and is capable of staying moist a little longer than the rocky hills, but there are no cacti on the flat, soil-rich areas, and we wonder what prevents them from growing there. We do not see any dense grass cover that would shade the cacti. It does not seem possible that there is enough sheet erosion every year to dislodge or cover or otherwise kill the seedling cacti. Could it be that the soil stays too wet too long, thus giving fungi a chance to attack the seedlings? This is such a common phenomenon in almost any cactus habitat that those of us who are lucky enough to study cacti in the field have learned that searching the hills produces cacti, but searching in the flat areas between the hills produces little more than opuntias and a sore back.

This area is home to both big and little cacti, including some of the very smallest cacti known. The big cacti are *Cereus forbesii*, tall, branched columnar cacti with narrow stems and large ripe fruits. But a cereus is a cereus, and there is not too much to say about one more *Cereus* species. It is the little cactus here, *Blossfeldia liliputana*, that does have a story. Plants of this species are only about 1/4 inch (0.6 cm) in diameter when fully grown. It may be worthwhile to take out a ruler and really see how little that is. A fully mature, blooming plant is probably about half the width of you little finger. Blossfeldias have extremely restricted localities, and they are almost always confined to very old, narrow cracks in boulders or cliff faces. We saw no blossfeldias in the new cracks; on road cuts in *Blossfeldia* territory, cracks exposed by road building never harbor blossfeldias, even though the road might have been built decades ago. Blossfeldias in the old crevices are lodged in dirt that is also clinging to the rock, and very often the plants are so shrunken and gray they blend in with the soil and are virtually invisible. They appear to spend most of their life in a dry state, only rarely receiving enough moisture to come out of dormancy, grow, and flower. Drs. Wilhelm Barthlott and Stefan Porembski have described them as poikilohydric, meaning that they have about the same moisture level as the air and soil, drying out when the environment dries out, and rehydrating when there is moisture. Rather than storing water like other cacti, blossfeldias tolerate extreme desiccation without

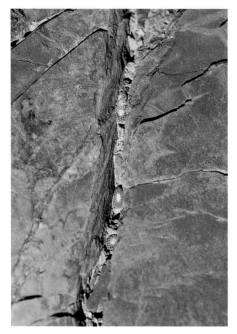

These are fairly typical plants of *Blossfeldia*
liliputana as they grow in an old,
natural rock fissure. This narrow cleft contains
an entire *Blossfeldia* grove of five fully mature
plants. Populations of *Blossfeldia* never contain
thousands or even hundreds of plants.
A plant must often rely on the same few
neighbors year after year for cross-pollination,
which may lead to genetic problems.

dying, then quickly rehydrate and grow when rain or dew is available. This same type of biology is used by mosses and lichens but it is a surprise to see it in an advanced plant like a cactus.

Typical pictures of *Blossfeldia liliputana* depict either a tiny, dried-up plant in habitat, or a big, fat, water-filled green blob, a growth form that occurs when it is grafted onto a strong rootstock. Almost any grafting stock will have more vigorous roots than *Blossfeldia* has, so when grafted, *Blossfeldia* receives an abnormal amount of water, minerals, and root-produced hormones, becoming grossly distorted. Grafting has therefore often been disparaged, and the idea that plants grown in culture look too good or too perfect has also been promoted.

Because Argentina, including north of Mendoza, has had a very wet spring and summer this year (1996), even the best gardeners and growers would have difficulty producing specimens that match the exquisite plants we have seen throughout the country. The blossfeldias are no exception. Although they are growing on bare rock as they like to do, they are big, fat, and as green as can be. Many are almost 1 inch (2.5 cm) in diameter, though several have 1¼-inch (3-cm) diameters, which is almost five times the normal size. They are so swollen with water that their areoles are widely separated. These plants are growing in a slightly shaded canyon (typically they are in full sunlight)

Blossfeldias are not permanently dry. This plant has enjoyed the unusually wet summer of 1996, and its two branches are both full of water. Notice that these blossfeldias are growing in the protection of a bromeliad that provides shade, helps retain moisture, and gives them a foothold on the cliff face.

that still has running water, so it may be that they will remain hydrated for weeks or even months. Could they remain hydrated for a year? We have no doubt that their metabolism is running at full speed as they carry out photosynthesis as fast as possible and make new tissues, wood, roots, flowers, and fruits. Like the armatocerei of Peru, these plants are probably accustomed to long periods of dormancy and rare, brief episodes of active metabolism immediately after a rain. Long-term field studies of many aspects of *Blossfeldia* biology are needed. Are there any plant physiologists out there interested in a species that holds intriguing secrets?

After a night in Andalgalá we proceed east. So far we have been passing through a high, intermountain plateau with two ranges to our west, the Sierra de Fiambalá and Sierra de Belén. The Sierra de Ambato is to the east of us. Throughout the morning we see the Nevados de Aconquija mountains in the distance (Nevado del Candado rises to a height of 16,350 feet [5030 m]), but here we pass through hot dry valleys that are more like little gullies, small

It is rare to find blossfeldias, and very rare to encounter them in flower,
but sometimes you are lucky. Although the flowers are tiny, they are as wide as
the rest of the body. We took this photograph in October 1988.

towns that turn out to be nothing more than a name and perhaps a single
house, and plenty of dust. There are cacti, but only species that we have
already seen. The dense, leafless thornshrubs discourage us from fighting our
way into the roadsides to look for any other cacti. We wind our way up one
steep hillside and down another for most of the morning. Then we begin
climbing another hillside that is taller and steeper than the others. The road
has frequent switchbacks, and our view becomes more extensive and magnificent with every turn. The plateau floor extends almost as far as we can see
to the west, and although it is interrupted at the horizon by mountains,
smaller ranges roughen the intervening terrain. At the top of our climb there
is no descent ahead. We have reached the top of a gigantic mesa that lies
tabletop flat as far to the east as we can see. The north of the mesa is bounded
by the Nevados de Aconquija that are, as their name indicates, snow-covered. We are only at 5100 feet (1569 m) altitude, but the air here is fresh and
cool. There is no sign of dust or scrub vegetation or even of cacti. We instead

Snow-covered mountains surround us once we reach the top of the plateau to the east of Andalgalá. The foreground is a potato field, and plants of *Gymnocalycium baldianum* occur everywhere that the ground has not been tilled.

see potato fields carpeting the entire mesa, their dark green leaves refreshing us even more than the air. Potatoes are certainly not desert plants, and they are not suffering from drought at all.

At this point we are almost at the top of the easternmost range of mountains, and nothing stands between us and the moist winds from the Atlantic. Weather systems dropped some of their moisture as they rose up to this high plateau, but they obviously continue to moisten this whole area. When the winds descend the slope we just climbed, they will compress and become warmer. The rains will stop, and a dry, hot wind will blow into the valley floor we just drove across. Only when the air reaches Chilecito and Tinogasta will it rise, cool, and once again provide rain, this time for *Gymnocalycium asterium*, *Trichocereus terscheckii*, and others.

An area full of potatoes seems an unlikely habitat for cacti. We thought the same thing when landing in Santa Cruz, Bolivia, however, and had been proven wrong. History repeats itself here. At the very top of our climb at a

Gymnocalycium baldianum are low, clustering plants.
They grow almost level with the soil surface and must be able to reach maturity quickly
if they are to survive here where the ground is periodically plowed.

place called the Cuesta de la Chilca, we find plants of *Trichocereus andal-galensis*, another of the small, lax, short-armed trichocerei that are similar to *T. candicans* and *T. strigosus*. Also here is that rare exception, a cactus that likes flat dirt. *Gymnocalycium baldianum* is everywhere that potatoes are not. Every patch of uncultivated soil supports a bit of grass and hundreds of little buttons of G. *baldianum*, all of which are perfectly healthy despite not grow-ing with their heads stuck far out of the ground. One plant has red flowers, and it is one of only a few species of *Gymnocalycium* that uses this color to attract pollinators.

We continue toward the northeast, and although the mountain peaks seem to come closer, they are always separated from us by a valley whose walls are so steep we never see the valley bottoms. Up ahead, the mesa becomes less flat. Real hills appear, and before long we see trees. Soon the road winds around even larger hills and we begin to climb. Trees are now tall enough to throw shade across us. They arch over the roadway to form a canopy. After climbing some distance, we pause before beginning our descent down the east-facing slope to the valley that contains the city of Tucumán. The mountainside that lies between us and the valley faces the rising Atlantic air and therefore receives the first real rainfall. At 27°S latitude, the Tucumán area is close enough to the equator not to be bothered with frost, and the altitude is only 3500 feet (1077 m). By way of comparison, 27°N runs through Laredo, Texas, and bisects Baja California, Mexico. At Tucumán in the plains below us, the annual rainfall is 40 inches (100 cm); up here it must be even greater. The region around Tucumán has a winter dry period, and during May through September, the average monthly rainfall is only about ½ inch (1.25 cm). Throughout the rest of the year, there is about 3 to 8 inches (7.5 to 20 cm) of precipitation per month in Tucumán. Real droughts never occur. June and July are the coldest months in Tucumán, with average temperatures of 54°F (12°C), and the altitude in the mountains is not great enough to put the plants in danger of freezing. A hot summer averages only a balmy 76°F (24°C). The region around Tucumán can support genuine rainforest, and indeed rainforest is everywhere around us. We collect samples of *Rhipsalis* and note that our pickup's odometer reads 3127 km. When we collected *Parodia microsperma* earlier in the day in the dry, desert valley, the odometer read 3061 km. Rainforest cacti are therefore separated from desert cacti by only 66 kilometers (40 miles).

From the trees that tower over us hang plants of *Rhipsalis floccosa* subsp. *tucumanensis* and *R. lorentziana*. All species of *Rhipsalis* are epiphytic, their roots clinging to the branches of large trees but not penetrating the bark or parasitizing the trees. As rainwater trickles down the rough bark of the host tree, roots of *Rhipsalis* absorb some of it. Along with the rainwater, the roots take up minerals that the water has dissolved out of the bark, dust, or decaying leaves that cling to the bark. Stems of these rhipsalises are round in cross-section, without ribs, and not strong enough to hold themselves upright. The stems may initially grow upward while young and light, but as they become larger and heavier, their weight overcomes the strength of their small amount of wood and they begin to droop. Although the stems may arch gracefully at

This is a medium-sized plant of *Rhipsalis* *lorentziana* dangling out of a moss-covered tree. Plants of *Rhipsalis* vary from a few scraggly branches to several healthy ones like this to hundreds of branches. Photographing rhipsalises is usually difficult because not only is the sky typically overcast (or raining), but the thick canopy of tree limbs and leaves also blocks out much of the light.

first, before long they dangle straight down. This is quite an advantage. A dangling stem can be supported more easily than an upright one, so pendent rhipsalises can get by without making much wood. It is, of course, easier to transport water down a stem than up it. When an ordinary, upright plant lifts water from its roots to its leaves, it has to go through the work of lifting that weight. Because plants of *Rhipsalis* have their roots above their stems, water runs downward through them, and the plant is relieved of any heavy lifting. We expected that plants of *Rhipsalis* could get away with producing a very weak wood, perhaps one with only a few fibers and very large water-conducting vessels, yet they have some of the toughest wood in the entire family. Not only is the wood full of fibers, but each fiber cell also has remarkably thick cell walls. For some reason, *Rhipsalis* stems make a small amount of very strong wood rather than a moderate amount of medium-strength wood. Perhaps it is not strength per se that is important, but flexibility and elasticity; the wood may not have to hold a stem upright, but it must resist breaking as the pendent stems sway and twist in the wind.

One sort of flexing that stems of *Rhipsalis* cannot survive is the flexing that results from being hit by a truck. This is a real problem for both the plants and us. Rhipsalises hang down from the branches that arch over the

Rhipsalises have small, juicy fruits with only a few seeds.
The seeds themselves do not have any sticky or adhesive layers, but probably enough
of the fruit remains on the seeds to allow them to adhere to a tree branch long enough
to germinate. If the seed falls on the ground, it will not survive.

roadway, but every stem has been broken off at about truck height. As it so happens, that height is a little beyond what we can reach while standing on top of our pickup. But since this is a mountain road, there is always a cliff on one side, and the big trees growing below us have their *Rhipsalis*-covered branches at about our level. For some mysterious reason, those branches are also always just out of reach. However, they are close enough to tempt us to lean way out, to stretch as far as possible for a specimen, but a quick look down shows us our foolishness. After much searching, we finally find small plants we can reach, but the big ones with old wood that would be good for anatomical studies elude us. If you have seen *Rhipsalis* in collections, you might be surprised at the idea of *Rhipsalis* having significant amounts of wood, but its species can become truly large plants. Some hang down at least 15 feet (4.5 m)—some are even longer—and as they branch repeatedly, they may end in hundreds of narrow, cylindrical stems. At their base where the stem meets the roots, there must be a great deal of wood, perhaps 1 inch (2.5 cm) in diameter or more. Plants like this decorate many of the trees around us, but not one is close enough for us to measure.

Flowers of *Rhipsalis* are small, and each is spectacular if viewed from up close. These plants can produce hundreds of flowers simultaneously, and each then develops into a pink or white berry (some berries are the color of red wine) that is the size of a pea and contains only a few seeds. For the next generation to have a chance, some seeds must germinate on a host tree and not on the ground. Mistletoes, whose fruits look much like those of *Rhipsalis*, use two tricks to ensure that birds are able to carry their seeds from one tree to another. Some species produce fruits that are sticky and messy enough to adhere to a bird's beak. When that bird cleans its beak by brushing it against the bark, the sticky seeds are wiped onto the tree. In other mistletoe species, the seeds have a tough, resistant seed coat so they pass through a bird undamaged, ending up on a branch in a little pile of bird fertilizer. Does *Rhipsalis* use either of these tricks? The fruits are juicy and sweet, not really sticky or messy, so the first method seems unlikely. We must conclude that *Rhipsalis* seeds pass through the birds' digestive system unharmed. However, our conclusion would take some field studies to validate, studies that would require the use of a long ladder and a lot of patience. In cultivation, *Rhipsalis* seeds germinate very easily and grow vigorously.

We descend to the plains and are close to Tucumán, but we skirt around it on the west side and instead head northwest toward the town of Tafí del Valle. We reenter mountains, but the forest quickly changes from a rainforest to a more mesic forest resembling those in Missouri or Ohio. At about 5700 feet (1754 m) elevation, the forest opens up into meadows of rolling hills, grassy slopes that converge on a lake, and trees confined to small groves nestled in ravines. As we leave the forest and are on its very edge, we discover *Trichocereus schickendantzii* growing as a drooping plant over rocky outcrops. Although it is not nearly as pendent as a *Rhipsalis*, we are nevertheless quite surprised to see *Trichocereus* hanging like this. At the Parque Los Menhires we encounter some curious little plants that are hybrids between *Lobivia schreiteri* and *Soehrensia bruchii*. These hybrids are strong evidence that these

This specimen of *Soehrensia bruchii* is growing on a relatively dry site on a rock outcrop, but even so there are mosses and herbs nearby, and water drains onto this site from the hill on the left. These plants do well in cultivation if given plenty of water during the growing season.

two genera are closely related. And in a pasture surrounding a stream, we find the plant that has brought us here, *Soehrensia bruchii* itself.

This is not our first visit to Tafi del Valle, but it is our driest. We were at this same pasture in 1985, and the fog was so thick we could barely see where we were walking. A drizzle was falling, and after two steps our shoes were soaked, then our pants. Groping through the fog and mist, we found the soehrensias. They were not on high ground or protected from the wet by a rocky outcrop, but instead were growing down beside the stream. Like the *Matucana aurantiaca* at Cajamarca, Peru, these plants of *Soehrensia* were covered in mosses. The mosses here had to be more vigorous, however, because these were big globular cacti, 12 inches (30 cm) tall and 11 inches (28 cm) in diameter.

On this visit there is no fog. The sky is bright and clear, but temperatures are cool since it is March, which is late summer or early autumn. Even in the summer, Tafi del Valle can be cool and wet, but what are the winters like?

With temperatures this cool now, does it freeze in winter? Globular cacti this large seem to be incompatible with a climate that drops below 32°F (0°C), but they also seem incompatible with sodden creek banks. On a day with no fog, we easily confirm our first impressions that for every plant of *Soehrensia* that is growing high up in a relatively dry, rocky outcrop, there is another plant at creek side or in a flat, almost marshy area. A few are solitary giants, but many occur in clusters. They are not columnar like the S. *formosa* near Uspallata, but they are very broad and slightly wider than tall.

Soehrensias are part of the *Echinopsis/Trichocereus* complex. In body shape they resemble members of *Echinopsis* but are much larger than is typical of that genus. On the other hand, they are a bit too short and broad to be closely related to *Trichocereus*. A fourth member of this complex of genera, *Lobivia*, differs from *Soehrensia* in body size and shape, but it is similar in an unusual feature, flower color. Flowers of S. *bruchii* range from red to orange and even yellow, as do those of some lobivias. Such colors are not typical of either *Echinopsis* or *Trichocereus*. The flowers of *Soehrensia* are short and wide, a shape that is not typical of any of the other three genera.

We still have *Soehrensia korethroides* to find, but that we will search for when we are in the far north of the country. After studying the S. *bruchii*, we find *Austrocylindropuntia verschaffeltii*, then set out for Cafayate, our stop for the night.

Our plans to get to town some time before dark go unrealized again, but for a good reason—*Trichocereus pasacana*. Plants of this species are some of the largest in South America. These columnar plants easily reach 12 feet (4 m) tall near Amaicha del Valle, and we have seen them over 45 feet (15 m) tall in Tilcara. In 2000, Marc Salak reported measuring a plant of *Pachycereus pringlei* at 63 feet (19 m) tall in Baja California (apparently it is the world's tallest cactus), but T. *pasacana* is a close second. The plants here are in a really healthy population, and we find a nice mix of very old plants that have survived many years, medium-sized plants that must be at middle age and are

These flowers of *Soehrensia bruchii* are a rather startling dark red,
a color that does not occur in *Echinopsis* or *Trichocereus*.
Photographed at the Jardin Exotique, Monaco.

probably reproducing well, and numerous young plants and seedlings that will keep this population thriving for many more years. We observe a nice phenomenon regarding the spines of *T. pasacana*. While they are young (less than about 4 to 5 feet [1.2 to 1.5 m] tall), the plants produce long, stout, spines—orange to red in color—that would ward off any animal, but when they are older they produce much finer, less ferocious white spines.

These plants of *Trichocereus pasacana* are some of the biggest plants of the entire family. They also have some of the most interesting wood, especially at their base where the plant is oldest and where some wood that was produced while the plant was just a seedling still exists. It is one thing to dissect a big *Matucana* or *Haageocereus* species, where *big* is not really very big, and quite another to dissect *T. pasacana*, a big plant that really is big. We debate for a long time about cutting down a whole plant to get a sample from the base. At last we realize we are surrounded by thousands of plants and that this is a widespread species that occurs in great abundance in Argentina. Sacrificing

This forest of *Trichocereus pasacana* at Amaicha del Valle in the late afternoon was a wonderful
sight. This is a healthy population with thousands of plants of all ages and sizes,
many of which are really gigantic.

one will not be the end of the world. We take our sample, still feeling some
regret, and get back in the pickup. Less than 2 miles (3250 m) down the road
we come to an area where a farmer is clearing a field—hundreds of plants of
T. pasacana have been chopped down and are lying every which way. We feel
foolish at having agonized needlessly. On we go to Cafayate, arriving at 8:30
P.M., well after dark.

Argentina is the home of the genus *Gymnocalycium*, one of the largest genera in the family with seventy species by a 1999 count. Here in the northwestern states we are passing through the western edge of a region of such
high diversity that there is another species in almost every valley or hillside
that we come to. The majority of gymnocalyciums are to our east in the
plains that extend to the Atlantic, and some species occur as far north as
Bolivia, Paraguay, Uruguay, and Brazil.

   Gymnocalycium is a favorite genus for many collectors for reasons that are
easy to understand. Many species thrive in cultivation because they are not

Humans 1, *Trichocereus* 0. This is one of hundreds of plants of *T. pasacana* cut down by a single farmer clearing land. Over-collecting has endangered some cacti, but habitat loss is the most critical danger.

particular about being given too little or too much water. They are also not picky about the amount of sun they get; they grow well in light shade but also develop attractive colors in stronger sunlight. Once you get to know a particular species and give it the conditions it really prefers, it will bloom enthusiastically and produce some of the most attractive flowers of the family. Plants of all species are globular and small (the size of an apricot) to moderate in size (about as big as an orange). Only a few become larger than a grapefruit. And all species are pretty. No cactus is ugly, of course, but some are, shall we say, ordinary. Gymnocalyciums are all pretty with beautiful skin, attractive spines, pleasant pigmentation, and exquisite flower buds.

Gymnocalyciums are easy to recognize, which probably contributes to their popularity. They are commonly called a chin cactus because each has a small projection—a chin—slightly below each areole. All flowers in the genus have elegant scales that overlap each other as the flower develops and that become individually arrayed once the flower has expanded to full size and opened. There are no gymnocalyciums that lack any of these features, so any given plant can be recognized as belonging to *Gymnocalycium*. The genus is distinctly set off from others, its only close relatives being *Brachycalycium tilcarense* (which is actually a member of *Gymnocalycium*) and *Neowerdermannia*, a genus with two species, one of which we will see a few days from now.

One question we have regarding *Gymnocalycium* is why so many species exist. Seventy species that all look remarkably alike suggest that this an evolutionarily dynamic genus because it is generating new species faster than old ones go extinct. Mutations early on must have given these plants a metabolism and physiology that is tolerant of minor changes in number, size, color, shape, and orientation of the spines, as well as of similar changes in features of their bodies, flowers, and fruits. In contrast, consider a genus like *Samaipaticereus* that we encountered in Bolivia. It has only two species, *S. corroanus* and *S. inquisivensis*. Over the several millions of years that the genus has existed, there must certainly have been many mutations that would cause variations in their features, variations that are marked enough for taxonomists to consider creating several species. And yet we have only the two (some taxonomists would even take away *S. inquisivensis* and put it in *Yungasocereus*). Possibly it is an old genus that was larger and more diverse in the past, and we just happen to live when everything has become extinct except these two species. Even so, why are plants of these two so unvarying, when genera such as *Gymnocalycium*, *Mammillaria*, and *Opuntia* generate such great variation?

We have already encountered *Gymnocalycium asterium*, *G. baldianum*, *G. ferrarii*, *G. gibbosum*, and *G. schickendantzii*, even though we are not searching specifically for gymnocalyciums. Leaving Cafayate and heading toward Salta and Jujuy, we soon encounter more gymnocalyciums. We find *Gymnocalycium spegazzinii* growing with *Acanthocalycium thionanthum* and *Parodia microsperma*, and another population of *G. saglionis* in a narrow, dry valley that has red sandstone similar to that of *Trichocereus terscheckii* near Chilecito. We spend much of the day driving across mountains and valleys, seeing constantly changing vegetation. At Ampascachi just south of Salta we enter another rainforest, and again there are plants of *Rhipsalis floccosa* subsp. *tucumanensis* cascading out of trees, dangling beyond our reach. Mixed in are plants of *R. lumbricoides* and an old friend from Bolivia, *Pfeiffera ianthothele*, although this latter plant is rarer and we see it only occasionally here. Perhaps it is more common than we think, but because it never becomes a large plant, we usually cannot see it unless we stop and scan tree branches carefully.

At Salta we are at only 3500 feet (1077 m) above sea level but have not entered desert. There are trees and greenery everywhere, and the roadsides support tall grasses bent down from morning rain. Rain occurs here almost every day during summer, and this same condition continues to Jujuy (its full name is San Salvador de Jujuy, and do not forget to pronounce the *j*'s as *h*'s: who who ee). Amazingly, climate records for both cities show that they have average annual rainfalls of only about 34 inches (85 cm) with low rainfall from May to September. As mentioned in chapter 1, this is also the same amount of rainfall that occurs in wet Seattle and dry Austin. Driving from Salta to Jujuy we are surrounded by low, moist forests with trees too small to support epiphytic cacti; rhipsalises are found only in big, old trees, never in young ones whose branches are still narrow.

It is raining in Jujuy when we arrive. We stay at the Hotel El Balcón, a pleasant hotel we are familiar with from previous travels in this area. The owner brings a large table onto the spacious balcony so we can work in comfort while enjoying a view of the city through the low and fast-moving clouds. After two weeks of travel, it is time to completely empty out the pickup and check all plants, all labels, all preserved specimens—not to mention it is well past time to wash some filthy clothes. We tried to dissect every specimen the same day we collected it, but that is not always possible, and cross-sections of big cacti like *Trichocereus pasacana* will keep for months in the back of a pickup. So the Hotel El Balcón is a perfect place to stop for a day, catch up on the dissecting, clean plants, record notes, and take a little time to relax. We even have lunch in a restaurant. Most days we buy bread, cold cuts, and

Parodia chrysacanthion grows among the bromeliads of the genus *Abromeitiella*, which hold plenty of water but at the same time are airy, light, and do not become waterlogged.

cheese, and as we drive along, someone cuts the bread, someone slices the meat and cheese, and we all eat on the move. It saves at least an hour each day, and exploring is more important to us than sitting in a restaurant.

When we depart from Jujuy and head north, we have nice, freshly laundered clothes—what a luxury. Since we will return to the Hotel El Balcón in a few days, we leave many of our boxes and bags here. We had the pickup washed and swept out, which more than makes up for the drizzle and gray weather that surrounds us. Rainforests certainly are important and we do need to conserve them, but to be honest, rainforests are wet. Some people may enjoy working in wet clothes, writing in a wet notebook, trying to keep rain off a camera lens, kneeling down in soaking grass to collect a plant. Some people may, but we do not. Dry sunny deserts make us come alive. So this drive north toward the Quebrada de Humahuaca, following the Río Grande, is not our cup of tea. The hills are covered with rain-soaked grass, although rocky outcrops here and there provide a place for cacti to keep dry, and cleistocacti, in particular *Cleistocactus hyalacanthus*, make a sporadic and welcome appearance. We climb slowly, and the wind carries fog and clouds up the valley with us. As we reach the town of Volcán, the sun breaks through and the clouds suddenly dissipate. We look back and see the two mountain ranges that create this valley, and we also see the clouds churning upward and flowing quickly our way, then evaporating just as rapidly. There is a point that the clouds simply do not cross. On some days the clouds must push farther up the valley, just as on others they probably do not make it this far. But here at Volcán, we are abruptly in desert again. And in cacti.

The hills around us are steep and rocky. Some are covered with soil, others are nothing but bare rock. Enough moisture reaches this area to support the growth of a terrestrial bromeliad, *Abromeitiella brevifolia*, that grows in mounds several feet across. Like plants of *Maihuenia poeppigii*, it branches so profusely that the short, pointed leaves of each branch are pressed against those of surrounding branches. Al-

Parodia stuemeri in Tastil, Argentina, grows in bare rock just next to but not actually in the cushions of *Abromeitiella* plants. It seems *P. stuemeri* plants need drier conditions than those of *P. chrysacanthion*.

though lacking wood, *Abromeitiella* shoots have so many fibers that the plants are almost solid. It turns out that this is an ideal nursery for several species of cacti, and here the plants of *Parodia chrysacanthion* take advantage of the airy, moist cushions. Seeds of *P. chrysacanthion* germinate almost anywhere, and seedlings can be found both on rocks and in the soil. The parodias we find in the stable, prickly mass of bromeliad leaves are flourishing, their bright yellow round bodies resembling Christmas tree ornaments, and yet there are no large plants of *P. chrysacanthion* anywhere except those nestling in the *A. brevifolia*. Our conclusion from both these observations is that any parodias that germinate outside the cushions only live a year or two before soil erosion or some other problem kills them. Other parodias do not require a seedbed of bromeliads, and *Parodia stuemeri*, for example, grows in dry, rocky soil.

This specimen of *Parodia microsperma* shows what can be expected from parodias in cultivation. We have had some trouble getting parodias established when they first arrive in the mail, but once they are rooted, they have been quite hardy. Jardin Exotique, Monaco.

The bromeliad leaves may offer some guidance to growing parodias in cultivation. There are probably some people who have no trouble with this genus at all, but we have often found that plants arrive healthy and happy from a nursery but then never recover from transplanting. Each plant follows one of three paths: it dies immediately, it dies slowly, or, after sitting around for a few months while we are tortured by their inactivity, it suddenly begins to grow well (though every once in a while, a perfectly healthy plant will die overnight). Perhaps some need an open, airy, well-drained potting mixture combined with frequent misting or light watering. Others, however, do not; they grow in rocky soil in bone dry deserts and likely could not tolerate misting or rich potting mixture. Compounding the uncertainty surrounding parodias' preferred growing conditions is the confusion over what exactly *Parodia* is. The latest count lists about 264 species, but this includes many species that most people would consider to be members of *Notocactus* and *Wigginsia*. These genera definitely appear closely related since they are mostly all small globular cacti with many fine spines rather than big, heavy, strong spines. Many seeds of these genera have a small food body that attracts ants, a feature that is so uncommon it must be an important criterion for showing that these genera are close. Whether these commonalities are sufficient to unite these genera is another matter. Like *Gymnocalycium*, both *Notocactus* and *Parodia* appear to be rapidly evolving and producing many new species, and as the lowlands that stretch from Argentina to southern Brazil are explored, more species are discovered every year. In general, the notocacti are very easy to grow in cultivation, and most grow enthusiastically, unlike the parodias.

At Volcán we also find *Austrocylindropuntia vestita*, *Lobivia densispina*, *Parodia stuemeri*, and *Rebutia wessneriana*. *Vestita* in the name *A. vestita* refers to the plants' *vestments*, its clothing of long white hairs that turns dense colonies into what appear to be patches of snow. Although it is much too warm for us to be fooled by *A. vestita* (it is early autumn), some of the high mountains that surround us on all sides do have snow on their peaks. We started our exploration for Argentina's cacti in the far southern Patagonian region because winter comes earlier there than it does closer to the equator, but during our two-week trek, we have rarely encountered any scorching days and instead enjoyed very pleasant, balmy temperatures. Despite our progress toward the equator, we are now later in the season, and we will be climbing to our highest altitudes yet in the next few days. Our ultimate destination is the frontier with Bolivia, at La Quiaca, home of *Oreocereus celsianus*. We wanted to examine this species during our trip in Bolivia, but the rains on the fragile mountain roads made that too risky. On this trip through Argentina, we are approaching *Oreocereus* habitat from the south on paved highways, but we will be back on dirt roads when we get closer to the frontier. The snow-covered peaks around us are beautiful, and although we could admire them for a long time, we know the snow is new and not left over from last spring. New snow means bad weather is racing us to the plants of *Oreocereus*. We are determined to get there first.

Continuing our climb from Volcán, we come to the drier, sunnier regions of the broad valley known as the Quebrada de Humahuaca. The Río Grande is never far away but it is often out of sight. At 6450 feet (1985 m), the road is flanked on one side by the river, on the other by steep rock cliffs that are almost entirely vertical and very fissured. Water and old rock crevices—the perfect formula for *Blossfeldia liliputana*. We do not have to do much searching to find them, and because they have not enjoyed an exceptionally moist summer like those we found earlier, they look more as we expected. They are small and shrunken, and because they are pulled flush with the surrounding clay, they are almost completely invisible with no sign of green tissue at all. But they are alive and well, merely biding their time.

At the town of Humahuaca we have climbed to 8817 feet (2713 m). The air here is thin, and even walking makes us breathe hard. Although we have been higher in both Peru and Bolivia, we have climbed to Humahuaca in a single day with no time for adjustment. Altitude sickness (called *puna* here and *soroche* in Peru) is only a risk, not necessarily a sure thing, and because we move slowly and do not bend over—and because we are free of heart problems—we have no trouble. It is at higher altitudes in the extremely high plains of Bolivia (also known as the Puna) that altitude sickness is almost inevitable. There is an old saying about altitude sickness: To cure an attack of *puna*, just lie down in the shade under a tree. In the Puna, of course, there are no trees and there is no shade.

Humahuaca is a beautiful, immaculately clean village, every building seemingly freshly painted and every street recently swept. After finding a hotel, we have plenty of afternoon light left and little dissecting or other work to do, so we head east on a side road toward Coctaca. The dirt road winds through low hills covered in scrub shrubs, rocks, and open soil. Cacti are everywhere. We find another *Austrocylindropuntia*, *A. shaferi* this time, a specimen of *Parodia maassii* larger than we imagined possible, and an example of *Lobivia ferox* that gives you a visceral understanding of the Latin word *ferox* meaning "wild and tough." Plants of *L. ferox*, unlike the seedlings from a nursery, are up to 16 inches (40 cm) tall and 8 inches (20 cm) in diameter. These big, fat bodies are protected by fierce spines 6 inches (15 cm) long that project in all directions and that can stop a thirsty animal from any side. This

This example of *Lobivia ferox* we found in a dry, high altitude desert
(almost 2 miles [3250 m] high) looks like a typical cactus, especially
with its full armor of spines. Plants almost 1 foot (30 cm) tall were common.

is another time where it might be worthwhile to take out a ruler and see how
long a 6-inch (15-cm) spine really is, and the next time you are around cacti,
pay attention to the spines and notice their size. These spines of L. *ferox* are
capable of doing significant damage. Yet despite their ferocious appearance,
most of the large plants are found in the shade of a nurse shrub. Those out in
the open tend to be shorter and smaller; it appears they are younger, as if
none of them survive to become as old as those growing in the shade.

As we continue toward Coctaca we know we are climbing a bit, but it
does not seem significant until we check the altimeter at 11,760 feet (3618
m). We are well over 2 miles (3250 m) high. The lobivias and parodias
increase in size with altitude, and they are here by the thousands. At some
points along the roadside, it would be difficult to walk among them without
stepping on them. *Austrocylindropuntia shaferi* too has become taller, proving
that its stems really can become cylinders under the right conditions. All the
plants of A. *shaferi* we have seen before tended to be so short that they

All lobivias are exquisite bloomers with richly pigmented flowers that open during the day.
In cultivation they produce many flowers, and although each lasts for only one day,
the whole display may last for over a week. This is *Lobivia famatimensis*.

seemed misnamed, but these are tall and proud-looking. They also have ripe fruits. The seeds are the big white seeds typical of all opuntias, and like the seeds of many opuntioid species, germination is slow, and a high percentage never show signs of life. The seedlings that do emerge elongate well for a few weeks, but then seem to go into a type of stasis. Although we cultivate them in full light, they stop elongating while spindly and weak. Perhaps they need some shock—maybe a cold winter—to get them going again. Years after collecting seedlings of this species, however, we have no mature or even good-sized plants.

Another real prize here is *Oreocereus trollii*, a relative of *O. celsianus* that we want so desperately. Plants of *O. trollii* are obviously close relatives of *O. celsianus* and of *O. hendriksenianus*, which we studied in Peru, because they have the same stout yellow spines and long white hair on their thick stems. There is also an obvious difference; plants of *O. trollii* are short, their stubby branches at most 3 feet (1 m) long as they lie along the ground with only their tips turned upward like hairy versions of *Trichocereus candicans*. Shoots of O. *trollii* do not put much effort into growing upright. They have only a thin ring of wood that is so soft the stems can be cut easily with a knife. We do not need a saw to get through this wood. There are a few dead stems where the cortex and pith have rotted away leaving tough skin over a delicate wood skeleton. The wood resembles the cholla wood used to make tourist items in the southwestern deserts of the United States, but this *Oreocereus* wood is like tissue paper. Only by handling it carefully can we avoid crushing it. In most of the dead stems, the wood, because it is not much tougher than the watery cortex, has also rotted away, and all that remains is skin and spines.

In mild climates, *Austrocylindropuntia shaferi* would make an attractive landscape plant with its many bright red flowers followed by fruits. They can take cool temperatures, probably even a hard frost, but they may find the summer heat and sun more stressful.

The low stature of *Oreocereus trollii* provides many advantages at this altitude. The air is calmer and warmer close to the ground, so prostrate stems are protected from the harsher conditions found just 1 to 2 feet (30 to 60 cm) higher up. All surrounding shrubs are diminutive as well, so O. *trollii* does not compete with them for light; even at only a foot (30 cm) tall, the oreocerei are giants here. Furthermore, because they are not upright, the plants need only enough wood to conduct the little bit of water that is available. If they were to produce larger amounts of hard wood to hold tall, heavy stems upright, they would simply be wasting scarce resources. As the sun moves down to the horizon, the air becomes chilly and our fingers grow stiff. We are

These plants of *Oreocereus trollii* are growing at an altitude of about 10,000 to 12,000 feet
(3075 to 3700 m) and are probably in cool to cold conditions all their life.
The air was already very cold when we took this photograph at sunset,
and night temperatures would certainly fall to nearly freezing.

reminded of the colonies of *O. hendriksenianus* near Puquio, Peru, that were
also standing in the cold, covered with snow.

We leave Humahuaca early in the morning and will arrive in La Quiaca later
that night. At Tres Cruces we pass through the guard station for the frontier
region with Bolivia and leave the pavement behind. Fortunately, the road is
well-packed dirt, nice and dry and solid with little washboarding, so we can
drive at 40 to 50 miles per hour (65 to 80 kph). We have entered altiplano
territory; there are mountains on either side of us, although they are miles
away, and the land between us and those mountains is more or less flat. Rain
and snow cannot wash this road off any mountain, so we should be safe.

The mountains around us here are free of snow, a reassuring sight.
Behind and above the mountains are huge cumulus clouds, the big fluffy kind
that you see only high in the sky, the kind you need to be in an airplane to
view up close. Up here, however, they are not simply brushing the tops of the

Photographed in full daylight, plants of *Oreocereus trollii* show their *Oreocereus* characteristics
of a thick coat of long white hairs penetrated by long, yellow spines.
Notice the habitat has only very short plants that are not even tall enough
to shade a prostrate plant like *O. trollii.*

mountains in the distance; they are the background visible through every gap in the mountains. The scene evokes an eerie feeling that the ancients were correct, that the world is a small, flat disk suspended in a void. If we were to drive to the mountains and look over, would anything be there? The high plains have a beauty like no other. It is a magical place.

There are no plants of interest to slow our progress, nothing but sparse bunch grasses forming clumps here and there. The wind is cold despite the clear blue sky. Once we arrive at La Quiaca (it is on the border with Bolivia), we decide not to stop to get a hotel. Instead, we immediately set out to the east and head toward a known locality of *Oreocereus celsianus*. It takes only minutes before we are surrounded by a forest of it. We are on top of the world at 11,100 feet (3415 m) in a forest of *Oreocereus* giants that tower over us. Although the wind blows, there is no sound. The stillness here is ghostly. We hear no sounds of birds, no rustling leaves as little animals scurry about. There are just the mountains, the wind, the quiet, oreocerei, and us.

Plants of *Oreocereus celsianus* branch repeatedly, and all branches grow upward.
None lie flat on the ground as branches of *O. trollii* do. This upward growth structure
exposes the branches to the wind, hail, frost, and freezing temperatures of these high altitudes.
Because all the plants of *O. celsianus* are perfectly healthy and have produced many fruits,
they must not be suffering.

Unlike many other high altitude cacti, plants of *Oreocereus celsianus* do not grow as low, compact hemispherical cushions like those of *Oroya* or *Austrocylindropuntia*. No, these are big columns up to 10 feet (3 m) tall; some must reach 12 feet (4 m). It has been a good year for them, and most branches bear clusters of big yellow fruits near their tops. To photograph them we must park the pickup beside them and climb onto its roof. Each fruit is about 2 inches (5 cm) across, about the size of a small plum, and filled with dozens of ripe, black seeds. There is no pulp surrounding the seeds (the fruits are hollow like a bell pepper), so cleaning the seeds is a snap—we simply cut open the fruit and pour the seeds out. This hollow fruit is the hallmark of *Oreocereus*, a characteristic used to unite it with the genus *Morawetzia* of Peru.

We are too late in the season to catch any of *Oreocereus*'s distinctive flowers. Red and tubular, the flowers do not project straight outward but

This forest of *Oreocereus celsianus* is somewhat deceiving because it appears as if there
are millions of plants, but by driving only a mile or two in any direction,
we find areas where there are none. However, the species is abundant
and not in danger of extinction. This forest is near Yavi, Argentina,
and other populations occur in various areas of Bolivia.

rather are curved. This ensures that only certain pollinators can fit into the
flower, and those pollinators—in this case they are giant hummingbirds
(*Patagonulas gigas*)—will probably visit only *Oreocereus* flowers. By using this
type of bent flower, *Oreocereus* pollen is carried only to other *Oreocereus* flowers rather than being wasted on flowers of some other species. This does not
seem like a particularly useful adaptation here in this barren altiplano where
pollinators do not have much choice in flowering plants. The oreocerei are
surrounded only by grasses which, being wind-pollinated, provide no nectar
to entice either birds or insects. This specialized flower of *Oreocereus* must be
a holdover from an earlier condition, when the ancestors lived in a richer
flora surrounded by other flowering plants that could distract the pollinators.
This type of flower is also found in *Arequipa*, *Borzicactus*, *Loxanthocereus*, and
Morawetzia, perhaps indicating that these have all descended from the same
ancestral plants that produced *Oreocereus*.

An important feature of *Oreocereus* is the hollow fruit that is similar to that of bell peppers.
Most of the seeds fell out of this fruit when we cut it for the photograph.
When we were in Yavi in March 1996, plants of *O. celsianus* and *O. trollii* bore up to fifteen
fruits on each stem, and each fruit had hundreds of seeds, all very fertile.

The temperature drops even though it is still a sunny afternoon, and we put on extra sweaters, sweatshirts, and jackets. Will it freeze tonight? The average temperature for La Quiaca in March is 54°F (12°C), but what temperature extremes does that average hide? We get our answer the next morning when we see that fresh snow has fallen on the mountains that surround us and feel the cold drizzle that falls on the oreocerei. If it does not freeze now, it certainly will in June and July, which is midwinter, when the average temperature is 38°F (3°C), only six degrees above freezing. There must be good, hard freezes many nights in those months, yet *Oreocereus celsianus* shows no obvious signs of adaptation to a cold habitat. Its plants do not have a dwarf stature and are not even short. Their stems are broad, up to 10 inches (25.5 cm) across, with twenty-nine ribs, so they are massive enough to hold some heat through the night if the day has been sunny enough to warm them. The plants are ensheathed with long hairs that, while much longer than those on most other cacti, are too sparse to adequately protect the plants from wind or hold in what little heat the cactus generates with its own metabolism. Instead, these cacti must have metabolic protections against freezing, perhaps producing antifreeze chemicals as do some trees of cold climates, such as maples.

An odd thing about South America is that mountains and high altitudes do not mean endless evergreen forests covered by snow in winter and raked by cloudbursts and thunderstorms in the summer. Unlike in the United States and Canada, high altitude areas are often as dry as low areas; they are cold deserts, home to cacti and sparse, low vegetation. The rainfall data for La Quiaca bear this out: average annual rainfall is only 13 inches (32.3 cm), with the wettest month being January (midsummer), when 3½ inches (9 cm) of rain might fall. Although that sounds okay, this amount of moisture is off-set by the average rainfalls of May, June, July, and August, which is zero inches. That is correct; on average, there is no rain at all for four months, and if the plants are lucky, this drought may be broken by a rain in September, which has an average rainfall of just ¹⁄₁₀ inch (0.25 cm). With such dry con-ditions, the plants are perhaps fortunate that it is so cold here because the low temperatures reduce the amount of water lost by evaporation from their epi-dermis. Winters must be terrible, both cold and dry. We could imagine that small, ground-hugging cacti might make a home here, but these big oreocerei seem completely out of place.

Indeed there is a small, ground-hugging cactus up here that seems more appropriately adapted, the plants of *Neowerdermannia vorwerkii*. These are short little plants that resemble flat-topped mammillarias. When full of water they become a small, bulging hemisphere, but in dry conditions, they con-tract until flat and level with the ground. Like punas and pterocacti, neower-dermannias have contractile roots. With further water loss, they actually pull down slightly under the soil surface where they are well protected from wind, cold, and other stresses. This makes them hard to see, but not hard to find because they are everywhere here. They seem to prefer hiding under bushes and grasses to being out in the open; perhaps the intensity of ultraviolet light is too great if they are fully exposed. Both animals and plants are protected in the lowland from the full impact of ultraviolet light by the atmosphere, but up here at 11,000 feet (3385 m), most of the atmosphere is far below us, and the thin air overhead permits UV rays to come streaming down. Ultraviolet light does its damage by causing mutations, altering the DNA of the cells. We animals and most plants can partially counteract this risk by throwing away the damaged parts. We humans shed our skin cells (they are always falling off us, day and night, unnoticed unless we sunburn ourselves), and plants shed their leaves, replacing them with new, fresh, undamaged leaves every spring. Cacti, however, cannot shed or replace their skin. They have to use it for their entire lifetime, so preventing UV damage by hiding under bushes is often necessary. Again and again we see plants of *Neowerdermannia* hunkering down into the soil and hiding under bushes out of harm's way. It is a strategy that works well for many cacti, including wigginsias and mammillarias that grow in sun-drenched areas.

After finishing with the neowerdermannias, we climb into the pickup and drive along the dirt road—just a trail really—back to La Quiaca. This is our most northerly point for this trip; we will not enter Bolivia, but instead turn around and head back toward Buenos Aires. The night is cold, and thunder crackles without letting up. In the morning there is drizzle, and we have many miles of dirt road ahead for our return to Tres Cruces. Our pickup should have no trouble as long as the road remains smooth and flat, but there are zinc and lead mines here, and trucks carrying heavy ore will soon be churning the road into one long mud pit. We leave immediately without waiting for breakfast, trying to cover as much distance as possible while the road is still solid. The surrounding mountains that were brown the day before are now white. Fortunately, the road runs through plains that are low enough not to get any snow, only drizzle. The weather had beaten us in Bolivia, but we have won this time.

Why such desperation to get one species? In 1990, a friend of ours, the nurseryman Hans Britsch, donated a large seedling of *Oreocereus celsianus* to us for study. At about 3 feet (1 m) tall, it was basically still a baby and years away from flowering. Knowing that plants of this species form tall, heavy columns that must be supported against leaning, we expected to find a hard fibrous wood similar to that in the big heavy plants of *Armatocereus*, *Pachycereus*, or *Pereskia*, cacti whose wood looks more or less like that of oaks but without the annual rings. Indeed, when we examined the plant we found such wood, but only in the outer part of the stem. The inner part had the spongy soft wood like that of *Echinopsis* and *Gymnocalycium* species, as well as of other short cacti whose bodies are so small they are really just water balloons and whose wood conducts water but does not act as a supporting skeleton. We concluded that the plant of *O. celsianus* we got from Hans was acting like a gymnocalycium when it was still a small seedling: it produced spongy wood during that phase of its life. Although a plant of *Gymnocalycium* never grows tall enough to need strong fibrous wood, plants of *O. celsianus* ultimately do become tall and heavy, and so must produce strong wood. At some point, this plant had changed the way it makes wood, switching from spongy to fibrous wood.

Every year, woody plants like pine trees, oaks, and cacti add a new layer of wood to the outside of the wood they had made the year before. When you cut a tree in cross section, the outermost ring of wood is what was formed that year, the next ring in is wood that was formed the previous year, and so on until you get to the center where you find the wood that was made in the plant's first year. Our plant of *Oreocereus celsianus* had within itself a record indicating that when it was small it made spongy wood, and when it became older it made fibrous wood. All this seemed reasonable, but we also considered other hypotheses. Since this plant came from a nursery, perhaps it was given special conditions while it was young, such as extra fertilizer, shade, or growth hormones that caused the change. Perhaps we were seeing something completely artificial. There were only two ways to be certain: plant a seedling, treat it uniformly for thirty or forty years, and then dissect it to see if it had one type of wood or two, or get a plant from nature. We are not young enough for method number one, so we are here in the highlands of northern Argentina looking for a mature plant of *O. celsianus*. We discover that the sample we take from La Quiaca does have both types of wood.

Dimorphic woods have since been discovered in about seventeen species of cacti (in chapter 3 we described another type for *Samaipaticereus* in the mountains of Bolivia). Surprisingly, the ability to make two types of wood seems confined to cacti. As we drive back from La Quiaca with our valuable specimen, we are struck by the fact that the two absolutely critical plants of this trip, *Maihuenia* and *Oreocereus*, live at opposite ends of one of the longest countries in the world.

What can this wood tell us about cacti? Is dimorphic wood merely a curiosity? Or is it an important feature in cactus evolution and adaptation? If the early cacti were indeed plants like pereskias, they were trees of medium size with hard fibrous wood. As cacti adapted both to drier, more xeric conditions and to high altitudes and colder habitats, their size tended to decrease. Small, low, globose plants like those of *Matucana*, *Neowerdermannia*, *Oroya*, or even prostrate, columnar plants like *Austrocylindropuntia tephrocactoides* or *Oreocereus trollii* are more protected from the environment simply by staying close to the ground, and they are often able to grow in the protection of nurse plants. We see an apparent trend in various groups of cacti in that tall plants like *Trichocereus* may have been the ancestors of shorter plants like *Echinopsis*. But how could plants with hard fibrous wood be ancestral to short ones with spongy wood? It may be that the intermediate plants had dimorphic wood, meaning that they produced spongy wood while young, and fibrous wood when older and bigger. What happens if the plants never become bigger? What if their growth rate is diminished so that even as old plants they are small? And just as importantly, what if they become adapted to flower while only two or three years old rather than at ten, twenty, or thirty years old as is the case with many big columnar cacti? If those changes occur, then the plants will start out life making spongy wood and never switch to fibrous wood. An adult plant of *Gymnocalycium*, for example, is small, able to reproduce, and has spongy wood; it is basically a seedling that has learned to flower.

When a plant or animal develops the ability to reproduce while still having juvenile features, we say the plant is neotenous, or that neoteny has occurred in its evolution. The dimorphic woods of *O. celsianus* may help us understand the history of this species. The many species of *Echinopsis*, *Lobivia*, *Soehrensia*, and *Trichocereus* that we are collecting are also important to determine if neoteny has been involved in the origin of these cacti.

That brings us to *Soehrensia*. This genus is also often united with *Echinopsis* and *Trichocereus*, and neoteny may be occurring in its evolution as well. Near Uspallata we collected samples of *S. formosa*, a species that has plants tall and heavy enough to need fibrous wood. At Tafi del Valle, medium-sized plants of *S. bruchii* are perhaps small and wide enough to survive without fibrous wood. And here near Purmamarca is *S. korethroides*, which has the smallest plants of the three soehrensias. Our guess is that we will find either only fibrous wood or dimorphic wood in *S. formosa*, and only spongy wood in *S. korethroides*, but it is hard to say what we expect to find in *S. bruchii*. And all we need to do now is collect *S. korethroides*.

We are lucky with the road because the mining trucks have not damaged it too badly. Before long we drop from 11,000 feet (3385 m) to 6000 feet (1840 m), but then we turn west from Purmamarca to the pass at Ronqui Angosto at 12,510 feet (3849 m). We find *Soehrensia korethroides* here, small spherical masses of spines wedged between rocks, the biggest plants measuring about 1 foot (30 cm) in diameter. Although adults are abundant, small plants are rare. They resemble the seedlings of *S. formosa*, but none even hints at becoming columnar. A fruit provides us with precious seeds.

From the pass we look west over a great salt desert, the Salinas Grandes, and to the north of that we see a salt lake, Laguna de Guayatayoc. The view is enticing, and it makes us wonder what cacti are at home in that valley. Cacti do not like salty soil, so near the salt desert itself there are probably no cacti. Simply by descending this mountain down to the valley we would probably see five or six more species, maybe even another genus. But time is short now, and we have to think not only about getting back to Jujuy, but also to Buenos Aires.

Soehrensia korethroides grows on a mountaintop with only *Lobivia* (*Mediolobivia*) *pygmaea* and *Maihueniopsis boliviana* for cactus company. These cacti all grow far above the valley plants of *Lobivia glauca*, *Oreocereus trollii*, and *Trichocereus pasacana*.

We make another rapid descent as we return to Purmamarca. Although we are driving and not exerting ourselves, we start to feel dizzy and a bit disorientated from spending the day repeatedly climbing and then dropping several thousand feet. This is not the best of conditions for negotiating a dirt road on the side of a precipice. Nevertheless, such a rapid descent allows us to take note of the effect of altitude on cactus distribution. At the highest altitude is *Soehrensia korethroides*, of course, and *Maihueniopsis boliviana* (it occurs even higher, up to 15,000 feet [4615 m] in protected areas). At 11,000 feet (3385 m) we see the last of the *S. korethroides*. At 10,500 feet (3231 m), the first plants of *Trichocereus pasacana* appear, but they look very bad; they are short, many of their tops have died, so causing the plants to branch repeatedly, and there are tillandsias, a type of bromeliad, clinging to their bodies. They are obviously not well adapted to this altitude. Finally at 10,200 feet (3138 m), *Oreocereus trollii* comes into view.

After rejoining the highway we have an easy drive back to Jujuy and the Hotel El Balcón. We stay at the hotel for an extra day or two to care for plants and seeds (and to do the laundry) before heading back to Buenos Aires. We will not see any spectacular new cacti along the way, but we will encounter some old friends that we had seen in southeastern Bolivia, such as *Stetsonia coryne*. Near Buenos Aires, the terrain is grasslands, and cacti drop out of the flora altogether.

We have met all our objectives of the trip, from *Maihuenia* to *Oreocereus celsianus*, with many others in between. The back of the pickup is full of samples for plant anatomy and the herbarium, and we carry the valuable packs of seeds in our pockets. Despite driving almost 5000 miles (8000 km), we managed not to fall off any cliffs. No road was washed out from under us by rain, and—this is the truly amazing part—none of us became impaled on a cactus spine.

We have collected enough specimens, photographs, and data to keep us busy in our clean, air-conditioned laboratories for years; but in a few months we will probably continue our journey along another dirt road—hungry, sweaty, and dirty—in search of more of these wonderful plants.

BIBLIOGRAPHY

Anderson, E. F. 2001. *The Cactus Family*. Portland, Oregon: Timber Press.

Anderson, M. 1998. *The Ultimate Book of Cacti and Succulents*. London: Lorenz Books.

Backeberg, C. 1958–62. *Die Cactaceae*. 6 vols. Stuttgart: Gustav Fischer Verlag.

———. 1976. *Cactus Lexicon*. Dorset, England: Blandford Press.

Barthlott, W. 1979. *Cacti: Botanical Aspects, Descriptions, and Cultivation*. Cheltenham, England: Stanley Thornes Publishers.

Barthlott, W., and N. P. Taylor. 1995. Notes towards a monograph of Rhipsalideae (Cactaceae). *Bradleya* 13: 43–79.

Bregman, R. 1996. *The Genus Matucana: Biology and Systematics of Fascinating Peruvian Cacti*. Rotterdam, Netherlands: A. A. Balkema Publishers.

Buxbaum, F. 1950. *Morphology of Cacti*. Pasadena, California: Abbey Garden Press.

Cullmann, W., E. Götz, and G. Gröner. 1986. *The Encyclopedia of Cacti*. Sherborne, England: Alphabooks; Portland, Oregon: Timber Press.

Diamond, J. 1997. *Guns, Germs, and Steel: The Fates of Human Societies*. New York: W. W. Norton.

Hunt, D. 1999. CITES *Cactaceae Checklist*. Second edition. David Hunt, 54 Priory Road, Richmond, England.

Innes, C., and C. Glass. 1991. *Cacti*. New York: Portland House.

Kattermann, F. 1994. *Eriosyce (Cactaceae): The Genus Revised and Amplified*. David Hunt, 54 Priory Road, Richmond, England.

Kiesling, R. 1978. El género *Trichocereus* (Cactaceae). 1. Las especies de la Rep. Argentina. *Darwiniana* 21: 263–330.

Leuenberger, B. E. 1993. The genus *Denmoza* Britton and Rose (Cactaceae): taxonomic history and typification. *Haseltonia* 1: 86–94.

———. 1986. *Pereskia* (Cactaceae). *Memoirs of the New York Botanical Garden* 41: 1–141.

Mauseth, J. D. 1989. Comparative structure—function studies within a single strongly dimorphic species, *Melocactus intortus* (Cactaceae). *Bradleya* 7: 1–12.

———. 1990. Morphogenesis in a highly reduced plant: the endophyte of *Tristerix aphyllus* (Loranthaceae). *Botanical Gazette* 151: 348–353.

———. 1993. Medullary bundles and the evolution of cacti. *American Journal of Botany* 80: 928–932.

———. 1996. Comparative anatomy of tribes Cereeae and Browningieae (Cactaceae). *Bradleya* 14: 66–81.

———. 1998. *Botany: An Introduction to Plant Biology*. Multimedia Enhanced Edition. Sudbury, Massachusetts: Jones and Bartlett Publishers.

———. 1999a. Anatomical adaptations to xeric conditions in *Maihuenia* (Cactaceae), a relictual, leaf-bearing cactus. *Journal of Plant Research* 112: 307–315.

———. 1999b. Comparative anatomy of *Espostoa*, *Pseudoespostoa*, *Thrixanthocereus*, and *Vatricania* (Cactaceae). *Bradleya* 17: 33–43.

Mauseth, J. D., and R. Kiesling. 1997. Comparative anatomy of *Neoraimondia roseiflora* and *Neocardenasia herzogiana* (Cactaceae). *Haseltonia* 5: 37–50.

Mauseth, J. D., and J. V. Landrum. 1997. Relictual vegetative anatomical characters in Cactaceae: the genus *Pereskia*. *Journal of Plant Research* 110: 55–64.

Mauseth, J. D., G. Montenegro, and A. M. Walckowiak. 1984. Studies of the holoparasite *Tristerix aphyllus* (Loranthaceae) infecting *Trichocereus chilensis* (Cactaceae). *Canadian Journal of Botany* 62: 847–857.

———. 1985. Host infection and flower formation by the parasite *Tristerix aphyllus* (Loranthaceae). *Canadian Journal of Botany* 63: 567–581.

Mauseth, J. D., and B. J. Plemons. 1995. Developmentally variable, polymorphic woods in cacti. *American Journal of Botany* 82: 1199–1205.

Mauseth, J. D., and M. Sajeva. 1992. Cortical bundles in the persistent, photosynthetic stems of cacti. *Annals of Botany* 70: 317–324.

Mauseth, J. D., Y. Uozumi, B. J. Plemons, and J. V. Landrum. 1995. Structural and systematic study of an unusual tracheid type in cacti. *Journal of Plant Research* 108: 517–526.

Nobel, P. S. 1988. *Environmental Biology of Agaves and Cacti*. New York: Cambridge University Press.

Ostolaza, C. 1996. Cactus de Churín y Ancash. *Quepo* 10: 83–90.

———— 1997. Cactus del sur de Cajamarca y del valle del Río Saña. *Quepo* 11: 57–68.

Rowley, G. D. 1997. *A History of Succulent Plants*. Mill Valley, California: Strawberry Press.

Sajeva, M., and M. Costanzo. 1994. *Succulents: The Illustrated Dictionary*. London: Cassell; Portland, Oregon: Timber Press.

————. 2000. *Succulents 2: The New Illustrated Dictionary*. Firenze, Italy: Le Lettre; Portland, Oregon: Timber Press.

Sajeva, M., and J. D. Mauseth. 1991. Leaflike structure in the photosynthetic, succulent stems of cacti. *Annals of Botany* 68: 405–411.

Salak, M. 2000. In search of the tallest cactus. *Cactus and Succulent Journal* (U.S.). 72: 162–166.

Schulz, R., and M. Machado. 2000. *Uebelmannia and their Environment*. Teesdale, Australia: Schulz Publishing.

Schulz, R., and A. Kapitany. 1996. *Copiapoa in their Environment*. Teesdale, Australia: Schulz Publishing.

Zappi, D. C. 1994. *Pilosocereus (Cactaceae). The Genus in Brazil*. David Hunt, 54 Priory Road, Richmond, England.

INDEX

Italicized page numbers refer to illustrations in the text.